Charlotte Brontë's
Jane Eyre

A CASEBOOK

Charlotte Brontë's

Jane Eyre

◆ ◆ ◆

A CASEBOOK

Edited by
Elsie B. Michie

OXFORD
UNIVERSITY PRESS

2006

OXFORD

UNIVERSITY PRESS

Oxford University Press, Inc., publishes works that further
Oxford University's objective of excellence
in research, scholarship, and education.

Oxford   New York
Auckland   Cape Town   Dar es Salaam   Hong Kong   Karachi
Kuala Lumpur   Madrid   Melbourne   Mexico City   Nairobi
New Delhi   Shanghai   Taipei   Toronto

With offices in
Argentina   Austria   Brazil   Chile   Czech Republic   France   Greece
Guatemala   Hungary   Italy   Japan   Poland   Portugal   Singapore
South Korea   Switzerland   Thailand   Turkey   Ukraine   Vietnam

Copyright © 2006 by Oxford University Press, Inc.

Published by Oxford University Press, Inc.
198 Madison Avenue, New York, New York 10016

www.oup.com

Oxford is a registered trademark of Oxford University Press

Library of Congress Cataloging-in-Publication Data
Charlotte Brontë's Jane Eyre : a casebook / edited by Elsie B. Michie.
p.   cm.
Includes bibliographical references and index.
ISBN-13 978-0-19-517778-7; 978-0-19-517779-4 (pbk.)
ISBN 0-19-517778-9; 0-19-517779-7 (pbk.)
1. Brontë, Charlotte, 1816–1855. Jane Eyre.   2. Governesses in literature.   I. Michie, Elsie B. (Elsie
Browning), 1948–
PR4167.J5C47 2006
823'.8—dc22   2005014213

1 3 5 7 9 8 6 4 2

Printed in the United States of America
on acid-free paper

Credits

✦ ✦ ✦

Bock, Carol, "Reading Brontë's Novels: The Confessional Tradition," in *Charlotte Brontë and the Storyteller's Audience* (Iowa City: University of Iowa Press, 1992), 155–65. Reprinted by permission of the University of Iowa.

Glen, Heather, " 'Dreadful to Me': *Jane Eyre* and History," in *Charlotte Brontë: The Imagination in History* (Oxford: Oxford University Press, 2002), 65–82. Reprinted by permission of Oxford University Press.

Kaplan, Cora, "Pandora's Box: Subjectivity, Class, and Sexuality in Socialist Feminist Criticism," in *Sea Changes: Culture and Feminism* (London: Verso, 1986), 170–76. Reprinted by permission of Verso Ltd.

Michie, Helena, " 'That Stormy Sisterhood': Portrait of the Brontës," in *Sororophobia: Differences among Women in Literature and Culture* (New York: Oxford University Press, 1992), 51–57. Reprinted by permission of Oxford University Press.

Newman, Beth, "Scopophilia, Art, and Distinction: The Psychical and Social Meanings of Jane's Paintings" and "The 'Divided Ideal of Social Duty,' " in *Subjects on Display: Psychoanalysis, Social Expectation, and Victorian Femininity* (Athens: Ohio University Press, 2004), 38–45. Reprinted by permission of Ohio University Press.

Oates, Joyce Carol, "Romance and Anti-Romance: From Brontë's *Jane Eyre* to Rhys's *Wide Sargasso Sea*," *Virginia Quarterly* 61:1 (1985): 44–58. Reprinted with permission from the author.

Sharpe, Jenny, "Slave as Emancipator" and "Sati as Feminine Ideal," in *Allegories of Empire: The Figure of the Woman in the Colonial Text* (Minneapolis: University of Minnesota Press, 1993), 39–55. First appeared as "The Unspeakable Limits of Rape: Colonial Violence as Counterinsurgency," *Genders* 10 (1991): 25–46. Reprinted by permission of the University of Texas Press.

Shuttleworth, Sally, "*Jane Eyre*: 'Lurid Hieroglyphics,' " in *Charlotte Brontë and Victorian Psychology* (Cambridge: Cambridge University Press, 1998), 148–63. Reprinted by permission of Cambridge University Press.

Stoneman, Patsy, "Jane Eyre in Later Lives: Intertextual Strategies in Women's Self-Definition," in *Fatal Attractions: Re-scripting Romance in Contemporary Literature and Film*, ed. Lynne Pearce and Gina Wisker (London: Pluto Press, 1998), 38–50. Reprinted by permission of Pluto Press.

Thomas, Ronald, "The Advertisement of *Jane Eyre*," in *Dreams of Authority: Freud and the Fictions of the Unconscious* (Ithaca, NY: Cornell University Press, 1990), 148–70. Reprinted by permission of Cornell University Press.

Contents

Charlotte Brontë's
Jane Eyre

A CASEBOOK

Introduction

ELSIE B. MICHIE

❖   ❖   ❖

WHEN *JANE EYRE* FIRST APPEARED IN 1847, the passionate voice of its first-person heroine took the Victorian literary world by storm. Contemporary reviewers called it "an extraordinary book," "unlike all that we have read," full of "originality and freshness" (Allott 78, 79, 87). Readers loved it even more than critics; "the public taste seems to have outstripped its guides in appreciating the remarkable power which this book displays" (Allott 88). An American journal characterized New England as suffering from "Jane Eyre fever" (Allott 97). Queen Victoria wrote in her diaries that she stayed up till half past eleven reading to Prince Albert out of "that melancholy, interesting book, *Jane Eyre*" (Allott 389). The energy that made Brontë's novel so compelling also meant it risked being unconventional, irreligious, improper, and revolutionary. One contemporary reviewer criticized it for "moral Jacobinism," a point expanded by Lady Eastlake, who described it as "pre-eminently an anti-Christian composition" that echoed "the tone of mind and thought which has overthrown authority and violated every code human and divine" (Allott 109–10). *Jane Eyre*'s combination of confident self-assertion and rebelliousness has intrigued readers and critics from the time the novel was first published to the present moment.

To grasp the historical and social contexts behind the language of rebellion in a Brontë novel, it helps to begin with the early life of Charlotte Brontë's father, the Reverend Patrick (Prunty) Brontë, who grew up in Ireland, one of ten children, the son of a hardworking farmer. Displaying early a love of books, Brontë established his own school at the age of sixteen, and in 1798, a year of rebellions in Ireland, became tutor to the family of the English Evangelical clergyman Thomas Tighe. Tighe helped Brontë cross the water to England to attend St. John's College Cambridge as a scholarship student. (There Brontë's recognizable Irish surname was changed from Prunty to Brontë.) Graduating from the university and being ordained in the Church of England, Brontë worked in West Riding, a region that, at the time of his tenure, was riddled with poverty and political unrest. From it arose the Luddites, a group of radical workers intent on destroying what they saw as their most visible enemy—the machines that, during the rise of the Industrial Revolution, were being installed in factories. Patrick Brontë was to remember and retell an event that E. P. Thompson has argued became legendary in the history of nineteenth-century English working-class rebellion, the attack on Rawfolds Mill and the mill owner William Cartwright's violent defense of his property. That incident remained so vivid in Charlotte's mind that she would retell it in *Shirley,* the novel she wrote immediately after *Jane Eyre.*

In 1812, not long after these political disruptions, Patrick Brontë married Maria Branwell of Penzance who gave birth to six children in six years: Maria (1814), Elizabeth (1815), Charlotte (1816), Patrick Branwell (1817), Emily (1818), and Anne (1820). Shortly after Anne's birth Patrick Brontë was offered a position as rector in Haworth, the town in the north of England where he and his children were to reside till their deaths. His wife Maria died soon after the family moved there, and her sister, Aunt Branwell, came to live with them and help raise the motherless children. In 1824, when Charlotte was eight, the Reverend Patrick

Brontë sent his four eldest daughters away to be educated at a school for clergymen's daughters run by the Evangelical minister Carus Wilson. While attending that school, located at Cowan Bridge, the two eldest Brontë daughters, Maria and Elizabeth, became seriously ill with consumption. When the Reverend Patrick Brontë realized the danger, he took the two girls home, but it was too late. Both died. (The school the girls attended was later assumed to be the model behind Lowood, the school depicted in the opening chapters of *Jane Eyre*. Charlotte was to assert that the portrait of suffering Helen Burns was based on her memories of her eldest sister, Maria.)

After the trauma of losing his two children, the Reverend Brontë determined that the remaining four—Charlotte, Branwell, Emily, and Anne—would be educated at home. Though the children did not have a formal tutor, they were exposed to an extraordinary range of reading material. As Mrs. Humphry Ward notes in her introduction to the 1899 Haworth edition of the Brontë novels:

> [They] were nourished upon the food of their elders: the Bible, Shakespeare, Addison, Johnson, Sheridan, Cowper, for the past; Scott, Byron, Southey, Wordsworth, Coleridge, *Blackwood's Magazine, Fraser's Magazine,* and Leigh Hunt for the moderns; on a constant supply of newspapers, Whig and Tory—Charlotte once said to a friend that she had taken an interest in politics since she was five years old—on current biographies, such as Lockhart's *Life of Burns*, Moore's lives of Byron and Sheridan, Southey's *Nelson*, Wolfe's *Remains*; and on miscellaneous readings of old Methodist magazines containing visions and miraculous conversions, Mrs. Rowe's *Letters from the Dead to the Living*, the *British Essayists*, collected from the *Rambler*, the *Mirror*, and elsewhere, and stories from the *Lady's Magazine*. (Allott 452)

Fascinated particularly by periodicals with their combination of political essays, reviews, and fiction, the Brontë children began in 1829 to issue their own publication based on *Blackwood's Edinburgh Magazine*, a "tiny magazine, only five and a half by three and a half centimeters, written in the special book print with . . . a quill pen" (Barker 159).

This was the period when the four Brontë children began to indulge in a lifelong passion they called " 'making out' interests for themselves." Elizabeth Gaskell explains in her 1857 biography of Charlotte that "the whole family used to 'make out' histories, and invent characters and events. I told [Charlotte] sometimes they were like growing potatoes in a cellar. She said, sadly, 'Yes! I know we are!' " (81). In 1826, the four had begun collaborating on plays: "the 'Young Men's Play' was inspired by a set of twelve wooden toy soldiers given to Branwell by Mr. Brontë on his return from a clerical conference in Leeds on 5 June 1826; 'Our Fellows Play' was derived from Aesop's Fables; and 'The Islanders' Play' was based on current political events" (Alexander xiii–xiv). Quickly abandoning "Our Fellows," the children merged the "Islanders" and "Young Men" into a fantastical account of an imaginary colony, Glass Town, founded on the delta of the river Niger in West Africa and ruled by both real and invented political heroes. They continued to write about this imaginary world well into adulthood but split it into two parts: the kingdom of Angria became the subject of Charlotte's and Branwell's inventions; Gondal of Emily's and Anne's.

Events taking place in these kingdoms were a vital part of the Brontës' daily lives. Thus Emily, writing in her diary in 1834 at age sixteen, describes how "Papa opened the parlour door and . . . gave Branwell a letter saying here Branwell read this and show it to your Aunt and Charlotte—The Gondals are . . . discovering the interior of Gaaldine Sally Mosley is washing in the back kitchen" (Wise and Symington 1:124). Charlotte's imagination continued to be engrossed with Angria even after she was once more attending school away from home, this time at the more congenial Roe Head where she formed her first friendships outside the family with Ellen Nussey and Mary Taylor. Writing in her journal when she was twenty and working as a teacher at Roe Head, Charlotte wonders whether "Branwell has really killed the Duchess" (Moglen 44). Listening to the winter wind, she is reminded of both Haworth and Angria and writes that "it has wakened a feeling that I cannot satisfy—a thousand wishes rose at its call which must die with me for they will never be fulfilled. Now I should be agonized if I had not the dream to repose on— its existence, its forms, its scenes do fill a little of the craving vacancy" (Moglen 45).

The painful dissatisfaction expressed here was characteristic of the girls' feelings as they were being trained to teach, to occupy professional positions each one experienced as painfully constraining. Charlotte describes how "my sister Emily is gone into a situation as teacher in a large school . . . hard labour from six in the morning until near eleven at night, with only one half-hour of exercise between. This is slavery" (quoted in Barker 294). Charlotte chafed against her own more congenial work at Roe Head: "the Thought came over me: Am I to spend all the best part of my life in this wretched bondage, forcibly suppressing my rage at the idleness, the apathy and the hyperbolical and most asinine stupidity of these fat-headed oafs, and on compulsion assuming an air of kindness, patience, and assiduity" (Moglen 45). Each of Charlotte's novels includes characters that experience the frustration of being dependent teachers. Similarly, Anne was to write her first novel, *Agnes Grey*, about a governess who has no power to control the wealthy and indulged children in her charge. That novel confirms Charlotte's assertion that "a private governess has no existence, is not considered as a living and rational being except as connected with the wearisome duties she has to fulfill" (quoted in Barker 310).

Finding a profession should have been easier for Branwell than for his sisters. Indeed, one of the early reviews of *Jane Eyre* suggests that that novel is about the difference between men's and women's abilities to find a place in the world. Eugene Forçade argues:

> The political, colonial, and mercantile activities of the English people, that spirit of enterprise that takes Anglo-Saxons to every corner of the world, do it is true redress for men, the effects of the law of primogeniture. It is not quite the same for women; they have not the same means

of winning a place in the sun. Among the middle classes
especially, how many girls belonging to the junior branch
of the family, must decline through poverty to dependence
and destitution! (Allott 102)

Certainly Branwell had more professional options than his sisters.
He attempted to make a living as a portrait painter and eventually
found employment with the Leeds and Manchester Railway. But
he was successful at neither of these occupations and ended up
working, like his sisters, as an educator of children, being hired
as a tutor for two families. He was dismissed from his first situation—perhaps, as Juliet Barker has speculated, for siring an il-
legitimate child—and from his second for having an affair with
his employer's wife, Lydia Robinson.

During this period Branwell began the habit of drinking that
was eventually to take his life. Yet it is hard to know whether
that behavior arose from his inability to hold a job. For Branwell,
as for his sisters, the most important preoccupation of the early
adult years was not work but writing. When he held posts as a
tutor, Branwell was submitting and publishing poems in local
newspapers and sending his translations of Horace to Samuel Taylor Coleridge's nephew Hartley. He accepted his first teaching job
primarily because it was in the Lake District near the Romantic
poets whose writings the Brontë children admired. This was the
period when Charlotte sent her own poetry to be judged by poet
laureate Robert Southey, who praised her abilities but warned:

The day dreams in which you habitually indulge are likely
to induce a distempered state of mind; and, in proportion
as all the ordinary uses of the world seem to you flat and
unprofitable, you will be unfitted for them without becoming fitted for anything else. Literature cannot be the business of woman's life, and it ought not to be. The more she
is engaged in her proper duties, the less leisure will she have
for it, even as an accomplishment and a recreation. To
those duties you have not yet been called, and when you
are you will be less eager for celebrity. (Wise and Symington
1:155)

Exquisitely sensitive to negative criticism, as would prove true her entire professional career, Charlotte Brontë perversely cherished this response, memorializing it as "Southey's advice to be kept for ever. My twenty-first birthday. Roe-Head, April 21, 1837" (Wise and Symington 1:156).

Frustrated in her attempts to establish herself as a writer, angry about having to work as a governess or teacher, Charlotte conceived the idea of the three sisters founding a school with financial help from their Aunt Branwell. But before they could do so, she argued, they needed more training in foreign languages. Charlotte and Emily would go to school in Brussels, where Mary Taylor, one of the two friends Charlotte had made at Roe Head, was also studying. That decision proved fortuitous. The director of the Belgian school Charlotte and Emily attended, Constantin Heger, recognized the talents of his new pupils. He freed them from conventional assignments, asking instead that they read famous French writers and write essays in French imitating what they had read. Though Charlotte had been writing since she was small, this was the first time her work had been critiqued by someone other than her siblings. Heger insisted that she pay attention to style, arguing:

> Man does not know what genius is, it is a gift from heaven, it is something one might call divine. It is the same as *force*. But imagine two men of the same strength, one without a lever, the other with a lever. The first will lift a thousand pounds, the second, in making the *same* effort, will uproot a plane tree. Is a lever worth nothing? Without a voice there is no singer—undoubtedly—but there will be no singer either without *art*, without study, without *imitation*. (quoted in Barker 415)

The letters Charlotte Brontë sent to Heger after she left Brussels suggest the importance of his relation to her. She writes of trying but failing to forget him: "That, indeed, is humiliating—to be unable to control one's own thoughts, to be the slave of a regret, of a memory, the slave of a fixed and dominant idea which lords it over the mind. Why can I not have just as much friendship for you, as you for me?" (quoted in Moglen 73). Juliet Barker has suggested that Heger had similarly intense relationships with others of his students, citing a letter in which he rhapsodizes:

> I often give myself the pleasure when my duties are over, when the light fades. I postpone lighting the gas lamp in my library. I sit down, smoking my cigar, and with a hearty will I evoke your image—and you come (without wishing to, I dare say) but I see you, I talk with you—you, with that little air, affectionate undoubtedly, but independent and resolute, firmly determined not to allow any opinion without being previously convinced, demanding to be convinced before allowing yourself to submit—in fact, just as I knew you . . . and as I have esteemed and loved you.

As Barker notes, "This could be Mr. Rochester talking to Jane Eyre" (419).

Whatever the relation between Heger and Charlotte Brontë, it bore fruit. She returned home from Brussels in 1844 more committed to becoming a published writer than ever, especially when plans to found the school proved impracticable. In the autumn of 1845, as Charlotte later explained:

> I accidentally lighted on a MS volume of verse in my sister Emily's handwriting. Of course, I was not surprised, knowing that she could and did write verse; I looked it over, and something more than surprise seized me—a deep conviction that these were not common effusions, nor at all like the poetry women generally write. I thought them condensed and terse, vigorous and genuine. To my ear, they had also a most peculiar music—wild, melancholy and elevating. (Bell 16)

Against the protests of her sister, Charlotte determined to publish those poems, together with a selection of Anne's verse and her own: "Averse to personal publicity, we veiled our names under those of Currer, Ellis, and Acton Bell; the ambiguous choice being dictated by a sort of conscientious scruple at assuming Christian names, positively masculine, while we did not like to declare ourselves women" (Bell 16). Readers were to know the Brontë sisters by these androgynous pseudonyms until 1850 when, after Emily's and Anne's deaths, Charlotte wrote a "Biographical Notice" to the second edition of *Wuthering Heights* and *Agnes Grey* in which she described the lives and personalities of the two authors.

Despite the failure of the volume of poems (only two copies sold), Charlotte was determined to continue. She proposed to submit three tales to publishers to be packaged as a three-volume unit: Emily's *Wuthering Heights,* Anne's *Agnes Grey,* and her own *The Professor.* While Emily's and Anne's novels were eventually accepted by Thomas Newby, Charlotte's *The Professor* was either withdrawn or rejected. She continued to send it out but became so discouraged she neglected even to cover the manuscript in a new wrapper, merely crossing out the name of the publisher who had rejected it and writing in the name of a new one. This round of unqualified rejections was interrupted when Smith and Elder wrote her back after receiving the manuscript, indicating that, while they were not interested in publishing *The Professor,* they would welcome the submission of a three-volume novel. Charlotte already had the beginnings of such a manuscript. In August of 1846, her father had had to go to Manchester for cataract surgery and Charlotte accompanied him. During the five weeks he lay in a dark room recovering, she began *Jane Eyre,* composing with the urgency others would experience in reading the novel. Victorian reviewer and novelist Margaret Oliphant called it "a force which makes everything real—a motion which is irresistible. We are swept on in the current, and never draw breath till the tale is ended" (Allott 313).

Charlotte later told Harriet Martineau that, even after she and her father returned to Haworth, "on she went, writing incessantly for three weeks; by which time she had carried her heroine away from Thornfield, and was herself in a fever, which compelled her to pause. The rest was written with less vehemence, and more anxious care" (Allot 303–4). When Smith and Elder asked for a three-volume novel, Charlotte sent them the manuscript of *Jane Eyre,* which was given to one of the firm's partners, George Smith. He has famously described how he took it to his study and began to read: "The story quickly took me captive. Before twelve o-clock my horse came to the door, but I could not put the book down.... Presently the servant came to tell me that luncheon was ready; I asked him to bring me a sandwich and a glass of wine, and still went on with 'Jane Eyre.' ... Before I went to bed that night I had finished reading the manuscript" (Barker 527). Smith and Elder accepted the novel but offered Charlotte only 100 pounds for her work and insisted on the rights of refusal for her next two novels. They had a hit. The first edition of twenty-five hundred copies sold out in three months; there were reprints three and six months later. By 1848, a year after the initial publication, a stage adaptation of Brontë's novel, *The Secrets of Thornfield Manor,* was running on the London stage, and there were requests to translate *Jane Eyre* into French.

Riding the wave of success, Charlotte quickly began work on a new novel, one that would answer criticisms that *Jane Eyre* was too narrow, too personal, "a story which contains nothing beyond itself" (Allott 75), the work of an author who has "artistic mastery over small materials" (Allott 84). In *Shirley,* Charlotte Brontë sets the story of her two heroines' passionate discontent with the limitations of their lives as women against the backdrop of the Luddite rebellions that her father had witnessed before she was born. Meanwhile, Charlotte's sister Anne published her second novel, *The Tenant of Wildfeld Hall,* the story of a woman's unhappy marriage to an alcoholic husband, perhaps based on the experiences of the wife of one of the local curates. But all writing from the Brontë household was shortly to be suspended. On September 24, 1848, Branwell, whose progressively worsening drinking had left him prone to violent fits of delirium tremens, entered into convulsions and died. For Charlotte, "the removal of our only brother must necessarily be regarded by us rather in the light of a mercy than a chastisement" (Wise and Symington 2:261). Such was not her reaction when, three months later, in December of 1848, Emily contracted consumption and died, and six months after that, Anne too died of consumption.

The only Brontë sibling left alive, Charlotte completed *Shirley* in a deep depression, writing about the valley of the shadow of death and rendering, in the form of the fictional character Shirley Keeldar, a portrait of her beloved sister Emily. The novel appeared to mixed reviews. Charlotte was particularly wounded by the response of George Henry Lewes, the essayist and literary critic who lived with the Victorian novelist George Eliot. One of *Jane Eyre*'s staunchest advocates, Lewes had corresponded with Charlotte Brontë ever since that novel's publication, giving her advice about writers she should read and encouraging her to attempt a broader subject. Charlotte experienced his negative review of *Shirley* as "brutal and savage" (Wise and Symington 3:66), a personal betrayal. She may have felt particularly vulnerable because, with the death of her siblings, she was for the first time without the presence of those who had surrounded her since childhood and shared her love of writing. She had also become, for the first time, a public personage whose identity was known and who could socialize in London with other literary successes like William Thackeray, Harriet Martineau, and Elizabeth Gaskell.

Public social occasions were often strained for Charlotte Brontë, in part because of her self-consciousness about her appearance, however. As her publisher George Smith noted: "She was very small, and had a quaint old-fashioned look. Her head seemed too large for her body. She had fine eyes, but her face was marred by the shape of the mouth and by the complexion. There was but little feminine charm about her; and of this fact she herself was uneasily and perpetually conscious" (quoted in Barker 559). Brontë had, of course, used this self-consciousness to good account in *Jane Eyre*, telling her sisters, "I will show you a heroine as small and plain as myself who shall be as interesting as any of yours" (Allott 303). She returned to this strategy in 1853 when she began her third novel *Villette*, which tells the story of a heroine, Lucy Snowe, who, aware of her own unattractiveness, watches with a satiric eye the fates of the more beautiful women who surround her. Darker in tone than *Jane Eyre*, *Villette* confirmed for contemporaries the stature of its author. George Eliot described the novel as "a still more wonderful book than *Jane Eyre*," with "something almost preternatural in its power" (Allott 192).

Sadly, *Villette* was to be Charlotte's last completed novel. In

1854, overcoming her father's objections she married his curate Arthur Nicholls, became pregnant at age thirty-eight, and died in 1855 before she gave birth. In the wake of that loss, the Reverend Patrick Brontë requested the Victorian novelist Elizabeth Gaskell to write his daughter's biography. (Gaskell also oversaw the posthumous publication of Charlotte's first novel, *The Professor.*) In the biography Gaskell defended Brontë against critics by emphasizing the isolation of the author's childhood. Describing the landscape in which the Brontës were raised, Gaskell characterizes those surroundings as "oppressive from the feeling which they give of being pent-up by some monotonous and illimitable barrier" (13). (This brooding portrait helped make Haworth the center of tourist pilgrimages that it remains to this day.) Of the children's upbringing, Gaskell argued that "the daughters grew up out of childhood into girlhood bereft, in a singular manner, of all such society as would have been natural to their age, sex, and station" (44). She even suggested the girls were small and sickly because their father didn't feed them meat when they were children, an assertion Patrick Brontë asked her to correct in later editions of the biography. Such descriptions triggered sympathy for the Brontës, inviting critics to view the three as enduring hardships rather than flouting conventions and to read the strange novels they produced as a reflection of their authors' lives.

In the first essay included in this anthology, the appendix to her book *Charlotte Brontë and the Storyteller's Audience*, Carol Bock catalogues the history of such responses to Charlotte Brontë's novels, noting that the early reviews of *Jane Eyre* discuss the novel not in terms of the author's biography but of its emotional power, its ability to engross its readers. It is only later, with the publication of Charlotte Brontë's biographical notice to the reissue of her sisters' novels and of Gaskell's biography, that the criticism of Charlotte Brontë shifts decisively in the direction of what Bock calls the "confessional tradition," where Charlotte's emotionally charged writings are read less as carefully structured artistic texts than as an outpouring of personal experiences and feelings. As John Skelton explained in reviewing Gaskell's biography, Charlotte Brontë's "life is transcribed into her novels. The one is the daguerrotype of the other" (Allott 331), a sentiment echoed in Emile Montégut's assertion that "the life of Charlotte Brontë is the very substance of her novels" (Allott 372). Almost twenty years later, Leslie Stephen would make virtually the same point: "The most obvious of all remarks about Miss Brontë is the close connection between her life and her writings. In no books is the author more completely incarnated" (Allott 415).

As Bock goes on to note, by the 1930s and 1940s, the tradition that led critics to read Charlotte Brontë's work as a reflection of her life meant that critics valued Emily's work over her sister's, reading *Wuthering Heights* as more carefully structured than *Jane Eyre*. Bock explains that there was a resurgence of interest in Charlotte Brontë in the 1970s when a number of new biographies were written. With the rise of feminist and psychoanalytic criticism, *Jane Eyre* came to be seen as the paradigmatic story of a woman's attempt to fight back against patriarchal oppression, what Sandra Gilbert and Susan Gubar were famously to call "Plain Jane's Progress." Gilbert and Gubar were not alone in reading *Jane Eyre* as a feminist text. There were powerfully evocative early essays by Adrienne Rich, Elaine Showalter, and Karen Rowe among others (essays which do not appear in this volume because they have been anthologized in such places as *The Norton Critical Edition of* Jane Eyre and Heather Glen's collection of essays on the novel). Brontë's novel was so important to Gilbert and Gubar's new woman-centered conception of literary history, however, that they entitled their volume *The Madwoman in the Attic* (after Edward Rochester's imprisoned first wife, Bertha Mason). For this generation of scholars, it was as if *Jane Eyre* provided a key to the struggles not just of the Brontës but of other nineteenth-century women writers—Mary Shelley, George Eliot, and Emily Dickinson.

Interestingly, *Jane Eyre* had been perceived as making a radical argument about the position of women since it was first published. Writing for *Blackwood's Magazine* in 1855 Margaret Oliphant asserted that "the most alarming revolution of modern times has followed the invasion of *Jane Eyre*." It was "a wild declaration of the 'Rights of Woman.' ... Here is your true revolution. France is but one of the Western Powers; woman is the half of the world" (Allott 312). The rebellious energy that troubled Oliphant is what interests Cora Kaplan in the second essay in this anthology. Citing the passage from *A Room of One's Own* where Virginia Woolf critiques the uncontrolled passion of Jane Eyre's assertion that "millions are condemned to a stiller doom than mine, and millions are in silent revolt against their lot. Nobody knows how many rebellions besides political rebellions ferment in the masses of life which people earth" (Brontë 96), Kaplan notes that here Jane allies her personal rebellion with the impulses that were fueling the working-class rebellions in both the early 1800s and the 1840s. Kaplan calls on critics to explore the ways in which the arguments Brontë makes about individual identity and women's resistance also implicitly involve other forms of social distinction. Terry Eagleton had already begun such an exploration in his 1975 study of the Brontës and class. Mary Poovey, Susan Fraiman, and Nancy Armstrong, among others, were later to analyze the way Brontë's novel combines feminist aspirations with middle-class anxieties.

Ronald Thomas's essay, "The Advertisement of *Jane Eyre*," could be read as following Kaplan's advice. Reading the novel, as is frequently done, as a version of *Pilgrim's Progress* in which the heroine moves through a series of stages that strengthen her identity, Thomas argues that each of these crises involves Jane struggling against someone in authority whom she resists through the agency of her dreams. When she is confined to the red room as a child, awaiting her marriage to Rochester at Thornfield, contemplating St. John Rivers's proposal at Moor Head, Jane falls asleep and dreams, only to awaken able to wrest the story of her life from the mouths of others and tell it in her own voice. Thomas's chapter complicates the tale of Jane's growing personal agency by insisting that "the novel conceives of and represents the self in essentially economic terms—specifically, in terms of a competitive marketplace of the mind." By showing how the novel links "psychological independence and financial success," Thomas demonstrates that Jane gains power by acquiring the wealth that allows her to become a member of the class that previously marginalized her. The novel's heroine is thus at once both rebellious and conservative.

In the 1980s and 1990s, as critics began to explore the role of class and property in Brontë's novel, they also began to view it in relation to the British Empire. This school of criticism was set in motion, at least in part, by Gayatri Spivak's well-known 1985 essay "Three Women's Texts and a Critique of Imperialism," which argues that Jane's triumphant emergence as a subject controlling her own destiny is only possible after the annihilation of her colonial other, Bertha Mason. A number of articles have since been written on *Jane Eyre*, race, and empire, including Susan Meyer's work linking the Brontës' childhood writings about Africa with *Jane Eyre* and Joyce Zonana's consideration of the novel's orient imagery. The selection included in this volume from Jenny Sharpe's *Allegories of Empire* reads Brontë's novel against the backdrop of early nineteenth-century Abolitionist writing about slave rebellions and of English arguments about the colonization of India and the abolition of "sati," or widow sacrifice. Sharpe argues that the self-assertive middle-class heroine of Brontë's novel is positioned between images of the rebellious Bertha Mason and of Indian women forced to accept the wills of their husbands even after death: "In *Jane Eyre*, a domestic form of social agency is established through a national and racial splitting of femininity, with the creole woman serving as a figure of self-indulgence and the Oriental woman, of self-immolation."

Stressing, as it does, the implicit contradictions of Jane's position, Sharpe's essay points toward the change that has taken place in recent criticism of *Jane Eyre*, which tends to read Brontë's heroine less as the coherent individual that she seemed to earlier critics and more as a battleground where readers can detect the play of conflicting impulses that also made themselves felt in other arenas of Victorian thought. As Sally Shuttleworth notes in her essay, "The difficulties of interpreting *Jane Eyre* lie in its internal contradictions, which in turn mirror those of the social, psychological and economic discourse of the age." Shuttleworth reads Brontë's depiction of the passionate rebelliousness of Jane Eyre as echoing the language of contemporary economists and

politicians who on the one hand praise the energies that drive
the desire for self-improvement and on the other hand fear those
energies will generate social unrest and revolution. Shuttleworth
reads the tension between self-assertion and loss of control in *Jane
Eyre* against the backdrop of mid-nineteenth-century psychology,
arguing that "medical texts of the era foregrounded the same
three concerns that dominate Bronte's novel: the mechanics of
self-control, the female body and sexuality, and the insurgence of
insanity."

Interested, like Shuttleworth, in "the Victorians' fears of the
passionate child," Heather Glen explores *Jane Eyre* in the context
of mid-nineteenth-century Evangelicism, not psychology. Quoting from an impressive array of religious tracts from the period,
Glen invites us to read *Jane Eyre* as echoing educational philoso-
phies that advocated breaking the will of children, exposing them
to death, catechizing them, and making them experience adult
authority that is "inquisitorial, judgemental, punitive." While *Jane
Eyre* has generally been read in more positive religious terms, the
story of an individual whose decision to avoid temptation is prov-
identially rewarded, Glen points to what she calls "the sense of
ever-present existential threat which attends Brontë's heroine,"
arguing that, read in the context of evangelical writings, it "seems
the stuff less of timeless fantasy than of historical actuality: not
a remote fairy tale, but the texture of life as it was actually presented to and experienced by hundreds of thousands of children
in the England of its time."

Like Shuttleworth and Glen, Beth Newman is interested in
"considering both the intrapsychical and social-historical forces
that incubate Jane's subjectivity." In her chapter "Excerpts from
Subjects on Display," Newman explores Jane Eyre's desire both to
avoid and receive what film critics have taught us to call the
"gaze." Analyzing the scenes in which Jane shows her paintings
to Rochester and in which she and Rochester shop for her wedding dress, Newman shows that Jane defines herself as different
from the showy, upper-class Blanche Ingram, in terms of her
willingness to be retiring, to wear the unobtrusive dress of the
puritan. However, Jane also enjoys the moment when contem-

plation of her art allows her to be on display, revealing, through the subjects of her paintings, "interior depths of which neither the dazzling Blanche nor the sweet but shallow foundry heiress Rosamond Oliver could ever dream." Newman's argument shows the inherent contradictions of Jane's position, the way the heroine's internal depths are defined simultaneously as something that comes to her naturally and as something she achieves through hard work. That doubleness marks the position of the middle classes who present themselves as both naturally better than those above and below them, and at the same time as working hard to secure their superiority.

The last three essays in the anthology provide external contexts for reading *Jane Eyre*. Helena Michie's short piece uses two of Branwell Brontë's paintings of the Brontë siblings to raise a series of questions about the relations between the brother and the three sisters. Patsy Stoneman's essay includes material from her longer book *Brontë Transformations,* which deals with the various ways in which Charlotte Brontë's *Jane Eyre* and Emily Brontë's *Wuthering Heights* have been transformed—made into plays or movies, referenced, rewritten, and illustrated—since their original publication. Like Michie, Stoneman is interested in the influence of sisterhood on writers. She considers, among many authors influenced by Brontë, two sisters, A. S. Byatt and Margaret Drabble, who "like Charlotte Brontë, shared a childhood fantasy world with siblings" and who responded to *Jane Eyre* in their novels. It includes quotations from Maya Angelou and references to a number of novels that show *Jane Eyre*'s influence on readers in India, Africa, Japan, and elsewhere.

In the concluding essay, a successful modern novelist, Joyce Carol Oates, reads *Jane Eyre* alongside the most famous of its colonial echoes, Caribbean novelist Jean Rhys's *Wide Sargasso Sea,* the story of Jane's double and rival, Rochester's first wife, the madwoman in the attic, Bertha Mason. Oates's and Stoneman's work confirms the international effect of Charlotte Brontë's novel; it has led to courses that explore the postcolonial world by considering *Jane Eyre* in relation to the various novels it has influenced—from Jeanette Winterson's *Oranges Are Not the Only Fruit* to Bharati

Mukherjee's *Jasmine* to Tsitsi Dangarembga's *Nervous Conditions.* In 1881 Peter Bayne asserted that Charlotte Brontë "has won for herself a place in our literature from which she cannot be deposed. Her influence will long be felt, as a strong plastic energy, in the literature of Britain and the world. The language of England will retain a trace of her genius" (Allott 326). He was right, of course, but he had no idea how far *Jane Eyre* would reach in the more than hundred and fifty years since it first appeared.

Works Referenced

Alexander, Christine, ed. *An Edition of The Early Writings of Charlotte Brontë.* Oxford: Basil Blackwell, 1987.

Allott, Miriam, ed. *The Brontës: The Critical Heritage.* London: Routledge and Kegan Paul, 1974.

Armstrong, Nancy. *Desire and Domestic Fiction.* Oxford: Oxford University Press, 1987.

Barker, Juliet. *The Brontës.* New York: St. Martin's Press, 1994.

Bell, Currer [Brontë, Charlotte]. "Biographical Notice of Ellis and Acton Bell." [1850]. In Emily Brontë, *Wuthering Heights,* 15–20. Edited by Linda H. Peterson. Boston: St. Martin's, 1992.

Brontë, Charlotte. *Jane Eyre: Authoritative Text, Backgrounds, Criticism.* Ed. Richard J. Dunn. New York: W. W. Norton, 1987.

Eagleton, Terry. *Myths of Power: A Marxist Study of the Brontës.* New York : Barnes and Noble, 1975.

Fraiman, Susan. *Unbecoming Women.* New York: Columbia University Press, 1993.

Gaskell, Elizabeth. *The Life of Charlotte Brontë.* London: Penguin, 1997.

Gilbert, Sandra, and Susan Gubar. *The Madwoman in the Attic: The Woman Writer and the Nineteenth-Century Literary Imagination.* New Haven: Yale University Press, 1979.

Glen, Heather, ed. *Jane Eyre: New Casebook.* New York: St. Martin's Press, 1997.

Meyer, Susan L. *Imperialism at Home: Race and Victorian Women's Fiction.* Ithaca: Cornell University Press, 1996.

Moglen, Helene. *Charlotte Brontë: The Self Conceived.* Madison: University of Wisconsin Press, 1984.

Poovey, Mary. "The Anathematized Race: The Governess and *Jane Eyre.*"

Uneven Developments: The Ideological Work of Gender in Mid-Victorian England, 126–64. Chicago: University of Chicago Press, 1988.

Rich, Adrienne. "*Jane Eyre:* The Temptations of a Motherless Woman." *On Lies, Secrets, and Silence: Selected Prose, 1966–1978*, 89–106. New York: Norton, 1979.

Rowe, Karen. "Fairy-Born and Human-Bred: Jane Eyre's Education in Romance." In *The Voyage In: Fictions of Female Development*, 68–89. Ed. Elizabeth Abel, Marianne Hirsch, and Elizabeth Langland. Hanover: University Press of New England, 1983.

Showalter, Elaine. *A Literature of Their Own: British Women Novelists from Brontë to Lessing.* Princeton: Princeton University Press, 1977.

Spivak, Gayatri Chakravorty. "Three Women's Texts and a Critique of Imperialism." *Critical Inquiry* 8(1986): 243–61.

Stoneman, Patsy. *Brontë Transformations: The Cultural Dissemination of* Jane Eyre *and* Wuthering Heights. London: Prentice Hall/Harvester Wheatsheaf, 1996.

Thompson, E. P. *The Making of the English Working Class.* New York: Vintage, 1966.

Wise, T. J., and J. A. Symington, eds. *The Lives, Friendships and Correspondence of the Brontë Family.* 4 vols. Oxford: Basil Blackwell, 1933.

Zonana, Joyce. "The Sultan and the Slave: Feminist Orientalism and the Structure of *Jane Eyre.*" *Signs* 18 (1993): 592–617.

Reading Brontë's Novels

The Confessional Tradition

CAROL BOCK

◆　◆　◆

S INCE *JANE EYRE* WAS PUBLISHED IN 1847, a set of expectations about what it means to read Brontë's novels has been fostered by reviewers, critics, teachers, and nonprofessional readers alike. These expectations have been passed from generation to generation, so that one can justifiably speak of a "tradition" in the reading of Brontë's novels: a set of interpretive assumptions we typically make about her work. To identify this tradition is to name our presuppositions and thereby understand how they direct and limit our reading responses. In tracing the history of the critical reception of Brontë's novels, this [essay] tries to account for the predominance of what I call "the confessional tradition" in reading her fiction and points out some of the interpretive constraints by which that tradition limits our understanding of her achievement as a narrative artist.

Perhaps the most striking feature of the history of response to Brontë's novels is a persistent concern with biographical background, what Miriam Allott aptly calls "the Brontë story" (1974, 2). Charlotte's life—or rather the various accounts of that life we have told each other—continues to have a significant effect on our interpretations of her work. Why is this the case? Do the texts of her novels contain features that inevitably point us in the direction of the life? Or does our familiarity with her life highlight certain qualities in her work and so point toward biography as an intrepretive key?

Though these questions cannot perhaps be answered conclusively, we should note that, until Brontë's identity became known, very few reviews of her work suggested a connection between the writer's life and the experience of her protagonists. Her narratives did not appear to most readers as self-evidently confessional.[1] Admittedly, the *Christian Remembrancer* concluded that the author of *Jane Eyre* was probably, "like her heroine, . . . a despised and slighted governess" (Review 1848, 397), and George Henry Lewes argued that the novel "*is* an autobiography,—not, perhaps, in the naked facts and circumstances, but in the actual suffering and experience" (1847, 691).

Most early appreciations of Brontë's writing, however, did not characterize it as autobiographical but rather stressed the writer's ability to engage the reader's attention and emotions. The *Atlas* described *Jane Eyre* as "a book to make the pulses gallop and the heart beat, and to fill the eyes with tears" (Allott 1974, 68), and the *People's Journal* praised the novel as "calculated to rivet attention, to provoke sympathy, to make the heart bound, and the brain pause" (Review, 1848, 269). *Era*'s anonymous reviewer was similarly struck by the "mode by which the writer engages you. . . . He fixes you at the commencement, and there is no flagging on his part—no getting away on your's [*sic*]—till the end" (Allott 1974, 79). Even Elizabeth Rigby, the most hostile of Brontë's critics, admitted that *Jane Eyre* immediately "takes possession of the reader's intensest interest" (1848, 163); and Lewes noted that the narrative "fastens itself upon your attention, and will not leave you" so that passages read "like a page out of one's own life" (1847, 691–92)—an interesting location of the novel's power in its apparent connection to the *reader*'s, rather than the *writer*'s, experience.

It would seem, then, that the initial appeal of Brontë's writing was that it offered readers an opportunity to be wholly absorbed in the narrative's fictional world. "This exhilaration," Virginia Woolf later explained,

> rushes us through the entire volume, without giving us time to think, without letting us lift our eyes from the page. So intense is our absorption that if some one moves in the room the movement seems to take place not there but up in Yorkshire. The writer has us by the hand, forces us along her road, makes us see what she sees, never leaves us for a moment or allows us to forget her. . . . Think of Rochester and we have to think of Jane Eyre. Think of the moor, and again there is Jane Eyre. Think of the drawing room, even, those "white carpets on which seemed laid brilliant garlands of flowers," that "pale Parian mantelpiece" with its Bohemia glass of "ruby red" and the "general blending of snow and fire"—what is all that except Jane Eyre? (1925, 156–57)

Woolf astutely draws a connection between the reader's absorption in the fictional world and the writer's method for making that realm the very embodiment of her protagonist—"what is all that except Jane Eyre?"—so that the reader's engagement in the novel is understood as an identification with its heroine. This interpretation echoes the responses of earlier readers like W. G. Clark, who "took up *Jane Eyre* one winter's evening . . . sternly resolved to be as critical as Croker," but found that "as we read on we forgot both commendations and criticism, identified ourselves with Jane in all her troubles, and finally married Mr. Rochester about four in the morning" (1849, 692). For the great majority of contemporary reviewers (an influential group of readers whose critiques helped establish Brontë's reputation and determine how other readers would respond to her books), the power of *Jane Eyre* lay in its irresistible claim on the reader's capacity for emotional involvement in the storyteller's experience.

But who was that storyteller? Not until the 1850s, when the circumstances of "Currer Bell's" life became the subject of vague literary gossip, did readers gradually began to evaluate her novels through reference to the author's own experience. Throughout the decade, reviewers continued to describe the activity of reading Brontë as one of complete absorption in another world and another personality.[2] But such comments were increasingly accompanied by remarks that traced the origin of the writer's power (and failings) to the autobiographical nature of her work. Initially, these comments tended to be apologetic in tone, attributing the pervasive melancholy of *Shirley* and *Villette* to the sorrowful events in Brontë's recent experience. Charlotte's own comments on Emily and Anne in her preface to the 1850 edition of *Wuthering Heights* and *Agnes Grey* encouraged this kind of response, and subsequent reviewers were noticeably reluctant to blame the writer too harshly for the excessive gloom they found in her books. The *Examiner*'s anonymous critic of *Villette*, for example, identified such morbidness as a defect common to all of Brontë's novels but would only "touch upon" this problem discreetly, "with respect, because we find it difficult to disconnect from it a feeling of the bitterness of experience actually undergone, and that a real heart throbs at such times under the veil of Lucy Snowe" (Review 1853, 84). Thus, "the spasms of heart-agony" in *Villette* came to be seen as "but fictitious in form, the transcripts of a morbid but no less real personal experience" (Review, *Spectator* 1853, 155), and Jane Eyre and Lucy Snowe were both increasingly accepted as "reflections of Currer Bell" (Review, *Guardian* 1853, 128).

In this critical climate, Peter Bayne noted the "perfect" verisimilitude of Brontë's writing (Allott 1974, 327), and Margaret Oliphant sweepingly attributed the arresting power of the novels to their dependence on actuality rather than artifice. "There is no fiction" in Brontë's writing, she asserts: "We feel no art in these remarkable books. What we feel is a force which makes everything real—a motion which is irresistible. We are swept on in the current and never draw breath till the tale is ended. Afterwards we may disapprove at our leisure, but it is certain that we have not had a moment's pause to be critical till we come to the end" (1855, 558–59). In claiming that Brontë's novels engage the reader by their mimetic realism, critics like Bayne and Oliphant prepared the way for the inestimable effect of [Elizabeth] Gaskell's biogra-

phy on the direction of Brontë criticism and on our understanding of what it is like to read Brontë's novels.

The reviews of *The Life of Charlotte Brontë* and the reconsiderations
of Charlotte's work that followed close on the heels of its publication show how at this time the author's life and art became
inextricably bound. Admitting that a writer's "experience can
never entirely explain the work," John Skelton nevertheless saw
Gaskell's biography and Brontë's novels as mutually illuminating.
Brontë's "life," he claimed, "is transcribed into her novels. The
one is a daguerrotype of the other. . . . When you read her life,
you read *Jane Eyre, Shirley, Villette*, in fragments" (1857, 570). This
excerpt is representative of the standard practice of reviewers at
this time, which was to use the fiction and the *Life* to perform a
kind of mutual exegesis on both, an interpretive strategy that
they encouraged in their own readers as well. The sensation
caused by Gaskell's biography was, according to the *Christian Remembrancer*, "indefinitely enhanced by the startling juxtaposition in
which it stands, to ordinary readers, with the preconceived conception of what the author of *Jane Eyre* must be. . . . What every
reader seeks to do, is to reconcile this seeming contradiction, and
unravel the mystery how can so bashful a woman be so unbashful
a writer?" (Review 1857, 90). To explain this apparent paradox,
readers increasingly identified the author with her protagonists—
"In the general outline of character she is herself . . . her own
heroine" (Dallas 1857, 92)—and it soon became unthinkable to
read her novels without reference to the biography. A reviewer
thus might begin a critique of Brontë's work, as Emile Montégut
did, with a by-then widely accepted claim— "The life of Charlotte
Brontë is the very substance of her novels" (Allott 1974, 372)—
and proceed to analyze each work as illustrating various aspects
of Brontë's personality and experience as Gaskell had described
them.

Charles Kingsley provides what is perhaps the most striking
testimony of the influence of Gaskell's *Life* on the way that readers
experienced Brontë's works. In a letter to Gaskell, he admits that
he had "hardly looked into" *Jane Eyre* and had put aside *Shirley*

because of its offensive "coarseness," but, now, having read the *Life*, he promises to return to Brontë's fiction with a new, and more favorable, set of preconceptions: "How I misjudged her! and how thankful I am that I never put a word of my misconceptions into print, or recorded my misjudgments of one who is a whole heaven above me. Well have you done your work, and given us a picture of a valiant woman made perfect by sufferings. I shall now read carefully and lovingly every word she has written" (Kingsley 1877, 2:25). Clearly revealing the expectations that Kingsley had formed on the basis of reading the *Life* (and such expectations are likely to be self-fulfilling), his letter demonstrates the powerful hold that "the Brontë story" now had on the reading public.

Indeed, a fascination with Brontë's life often exceeded interest in the novels themselves. This was certainly true for Kingsley and for the critic who compared "the wondrous story of *Jane Eyre*" with the even "more wondrous . . . life-drama of Charlotte Brontë" (Review *Athenaeum* 1857, 755). The popularity of Gaskell's biography ensured that the primary interpretive strategy for reading Brontë's texts would be to use the *Life* to illuminate her art. Thus, twenty-two years after Charlotte Brontë's death, Leslie Stephen would comment that "the most obvious of all remarks about Miss Brontë is the close connection between her life and her writings" (1877, 726). Forty-eight years later, this judgment remained entirely unchanged as Stephen's daughter [Virginia Woolf] described Brontë as a "self-centred and self-limited" author whose work is distinctly characterized by the writer's forceful assertions, " 'I love,' 'I hate,' 'I suffer' "—always, Woolf implies, with an emphasis on the autobiographical "I" (1925, 157).

Readers thus generally accepted that the storyteller with whom we identify in Brontë's novels is the author herself and that the emotional experience in which we become so thoroughly engrossed is, almost literally, Charlotte Brontë's. This widely shared assumption helps explain why critics have so often referred indiscriminately to Jane Eyre or Charlotte Brontë as though they did not know the difference between a novelist and a first-person narrator. In principle, of course, they do. But in the practice of reading her novels, the difference is obscured, even made invisible, by what has long been a convention of reading Brontë's fiction: the assumption that her work is fundamentally confessional in nature.

In the latter half of the nineteenth century, the event of reading Brontë's novels continued to be explained as an act of imaginative and emotional engagement in the author's experience, but increasingly, reviewers drew attention to the limitations of such reading. "We cannot sit at her feet as a great teacher," Leslie Stephen wrote, "nor admit that her view of life is satisfactory or even intelligible. But we feel for her as for a fellow-sufferer" (1877, 739). Stephen's remark that Brontë was not "a philosophical thinker" (725) was echoed later by his daughter, who explained that her novels are "poetry" conveying the author's "authentic voice" and "overpowering personality" rather than "a philosophic view of life" (Woolf 1925, 158). For Mrs. Humphry Ward, as for Stephen and Woolf, "the sole but sufficient spell of [Brontë's] books" is "the contact which they give us with her own . . . personality" (1902, I:xx–xxi). To be a contented Brontë reader, in other words, is to identify with the author, to view life temporarily from this fascinating but narrow perspective, and to do so without questioning its accuracy or hankering after a wider and wiser vision.

Such judgments anticipated the widespread defection of critics from Charlotte's camp to Emily's during the 1940s and 1950s. Though *Jane Eyre* continued to have popular appeal, professional readers during this time increasingly allied themselves with the implied audience they saw inscribed in *Wuthering Heights* and thought Charlotte's novels less worthy of serious consideration. Now the fault in Charlotte's writing was not the narrowness of her vision—for surely Emily's was at least as idiosyncratic—but the supposed lack of aesthetic coherence in her texts. This shift in critical activity from making judgments about an author's philosophical conceptions to exploring her texts for evidence of artistic unity reflects the growing influence of formalist theory at this time, a trend that was forecast in Brontë studies by the appearance of David Cecil's essays on Charlotte and Emily in *Early*

Victorian Novelists. Cecil's essays demonstrate the reading conventions that had come into play for modern professional audiences by 1935 and consequently help us envision the implied audience of Brontë's fiction as they appeared to literary critics at that time.

Cecil first reiterates the accepted view of Brontë as a confessional writer who uses fiction as a "vehicle of personal revelation" and whose protagonists are stand-ins for the author: "She is our first subjective novelist," he claims; her protagonists "are all the same person; and that is Charlotte Brontë" (1935, 121–22). He assumes, like others before him, that "any description of her achievement . . . resolves itself into a description of her personality" (136). Indeed, Brontë's ability to saturate her narratives with her own character is, in Cecil's mind, what saves her work from its "colossal defects" (152) and "sweeps the reader away with the compelling force of genius" (152). But granting the power of her novels to absorb readers in the life of the narrating protagonist, Cecil makes clear that this effect is *not* due to the author's artistic skill or conscious intent. A confessional narrative by Charlotte Brontë is not, according to Cecil, "a deliberate self-diagnosis, but an involuntary self-revelation" (122) because the author lacked the detachment necessary to analyze the inner life her novels so powerfully describe. "She feels rather than understands" (132), and any insight into human psychology or character that her fiction reveals is, presumably, the product of strong emotion and mere intuition.

In addition to considering Brontë a weak thinker, Cecil thought she was "hardly a craftsman at all" (148). She was, rather, "a very naive writer" (124) who "did not know the meaning of the word restraint" (128) and consequently wrote books that are "badly constructed" and "incoherent" (124). Her "incapacity to make a book coherent" (126) he attributes to the confessional nature of her writing: "Once fully launched on her surging flood of self-revelation, Charlotte Brontë is far above pausing to attend to so paltry a consideration as artistic unity" (126). With *The New Criticism* about to be published in 1941, no more damaging judgment could have been made of Brontë's writing and of the reading experience her novels afford.

In spite of this sweeping dismissal of Brontë's artistry, many critics attempted to apply the formalist method to the interpretation of her work during the 1960s; and some of these readings have been most illuminating. [Robert] Martin's *Charlotte Brontë's Novels: The Accents of Persuasion* (1966), [W. A.] Craik's *Brontë Novels* (1968), and [Earl] Knies's *Art of Charlotte Brontë* (1969) are the most notable full-length studies of this sort. A proliferation of essays that demonstrate the aesthetic and thematic unity of Brontë's novels, especially of *Jane Eyre*, also contributed to this trend in the 1960s to counter Cecil's assessment of the author as an entirely subjective novelist and "hardly a craftsman at all."[3] The fact that Cecil later retracted his criticism and conceded that there is a "fundamental coherence" in Brontë's work (quoted in Rosengarten 1978, 183) illustrates the power of trends in literary criticism and theory to shape the responses of professional readers.

The 1970s marked a return to interest in biographical studies, largely due to the decline of formalism and the emergence of feminism and psychoanalysis as important critical tools for understanding Brontë's fiction.[4] At least seven biographies and bio-critical studies have appeared since the publication of [Margot] Peters's *Unquiet Soul* in 1975 (Moglen 1976; Gilbert and Gubar 1979; Keefe 1979; Maynard 1984; Nestor 1987; Fraser 1988; Winnifrith and Chitham 1989), a scholarly trend necessitated by the interpretive methods through which feminist and psychoanalytic criticisms operate. Having psychological rather than moral orientations, these studies are otherwise remarkably similar to Gaskell's, for they, too, emphasize the tragedy of Brontë's experience and interpret her work as a reflection of, or reaction to, the oppressive limitations of her life.

Nearly all of the many readings of Brontë's novels that rely on this current version of "the Brontë story" also depend on common premises about the location of textual authority and about Charlotte's achievement as a narrative artist. Employing various combinations of Freudianism (Keefe 1979), Freudianism and feminism (Moglen 1976), feminism and "Bloomian" method (Gilbert and Gubar 1979), feminism and French psychoanalysis (Sadoff 1982; Homans 1983), and feminism, French psychoanalysis, and deconstructionism (Jacobus 1978), such readings find the significance of Brontë's novels in their covert, or subtextual, messages and assume that the authorial expression of such ideas was largely involuntary. For example, [Sandra] Gilbert and [Susan] Gubar—whose views on Brontë have been widely disseminated through their popular study of nineteenth-century women writers (1979) and through their introduction to *Jane Eyre* in the *Norton Anthology of Literature by Women* (1985)—describe Brontë as "essentially a trance-writer" who expressed "her anxiety" by writing in a state of "entranced obsessiveness" (1979, 311–12). They thus present her narratives as displaced confessions of the writer's own fears and fantasies and ally themselves (perhaps unwittingly) with Cecil's view of Brontë as riding helplessly on the "surging flood of [unconscious] self-revelation."

Marxist (Eagleton 1975; Marxist-Feminist Literature Collective 1978) and historicist critics (Chase 1984; Kucich 1987; Newton 1981) have usefully expanded our understanding of the social and cultural contexts from which Brontë's writings emerged, but they too, have depended heavily on the assumption that the repressed "not said" in her fiction is of most value. Thus, while there has been a strong resurgence of interest in Charlotte's novels since the decline of formalism in the early 1970s, Cecil's judgment of her, as "hardly a craftsman at all" remains tacitly accepted. The assessment now lacks some of its pejorative value, of course, since contemporary critics are rarely concerned to evaluate the aesthetic merits of her work as Cecil was, and because a privileging of authorial "authenticity" over deliberate artistry has sometimes reversed the criteria by which we judge literary achievement today. But whether we agree with Cecil that Brontë's supposed lack of control of her art was a weakness or contend that precisely this spontaneity allowed her to express forbidden truths, this view of her creative process commits us to reading her novels as largely involuntary confessions by the author herself. That is, it carries on the confessional tradition in reading Brontë's fiction.

In the past decade, however, the appearance of several studies suggests a movement away from this approach to her novels. In 1977 [Tom] Winnifrith had warned against facile biographical interpretation of the Brontës' fiction, and though Kathleen Blake noted in 1982 that his "hopes for relative 'de-biographicalization' of Brontë studies have not been realized" (224), a number of subsequently published works show a new cautiousness about relying on "the Brontë story" as it has been formulated by the critics mentioned above. [John] Maynard takes particular issue with the commonly invoked assumption that Brontë was neurotically fearful of pregnancy, and he attempts to prove both her psychological health and artistic maturity. "It simply won't do," he contends, "to speak of her work . . . as merely the output of a neurotic unconsciousness writing ignorantly and compulsively" (1984, 71).

Similarly, [Shirley] Foster argues that Brontë is "*openly* ambivalent" rather than psychologically conflicted about the topics she addresses in her novels, which we should therefore regard "as *conscious* explorations of personally important issues with whose complexities she was trying to come to terms." In this way, Foster urges, we can see "the contradictory elements in [Brontë's] work . . . as avowed declarations of her ambivalence, and the ambiguities as an acknowledgment of the insolubility of the problems she depicts" (1985, 71, 79; emphasis added). Blake also expresses a wariness about "Freudian and feminist" readings that infuse "supposed unwitting subtexts" into Brontë's novels (1989, 392), and both [Annette] Tromly (1982) and [Maggie] Berg (1987) point to the deliberate ironies in her writing, arguing that the author handled her material with far greater aesthetic detachment than she is generally given credit for.

Though still in the minority, such readings point the way, I believe, to a more appreciative understanding of Brontë's literary achievement. In urging us to see the ambiguities in her novels as intentional —the apparent contradictions as a sign of complexity rather than a symptom of confusion —these critics ask us to take Brontë seriously both as a thinker and as a writer. Crediting her with aesthetic control of her material allows us, in particular, to see Brontë as a conscious narrative artist, a storyteller aware of the tools of her trade and concerned with the problematics of her craft. . . . Attributing such awareness to Brontë seems amply justified by what we know of her early literary experience and by the insistent concern with reading and storytelling that her novels display.

Granting that Brontë was in control of her art also significantly affects our understanding of the role we are to play as readers of her work. In acknowledging the author's aesthetic distance from her fictional narrators, we begin to see that a corresponding distinction holds between her fictitious narratees and the implied audience that we must try to join.[5] Recognizing our difference from the intradiegetic readers addressed, we allow ourselves to attend to the cues provided by an extradiegetic narrator, the implied author who tells us how to behave as implied readers. As such, we approach Brontë's texts more modestly than those who assume that they have access to subtextual meanings that the author has unconsciously conveyed. We pick up a novel by Brontë looking for our interpretive equal—a companion and guide in the literary experience—and thus adopt the role that Brontë seems to have conceived for her readers as she conceptualized the storytelling experience itself.

Notes

1. Claims that Brontë's contemporaries immediately recognized the autobiographical elements in *Jane Eyre* are based largely on subsequent assessments of the author's career rather than on the contemporary reviews themselves. Charles Burkhart, for example, states that "contemporary critics treated *Jane Eyre* as the 'Autobiography' . . . its title page proclaimed it to be," but he offers only one contemporary review in support of that argument. He draws other evidence from critical responses written after the publication of Gaskell's biography, and these reviews clearly reflect the influence of the *Life*. Burkhart's emphasis on the so-called "purity of the autobiographical impulse in [Brontë's] creativity" is also necessitated by his psychoanalytic method, which must "of course [insist] on the autobiographical element in the novels," as he himself admits (1973, 17–18).

2. George Eliot's comment to Charlotte Bray typifies this reaction: "I am only just returned to a sense of the real world about me for I

have been reading *Villette*, a still more wonderful book than *Jane Eyre*. There is something almost preternatural in its power" (1954, 2:87). Less famous critics were similarly affected: "Brain and heart are both held in suspense by the fascinating power of the writer" (Review, *Literary Gazette* 1853, 123) whose "style . . . never permits the attention of the reader to flag" (Review, *Critic* 1853, 95).

3. See, for example, [David] Lodge's discussion of elemental imagery in *Jane Eyre* (1970), [Thomas] Langford's "Three Pictures in *Jane Eyre*" (1967), [Donald] Ericksen's "Imagery as Structure in *Jane Eyre*" (1966), and F.D.H. Johnson's article on the image of the ghostly nun in *Villette* (1966).

4. See Blake (1982, 240; 1989, 383, 393).

5. Readings of *Villette* and *Jane Eyre* by [Brenda] Silver (1983), [Gregory] O'Dea (1988), [Rosemarie] Bodenheimer (1980), [Mark] Hennelly (1984), and [Carla] Peterson (1986) demonstrate a recent interest in the role of the audience in Brontë's fiction. Silver provides the only sustained account of the intradiegetic narratee, however, and she gives little attention to the way in which readers make use of the narratee in defining their role as narrative recipients.

Works Cited

Allott, Miriam. *The Brontës: The Critical Heritage.* London: Routledge and Kegan Paul, 1974.

Berg, Maggie. *Jane Eyre: Portrait of a Life.* Boston: Twayne, 1987.

Blake, Kathleen. "Review of Brontë Studies, 1975–1980." *Dickens Studies Annual* 10 (1982): 221–40.

———. "Review of Brontë Studies, 1981–1987." *Dickens Studies Annual* 18 (1989): 381–402.

Bodenheimer, Rosemarie. "Jane Eyre in Search of Her Story." *Papers on Language and Literature* 16 (1980): 155–68.

Burkhart, Charles. *Charlotte Brontë: A Psychosexual Study of Her Novels.* London: Victor Gollancz, 1973.

Cecil, Lord David. *Early Victorian Novelists: Essays in Reevaluation.* New York: Bobbs-Merrill, 1935.

Chase, Karen. *Eros and Psyche: The Representation of Personality in Charlotte Brontë, Charles Dickens, and George Eliot.* London: Methuen, 1984.

[Clark, W. G.?] "New Novels." *Fraser's Magazine* 40 (1849). 691–702.

Craik, W. A. *The Brontë Novels.* London: Methuen, 1968.

[Dallas, E. S.] "Currer Bell." *Blackwood's Magazine* 82 (1857): 77–94.

Eagleton, Terry. *Myths of Power: A Marxist Study of the Brontës.* London: Macmillan, 1975.

Eliot, George. *The George Eliot Letters.* Vol. 2. Edited by Gordon S. Haight. New Haven: Yale University Press, 1954.

Ericksen, Donald H. "Imagery as Structure in *Jane Eyre.*" *Victorian Newsletter* 30 (1966): 18–22.

Foster, Shirley. "Charlotte Brontë: A Vision of Duality." In *Victorian Women's Fiction: Marriage, Freedom, and the Individual,* 71–109. London: Croom Helm, 1985.

Fraser, Rebecca. *Charlotte Brontë.* London: Methuen, 1988.

Gilbert, Sandra, and Susan Gubar. *The Madwoman in the Attic: The Woman Writer and the Nineteenth-Century Literary Imagination.* New Haven: Yale University Press, 1979.

———, eds. *The Norton Anthology of Literature by Women: The Tradition in English.* New York: Norton, 1985.

Hennelly, Mark M., Jr. "*Jane Eyre*'s Reading Lesson." *English Literary History* 51 (1984): 693–717.

Homans, Margaret. "Dreaming of Children: Literalization in *Jane Eyre* and *Wuthering Heights.*" In *The Female Gothic,* 257–79. Edited by Juliann E. Fleenor. Montreal: Eden Press, 1983.

Jacobus, Mary. "*Villette's* Buried Letter." *Essays in Criticism* 28 (1978): 228–44.

Johnson, E. D. H. " 'Daring the Dread Glance': Charlotte Brontë's Treatment of the Supernatural in *Villette.*" *Ninteenth Century Fiction* 20 (1966): 325–36.

Keefe, Robert. *Charlotte Brontë's World of Death.* Austin: University of Texas Press, 1979.

Kingsley, Charles. *Charles Kingsley: His Letters and Memories of His Life.* Vol. 2. London: Henry S. King, 1877.

Knies, Earl A. *The Art of Charlotte Brontë.* Athens: Ohio University Press, 1969.

Kucich, John. *Repression in Victorian Fiction: Charlotte Brontë, George Eliot, and Charles Dickens.* Berkeley: University of California Press, 1987.

Langford, Thomas. "Three Pictures in *Jane Eyre.*" *Victorian Newsletter* 31 (1967): 47–48.

[Lewes, George Henry.] "Recent Novels: French and English." *Fraser's magazine* 36 (1847): 686–95.

Lodge, David. "Fire and Eyre: Charlotte Brontë's War of Earthly Elements." In *The Brontës: A Collection of Critical Essays,* 110–36. Edited by Ian Gregor. Englewood Cliffs, N.J.: Prentice-Hall, 1970.

Martin, Robert Bernard. *Charlotte Brontë's Novels: The Accents of Persuasion.* New York: Norton, 1966.

Marxist-Feminist Literature Collective. "Women's Writing: 'Jane Eyre,' 'Shirley,' 'Villette,' 'Aurora Leigh.' In *1848: The Sociology of Literature,* 112–20. Edited by Frances Barker, John Coombes, Peter Hulme, Colin Mercer, and David Musselwhite. Essex: University of Essex, 1978.

Maynard, John. *Charlotte Brontë and Sexuality.* Cambridge: Cambridge University Press, 1984.

Moglen, Helene. *Charlotte Brontë: The Self Conceived.* Madison: University of Wisconsin Press, 1976.

Nestor, Pauline. *Charlotte Brontë.* Totowa, N.J.: Barnes and Noble, 1987.

Newton, Judith Lowder. *Women, Power, and Subversion: Social Strategies in British Fiction, 1778–1860.* Athens: University of Georgia Press, 1981.

O'Dea, Gregory S. "Narrator and Reader in Charlotte Brontë's *Villette.*" *South Atlantic Review* 53 (1988): 41–57.

[Oliphant, Margaret.] "Modern Novelists—Great and Small." *Blackwood's Magazine* 77 (1855): 554–68.

Peters, Margot. *Unquiet Soul: A Biography of Charlotte Brontë.* New York: Doubleday, 1975.

Peterson, Carla L. "*Jane Eyre* and *David Copperfield*: Nature and Providence." In *The Determined Reader: Gender and Culture in the Novel from Napoleon to Victoria,* 82–131. New Brunswick, N.J.: Rutgers University Press, 1986.

Review of *Jane Eyre: An Autobiography,* edited by Currer Bell. *Christian Remembrancer* 15 (1848): 396–409.

Review of *Jane Eyre: An Autobiograpy,* edited by Currer Bell. *People's Journal* 4 (1848): 269–72.

Review of *The Life of Charlotte Brontë,* by Mrs. Gaskell. *Christian Remembrancer* 97 (1857): 87–145.

Review of *The Professor; A Tale,* by Currer Bell. *Athenaeum,* 13 June 1857, 755–57.

Review of *Villette,* by Currer Bell. *Critic,* 15 February 1853, 94–96.

Review of *Villette,* by Currer Bell. *Examiner,* 5 February 1853, 84–85.

Review of *Villette,* by Currer Bell, *Guardian,* 23 February 1853, 128–29.

Review of *Villette,* by Currer Bell, *Literary Gazette,* 5 February 1853, 123–25.

Review of *Villette,* by Currer Bell, *Spectator,* 12 February 1853, 155–56.

[Rigby, Elizabeth.] Review of *Vanity Fair,* by William Makepeace Thackeray, and *Jane Eyre: An Autobiography,* edited by Currer Bell. *Quarterly Review* 84 (1848): 153–85.

Rosengarten, Herbert J. "The Brontës." In *Victorian Fiction: A Second Guide to Research*, 172–203. Edited by George H. Ford. New York: Modern Language Association, 1978.

Sadoff, Dianne F. *Monsters of Affection: Dickens, Eliot, and Brontë on Fatherhood.* Baltimore: Johns Hopkins University Press, 1982.

Silver, Brenda R. "The Reflecting Reader in *Villette.*" In *The Voyage In: Fictions of Female Development*, 90–111. Edited by Elizabeth Abel, Marianne Hirsch, and Elizabeth Langland, Hanover: University Press of New England, 1983.

Skelton, John [Shirley, pseudo.]. "Charlotte Brontë." *Fraser's Magazine* 55 (1857): 569–82.

[Stephen, Leslie.] "Charlotte Brontë." *Cornhill Magazine*, December 1877, 723–39.

Tromly, Annette. *The Cover of the Mask: The Autobiographers in Charlotte Brontë's Fiction.* Victoria, Canada: University of Victoria Press, 1982.

Ward, Mrs. Humphry [Mary Ward]. Introduction to *The Life and Works of Charlotte Brontë and Her Sisters.* Vol. 1. London: Smith Elder, 1902.

Winnifrith, Tom. *The Brontës.* London: Macmillan, 1977.

Winnifrith, Tom, and Edward Chitham. *Charlotte and Emily Brontë.* New York: St. Martin's Press, 1989.

Woolf, Virginia. " 'Jane Eyre' and 'Wuthering Heights.' " In *The Common Reader*, 196–204. Edited by Andrew Mcnellie. First Series. New York: Harcourt Brace Jovanovich, 1925.

———. *A Room of One's Own.* New York: Harcourt Brace Jovanovich, 1929.

Pandora's Box

Subjectivity, Class, and Sexuality in
Socialist Feminist Criticism

CORA KAPLAN

◆　◆　◆

STORIES OF SEDUCTION AND BETRAYAL, of orphaned, impoverished heroines of uncertain class origin, provided a narrative structure through which the instabilities of class and gender categories were both stabilized and undermined. Across the body and mind of "woman" as sign, through her multiple representations, bourgeois anxiety about identity is traced and retraced. A favorite plot, of which *Jane Eyre* is now the best-known example, sets the genteel heroine at sexual risk as semi-servant in a grand patriarchal household. This narrative theme allowed the crisis of middle class femininity to be mapped on to the structural sexual vulnerability of all working-class servants in bourgeois employment. Such dramas were full of condensed meanings in excess of the representation of sexuality and sexual difference. A doubled scenario, in which the ideological and material difference between working-class and bourgeois women is blurred through condensation, it was popular as a plot for melodrama with both "genteel" and "vulgar" audiences.

We do not know very much so far about how that fictional

narrative of threatened femininity was understood by working-class women, although it appeared in the cheap fiction written for servant girls as well as in popular theatre. Nineteenth-century bourgeois novels like *Jane Eyre* tell us almost nothing about the self-defined subjectivity of the poor, male or female. For, although they are rich sources for the construction of dominant definitions *of* the inner lives of the working classes, they cannot tell us anything about how even these ideological inscriptions were lived *by* them. For an analysis of the subjectivity of working-class women we need to turn to non-literary sources, to the discourses in which they themselves spoke. That analysis lies outside the project of this paper but is, of course, related to it.

I want to end this chapter with an example of the kind of interpretative integration that I have been demanding of feminist critics. No text has proved more productive of meaning from the critic's point of view than Charlotte Brontë's *Jane Eyre*. I have referred to the condensation of class meanings through the characterization and narrative of its heroine, but now I want to turn to that disturbing didactic moment in volume 1, chapter 12, which immediately precedes the entry of Rochester into the text. It is a passage marked by Virginia Woolf in *A Room of One's Own*, where it is used to illustrate the negative effect of anger and inequality on the female imagination. Prefaced defensively— "Anybody may blame me who likes"—it is a passage about need, demand, and desire that exceed social possibility and challenge social prejudice. In Jane's soliloquy, inspired by a view reached through raising the "trap-door of the attic," the Romantic aesthetic is reasserted for women, together with a passionate refusal of the terms of feminine difference. Moved by a "restlessness" in her "nature" that "agitated me to pain sometimes," Jane paces the top floor of Thornfield and allows her "mind's eye to dwell on whatever bright visions rose before it": "to let my heart be heaved by the exultant movement which, while it swelled it in trouble, expanded it with life; and, best of all, to open my inward ear to a tale that was never ended—a tale my imagination created, and narrated continuously; quickened with all of incident,

life, fire, feeling, that I desired and had not in my actual existence."[1]

This reverie is only partly quoted by Woolf, who omits the
"visionary" section, moving straight from "pain . . ." to the paragraph most familiar to us through her citation of it:

> It is in vain to say that human beings ought to be satisfied
> with tranquility; they must have action; and they will make
> it if they cannot find it. Millions are condemned to a stiller
> doom than mine, and millions are in silent revolt against
> their lot. Nobody knows how many rebellions besides po-
> litical rebellions ferment in the masses of life which people
> earth. Women are supposed to be very calm generally: but
> women feel just as men feel; they need exercise for their
> faculties, and a field for their efforts as much as their broth-
> ers do; they suffer from too rigid a restraint, too absolute a
> stagnation, precisely as men would suffer; and it is narrow-
> minded in their more privileged fellow-creatures to say that
> they ought to confine themselves to making puddings and
> knitting stockings, to playing on piano and embroidering
> bags. It is thoughtless to condemn them, or laugh at them,
> if they seek to do more or learn more than custom has
> pronounced necessary for their sex.
>
> When thus alone I not unfrequently heard Grace Poole's
> laugh . . .[2]

This shift from feminist polemic to the laugh of Grace Poole is
the "jerk," the "awkward break" of "continuity" that Woolf crit-
icizes. "The writer of such a flawed passage will never get her
genius expressed whole and entire. Her books will be deformed
and twisted. She will write in a rage where she should write
calmly. She will write foolishly where she should write wisely.
She will write of herself when she should write of her characters.
She is at war with her lot. How could she help but die young,
cramped and thwarted?"[3]

It is a devastating, controlled, yet somehow uncontrolled in-
dictment. What elements in this digression, hardly a formal in-

novation in nineteenth-century fiction, can have prompted Woolf to such excess? Elaine Showalter analyzes this passage and others as part of Woolf's "flight into androgyny,"[4] that aesthetic chamber where masculine and feminine minds meet and marry. Showalter's analysis focuses on Woolf's aesthetic as an effect of her inability to come to terms with her sexuality, with sexual difference itself. Showalter's analysis is persuasive in individual terms, but it does not deal with all of the questions thrown up by Brontë's challenge and Woolf's violent response to it. In the sentences that Woolf omits in her own citation, Brontë insists that even the confined and restless state could produce "many and glowing" visions. Art, the passage maintains, can be produced through the endless narration of the self, through the mixed incoherence of subjectivity spoken from subordinate and rebellious positions within culture. It was this aesthetic that Woolf as critic explicitly rejected.

However, the passage deals with more than sexual difference. In the references to "human beings" and to unspecified "millions," Brontë deliberately and defiantly associates political and sexual rebellion even as she distinguishes between them. In the passage the generic status of "men" is made truly trans-class and trans-cultural when linked to "masses," "millions," and "human beings," those larger inclusive terms. In 1847, on the eve of the second great wave of modern revolution, it was a dangerous rhetoric to use.

Its meaningful associations were quickly recognized by contemporary reviewers, who deplored the contiguous relationship between revolution and feminism. Lady Eastlake's comments in the *Quarterly Review* of 1849 are those most often quoted: "We do not hesitate to say, that the tone of mind and thought which has overthrown authority and violated every code human and divine abroad, and fostered chartism and rebellion at home is the same which has also written *Jane Eyre*."[5]

Yet Charlotte Brontë was no political radical. How is it then that she is pulled towards the positive linking of class rebellion and women's revolt in this passage, as she will be again in *Shirley*? Perhaps my earlier example of the process through which class meaning is transformed for class subjects during a strike is helpful here. For this passage does not mark out a moment of conscious reformulation of Brontë's class politics. Rather it is a significant moment of incoherence, where the congruence between the sub ordination of women and the radical view of class oppression becomes, for a few sentences, irresistible. It is a tentative, partial movement in spite of its defiant rhetoric, a movement which threatens to break up the more general, self-conscious class politics of the text. And it brings with it, inexorably, its own narrative reaction which attempts, with some success, to warn us quite literally that the association of feminism and class struggle leads to madness. For Jane's vision is checked, instantly, by the mad mocking female laughter, and turned from its course a few pages later by the introduction of Rochester into the narrative.

For Woolf, Jane's soliloquy spoils the continuity of the narrative with its "anger and rebellion." Woolf turns away, refuses to comprehend the logical sequence of the narration at the symbolic level of the novel.

Jane's revolutionary manifesto of the subject, which has its own slightly manic register, invokes that sliding negative signification of women that we have described. At this point in the story the "low, slow ha' ha!" and the "eccentric murmurs" that "thrilled" Jane are ascribed to Grace Poole, the hard-featured servant. But Grace is only the laugh's minder, and the laugh later becomes correctly ascribed to Rochester's insane wife, Bertha Mason. The uncertain source of the laughter, the narrator's inability to predict its recurrence—"There were days when she was quite silent; but there were others when I could not account for the sounds she made"—both mark out the "sounds" as the dark side of Romantic female subjectivity.[6]

Retroactively, in the narratives the laughter becomes a threat to all that Jane had desired and demanded in her roof-top reverie. Mad servant, mad mistress, foreigner, nymphomaniac, syphilitic, half-breed, aristocrat, Bertha turns violently on keeper, brother, husband, and, finally, rival. She and her noises become the condensed and displaced site of unreason and anarchy as it is metonymically figured through dangerous femininity in all its class, race, and cultural projections. Bertha must be killed off, narratively speaking, so that a moral, Protestant femininity, licensed sexuality, and a qualified, socialized feminism may survive. Yet the text cannot close off or recuperate that moment of radical association between political rebellion and gender rebellion, cannot shut down the possibility of a positive alliance between reason, passion, and feminism. Nor can it disperse the terror that speaking those connections immediately stirs up—for Woolf in any case.

Woolf was at her most vehement and most contradictory about these issues, which brought together for her, as for many other feminists before and after, a number of deeply connected anxieties about subjectivity, class, sexuality, and culture. Over and over again in her critical writing, Woolf tries to find ways of placing the questions inside an aesthetic that disallows anger, unreason, and passion as productive emotions. Like Wollstonecraft before her, she cannot quite shake off the moral and libidinal economies of the Enlightenment. In "Women and Fiction" (1929) she frames the question another way:

> In *Middlemarch* and in *Jane Eyre* we are conscious not merely of the writer's character, as we are conscious of the character of Charles Dickens, but we are conscious of a woman's presence—of someone resenting the treatment of her sex and pleading for its rights. This brings into women's writing an element which is entirely absent from a man's, unless, indeed, he happens to be a working man, a Negro, or one who for some other reason is conscious of disability. It introduces a distortion and is frequently the cause of weakness. The desire to plead some personal cause or to make a character the mouthpiece of personal discontent or grievance always has a distressing effect, as if the spot at which the reader's attention is directed were suddenly two-fold instead of single.[7]

Note how the plea for a sex, a class, a race becomes reduced to individual, personal grievance, how subordinate position in a group becomes immediately pathologized as private disability, weakness. Note too how "man" in this passage loses its universal connotation, so that it only refers normatively to men of the ruling class. In this passage, as in *Jane Eyre*, degraded subjectivities are metonymically evolved—"disability," "distortion"—and degradation is expressed as an effect of subordination, not its rationale nor its cause. But the result is still a negative one. For the power to resist through fictional language, the language of sociality and self; the power to move and enlighten, rather than blur and distress through the double focus, is denied. Instead, Woolf announces the death of the feminist text, by proclaiming, somewhat prematurely, the triumph of feminism. "The women writer is no longer bitter. She is no longer angry. She is no longer pleading and protesting as she writes. . . . She will be able to concentrate upon her vision without distraction from outside."[8] This too is a cry from the roof-tops of a desire still unmet by social and psychic experience.

Although the meanings attached to race, class, and sexuality have undergone fundamental shifts from Wollstonecraft's (and Woolf's) time to our own, we do not live in a post-class society any more than a post-feminist one. Our identities are still constructed through social hierarchy and cultural differentiation, as well as through those processes of division and fragmentation described in psychoanalytic theory. The identities arrived at through these structures will always be precarious and unstable, though *how* they will be so in the future we do not know. For the moment, women still have a problematic place in both social and psychic representation. The problem for women of woman-as-sign has made the self-definition of women a resonant issue within feminism. It has also determined the restless inability of feminism to settle for humanist definitions of the subject, or for materialism's relegation of the problem to determinations of class only. I have emphasized in this chapter some of the more negative ways in which the Enlightenment and Romantic paradigms of subjectivity gave hostages to the making of subordinate identities, of which femininity is the structuring instance. Although psychoanalytic theories of the construction of gendered subjectivity stress difficulty, antagonism, and contradiction as necessary parts of the production of identity, the concept of the unconscious and the psychoanalytic view of sexuality dissolve in great part the binary divide between reason and passion that dominates earlier concepts of subjectivity. They break down as well the moralism attached to those libidinal and psychic economies. Seen from this perspective, "individualism" has a different and more contentious history within feminism than it does in androcentric debates.

That is the history we must uncover and consider, in both its positive and its negative effects, so that we can argue convincingly for a feminist rehabilitation of the female psyche in non-moralized terms. Perhaps we can come to see it as neither sexual outlaw, social bigot, nor dark hiding-place for treasonable regressive femininity waiting to stab progressive feminism in the back. We must redefine the psyche as a structure, not as a content. To do so is not to move away from a feminist politics that takes race and class into account, but to move towards a fuller understanding of how social divisions and the inscription of gender are mutually secured and given meaning. Through that analysis we can work towards change.

Notes

1. Charlotte Brontë, *Jane Eyre*, Margaret Smith ed., London 1976, p. 110.

2. Ibid., p. 110–11.

3. Virginia Woolf, *A Room of One's Own*, Harmondsworth 1973, p. 70.

[4. Elaine Showalter, *A Literature of Their Own: British Women Novelists from Brontë to Lessing* Princeton, NJ., 1977, pp. 263–297.]

[5. Eastlake, Elizabeth, Lady. "*Vanity Fair* and *Jane Eyre*." *Quarterly Review* 84 (1848): 153–185, p. 174.]

6. Brontë, *Jane Eyre*, p. 111.

7. Virginia Woolf, "Women and Fiction," in *Women and Writing*, Michèle Barrett, ed., London 1979, p. 47.

8. Ibid., p. 48.

The Advertisement of *Jane Eyre*

RONALD THOMAS

❖ ❖ ❖

I shall advertise.
—JANE EYRE

Promise me one thing. . . . Not to advertise: and trust
this quest of a situation to me. I'll find you one in time.
—EDWARD ROCHESTER

You, sir, are the most phantom-like of all: you are a
mere dream.
—JANE EYRE

"WE HAD VERY EARLY CHERISHED THE DREAM of one
day becoming authors," Charlotte Brontë wrote about
herself and her two younger sisters in a preface for *Wuthering
Heights*. "This dream never relinquished," she added, "it took the
character of resolve."[1] The dream was especially dear to Charlotte
Brontë, whose persistent and aggressive marketing of her own
and her sisters' manuscripts to publishers—sometimes in direct
opposition to Emily's wishes—was largely responsible for making
the dream come true. Even after her considerable efforts as literary "agent" managed to secure an agreement with a publisher,
Brontë insisted that more than the normal amount of money be
spent on advertising, agreeing to deduction of that amount from
the authors' expected royalties.[2] But this dream of authorship was
not the only one that drove her. Through much of her life her
sleep was disturbed by a recurrent dream of her two elder sisters,
Maria and Elizabeth, both of whom had died at Cowan Bridge
School, the model for what would become the Lowood School

of *Jane Eyre*. This dream and Charlotte Brontë's response to it are not unrelated to her consciously cultivated "dream" of becoming an author, and they may even provide a basis for understanding that dream and the dreams she later introduced into the book that made her the successful writer she so deeply desired to be.

Brontë first gave an account of her dream as a young girl, to her friend Mary Taylor, who later described the incident to Elizabeth Gaskell:

> She had told me, early one morning, that she had just been dreaming: she had been told that she was wanted in the drawing room, and it was Maria and Elizabeth. I was eager for her to go on, and when she said there was no more, I said, "But go on! *make it out.* I know you can." She said she would not; she wished she had not dreamed, for it did not go on nicely; they were changed; they had forgotten what they used to care for. They were very fashionably dressed, and began criticizing the room, etc.[3]

Brontë's refusal—or inability—to relate this dream fully was finally overcome when she wrote *Jane Eyre*, the novel she subtitled *An Autobiography*. Writing *Jane Eyre* provided Brontë with the opportunity to express her anger at the role the Cowan Bridge School played in her sisters' deaths. She was able to expose the cruelty of the institution and to purge it through its fictional incarnation as Brocklehurst's Lowood School. But in writing *Jane Eyre* Brontë was also able to tell a story in the first person of a young woman who—like her sisters in the dream—became rich and independent after lowly beginnings. By the end of the novel, Jane Eyre is not only an heiress; she is an entrepreneur as well, who has earned and advertised her way to financial and psychological independence. "I shall advertise," Jane informs Rochester when she mistakenly believes she will have to get another situation because he is to marry someone else (197). She had come to Thornfield by advertising herself, and by advertising herself she would leave it. But though Jane never has to take out another advertisement in the newspaper, when she returns to Rochester at the end of the novel, she is still advertising her independence to him: "I told you I am independent, sir, as well as rich," she says. "I am my own mistress" (383).

Jane's story of becoming her own mistress consistently links psychological independence and financial success. The literal accumulation of wealth becomes a metaphor for Jane's psychic development; she increasingly conceives of her own psychological processes in terms of an economic system. Jane's success on both counts turns on one critical avoidance: the marriage to Rochester does not take place, presumably because Jane discovers that Rochester is already married. For her to marry him would be a violation of law, and in terms of the dream of authorship and the hidden narrative plot, the marriage would also violate Jane's struggle to gain authority over her life by winning psychological and economic independence from all her "masters." Jane's equation of psychological well-being with financial security is evident in her declaration to Rochester about how she will function once they are married. "I will not be your English Céline Varens," she declares. "I shall continue to act as Adèle's governess; by that I shall earn my board and lodging, and thirty pounds a year besides. I'll furnish my own wardrobe out of that money, and you shall give me nothing but . . . your regard: and if I give you mine in return, that debt will be quit" (237). Whether she is describing her material or her moral disposition, Jane consistently represents her life as a series of such debts and payments, for which she makes the terms. Her dreams—two of which she insists on telling Rochester on the eve of the ill-fated wedding day—become the private capital upon which she draws to settle those bargains. They are an "inward treasure," providing her with the self-knowledge that ensures her own regard for herself and acquits her of any debts to anyone else (177).

Jane Eyre's dreams can become useful in the project of self-authorship only when she converts them into verbal representations of herself, when she makes them into personal "accounts." Jane's determination to tell her dreams to Rochester before marrying him contrasts dramatically with Charlotte's reluctance to tell a friend her childhood dream about the visit of her fashionable and contemptuous sisters. Whereas Charlotte's friend had to urge her to "go on" and "make it out," Jane demands that Rochester allow her to tell him her dreams, despite his active interference. "Let me talk undisturbed," she warns him; "hear me to the end" (246, 248). It is as if in *Jane Eyre* Charlotte Brontë was finally able to "make out" the dream that remained so unapproachable to her through much of her life. In writing her novel, she realizes with Jane that her most precious possession is her voice, her power to articulate her own story of herself from beginning to end without fearing competition from those who would disturb her tale or sell it short.[4] Brontë's reluctance to tell her disturbing dream seems to be rooted in the shame she felt when her apparently affluent sisters judged her as inadequately "fashionable." Brontë worked through that shame by writing this autobiography as a Cinderella story and a capitalist myth, the story of the dispossessed orphan child who earns her way to respectability and learns to give voice to the unconscious desires encoded in her dreams.

Critics have viewed Jane Eyre's story of acquiring power and independence from a number of perspectives. Terry Eagleton links the dialectical patterns of Jane's desire for mastery and her resistance to it with the social structures of capitalism. Helene Moglen has connected these desires to specific relationships in Brontë's family, and Dianne Sadoff has extended the analysis to the larger oedipal structures of desire operating in the nineteenth-century family. Sandra Gilbert and Susan Gubar, Margaret Homans, and other feminist critics have interpreted these issues as expressions of a feminist counterattack on an oppressive patriarchal system. Gayatri Spivak, however, interprets the politics of the novel as essentially repeating the model of imperial conquest practiced economically by the Masons and personally by Rochester's family in Jamaica.[5] I believe that the critique of desire central to all these interpretations is made possible because the novel conceives of and represents the self in essentially economic terms—specifically, in terms of a competitive marketplace of the mind. Over the course of her narrative, Jane increasingly comes to think of the dreams and desires of her "inner self" as entities in a marketplace over which she struggles to gain entrepreneurial control. This thinking not only reflects the dominant economic realities of Jane's life; it also anticipates the bourgeois model of the psyche which will be formalized by Freud at the end of the century.

The now-famous December 1848 review of *Jane Eyre* in the *Quarterly Review* condemned the author's "tone of mind and thought" as the same kind of thinking that had "overthrown authority" abroad and "fostered Chartism and rebellion at home."[6] This description of the author's psychology in terms of a radical economic movement is useful for understanding the dream psychology implicit in *Jane Eyre*. In the 1840s the debate over the English economy led to a controversy that eventuated in, among other things, the transformation of the problem of poverty from a social condition to a psychological state. Increasingly in this debate, the discourse of the mind became intertwined with the discourse of money. In *The Idea of Poverty* Gertrude Himmelfarb demonstrates how developing *ideas* about the meaning of poverty largely eclipsed the *material fact* of poverty in nineteenth-century England. She traces an intricate ideological conflict that raged through the first half of the century among moralistic, sentimental, and scientific treatments of economic problems and among the competing models of Adam Smith, Thomas Malthus, and Henry Mayhew for what was more and more regarded as the wasted productive resource of the poor. Ironically, Himmelfarb concludes, "just at the time when the poor were finally relieved of the stigma of pauperism," Mayhew came along at midcentury "with the most laudable of intentions and the most generous of sympathies" and "inflicted upon the poor a new stigma," the interpretation of economic poverty as a "moral, psychological, and cultural poverty" that was even more debilitating than the harsh material conditions the poor suffered.[7] This conception of one's economic condition as a state of mind led directly to the conception of one's state of mind as an economic condition. In *Jane Eyre*, the "tone of mind and thought" adopted by the narrative voice in making her life story out of her dream accounts, reflects (as Freud would later say) "an *economic* view of mental processes."[8]

Jane's identification of herself as a figure in the marketplace—

at once capital, labor, and commodity in a series of economic exchanges—not only acts as a representation of a material fact and as a metaphor for the psyche. It is expressed in the narrative form her novel assumes as well. In each of the settings where her story takes her, Jane is confronted with a narrative competitor who attempts to take her story from her. In every case those narrators seek to silence Jane and assign her a passive role in the story of her life, subordinating her to their own designs, absorbing her in narratives in which she serves their ends. Like Rochester, these linguistic competitors are also always economic superiors who wield their verbal power over her by virtue of some financial advantage they possess.

Jane is first abused by her "benefactress" Aunt Reed, then maligned by the "treasurer and manager" of Lowood School, deceived and exploited by her master and employer, and finally manipulated by her "charitable" clergyman cousin. Jane's resistance to these narrative competitors and her reversal of their financial advantage constitute the hidden plot of *Jane Eyre*. She overpowers each of them when she refuses and exposes their false narratives and, at the same time, reconfigures the terms of their economic relationship with her. In every case, the reversal is accompanied by a dream or dreamlike vision to which Jane gives voice and by which she defines herself.[9] The business of Jane's self-narrated novel aims at giving an account of these dreams and thereby taking and retaining possession of the privilege of telling her own story. In the dream of her dead sisters, Charlotte Brontë is "told that she is wanted" in the drawing room. In the dream accounts of *Jane Eyre*, the dreamer does the telling and finally determines where she is wanted and what she wants. Just before Jane recounts her two disturbing dreams to Rochester on the eve of the wedding that will not take place, she tells him that he is "a mere dream" (245). By so identifying him, she takes control over him and his mystifications of her. But she also takes control of her own unconscious, implicitly recognizing that Rochester is the embodiment of her desires as well as the obstacle to achieving them. In his present position of mastery, he is a force she must manage if she is not to be managed by him.

The hidden plot of competition for the right to be the author of the story is made known on the very first page of the novel when Jane is ostracized by her adoptive family for the things she says and the way she says them. Mrs. Reed identifies herself as the first narrative competitor in the first words spoken to Jane in the novel, when her aunt reprimands Jane for being a "caviller" and a "questioner," commanding her: "Until you can speak pleasantly, remain silent" (5). The injunction to silence is the fundamental threat Jane faces throughout the novel, and it is consistently tied to her financial dependency. "You are less than a servant," one of the servants reproves her, "for you do nothing for your keep" (9). Another servant immediately reinforces the reproof and urges Jane to keep her thoughts to herself. "You ought to be aware, Miss, that you are under obligations to Mrs. Reed: she keeps you: if she were to turn you off, you would have to go to the poor-house" (10). "They will have a great deal of money," Jane is told of the Reed children, "and you will have none: it is your place to be humble, and to try to make yourself agreeable to them" (10).

For Jane, this "reproach of my dependence" is "painful and crushing." She recognizes from the start that her silencing is a function of this impoverishment. So she resolves very early that she will neither "do nothing" nor be "kept." She will live her life on her own terms, whatever the cost. Eventually, she reverses the prophecy of her poverty. Jane returns to this household when her benefactress is dying and her tyrannical cousin John has already died in bankruptcy. Her summons to the house comes after she dreams a recurrent dream in which she is accompanied by a phantom infant whose wailing she silences. When she arrives at Gateshead, her tormenting cousin, John Reed, has been silenced; he has slit his own throat. Driven to distraction by her dissolute son's incessant demands for money, Mrs. Reed confesses her cruelty to Jane and dreams on her own deathbed of her son with that mortal wound in his throat. Jane's fortunes, however, are on the rise; and she proceeds to dream of her own increasing eloquence as the Reeds are rendered more and more silent. Throughout the novel, this pattern of a dream of silence, an articulated dream account, and a financial reversal by Jane continues to bring her into possession of her own voice and fortune. Like the dreams of *Frankenstein* or *Wuthering Heights*, Jane Eyre's dreams embody the desire for a language to express them. Unlike the dreams of those novels, however, these manifest a desire for a language that profits the dreamer instead of merely healing her.

As is the case with all of Jane's narrative rivalries, her battle with the Reeds takes place most profoundly on the level of language. When Jane rebels against their mastery, she is reproved by Mrs. Reed's "emphatic voice," which confines her to her room and forbids her to "utter one syllable" (23). Jane cannot bear this unjust prohibition; she challenges Mrs. Reed "as if my tongue pronounced words without my will consenting to their utterance: something spoke out of me over which I had no control" (23). The whole of Jane Eyre's story relates how she gains control over this "something," how she comes into possession of this voice that speaks out of her unconscious. Here at the outset of her tale, Jane seems already to be naturally aware of the issue that will form the center of her dreams—the importance of preserving her own voice and of refusing others' descriptions of her and her experience.

Later, when Jane is interrogated by Brocklehurst, and Mrs. Reed banishes her once more to silent confinement in her room, Jane again "retaliates" with words. "*Speak* I must," she declares, and she "launches" a single "blunt sentence" that asserts the truth of her own self-description and the deceit of the Reeds (30–31). Jane describes this verbal counterattack in military terms as "the hardest battle I had fought and the first victory I had gained" (32). She is provoked into it, she says, by Brocklehurst's presentation to her of a book about the "awfully sudden death" of a young girl who is "addicted to falsehood and deceit" (30). By rejecting this book, which Brocklehurst and her aunt imply is a prospective narrative of her own fate, Jane rejects both their accusations and their threats to reform her. "I am not deceitful," she declares to Mrs. Reed. "If I were, I should say I loved you; but I declare I do not love you . . . and this book about the liar, you may give to your girl, Georgiana, for it is she who tells lies,

and not I" (30–31). Throughout her story, Jane insists on being
the only source of truth about herself. This incident is fundamental because in it she refuses a book in which her life is threatened and the truth of her voice is questioned. In the psychological
terms of Jane's story, these two things are equivalent. When Jane
declares that Georgiana must play the character of the liar in this
book, she assumes authority over her usurpers. Then, having
made her eloquent defense by telling a narrative of her life in
which she accuses her "benefactress" of cruelty and deception,
Jane explicitly declares her narrative power and warns her accus-
ers, "I will tell anybody who asks me questions this exact tale"
(31). "This exact tale" becomes a chapter in the book Jane writes
and in which she plays the truth-telling hero rather than the
lying victim.

This successful claim to authority is preceded by a dream, setting the pattern for the rest of Jane's story. At the climax of her
panic when she is confined in the red room by Aunt Reed, Jane
falls asleep and has the first of her dreams, a terrifying nightmare
of which she never gives a complete account. "I suppose I had a
species of fit," she says at the end of the second chapter; "unconsciousness closed the scene." "The next thing I remember,"
she says in opening the following chapter, "is waking up with a
feeling as if I had had a frightful nightmare, and seeing before
me a terrible red glare, crossed with thick black bars" (15). The
nightmare Jane refers to but does not tell is locked behind those
bars, inaccessible even to her. Its content is hidden in the blank
space between these two chapters of her life. But Jane's verbal
assault on the Reeds after she awakens may be regarded as the
displaced account of this dream. A voice, Jane says, "spoke out
of me over which I had not control" (23). The fantasies Jane
indulges in immediately before her dream suggest that her suppressed dream is concerned with the preservation of this voice.
As she is about to go to sleep in the dreamlike space of the red
room, Jane sees a beam of light move across the wall: "I began
to recall what I had heard of dead men, troubled in their graves
by the violation of their last wishes, revisiting the earth to punish
the perjured and avenge the oppressed. . . . I wiped my tears and

hushed my sobs, fearful lest any sign of violent grief might waken a preternatural voice to comfort me. . . . This idea, consolatory in theory, I felt would be terrible if realised: with all my might I endeavored to stifle it—I endeavored to be firm" (13–14). What Jane fears most in this fantasy is a voice, an alien voice, which, even though theoretically reassuring, in fact threatens her. Jane "endeavored to stifle" the voice that would direct her like Hamlet's ghost, just as she stifles the dream that follows it. Since she has been the victim of so many tyrannical voices already, she instinctively refuses the wishes even of a benevolent voice here. Unlike Hamlet, who pursues his ghost and bids it, "Speak, I am bound to hear" (1.5.7), Jane will be bound by no speech but her own. She censors the content of this alien, "preternatural voice" from her consciousness as well as from her readers.

Jane begins the chapter that recounts her exile and nightmare in the red room by saying, "I resisted all the way" (9). This resistance to authority provokes the dream, and it also causes her to censor it. Whatever the manifest content of the dream, the entire dream event bespeaks Jane's resistance to an authoritative voice from outside herself and the assertion of her own. Specifically, Jane resists the interpretation of her dream as a *ghostly* voice, as the utterance of some "spirit" or "preternatural voice" that originates "in the church vault, or in the unknown world of the departed" (13).[10] The meaning of the nightmare for Jane is clear even though it remains unspoken: she refuses the gothic dream of an alien presence and transforms it into an expression from her own "unconsciousness" which empowers her to speak for herself. Jane proleptically identifies this as a dream of her own authority when she sees herself in the mirror, immediately before the dream, in the form of a fiction to be narrated: "All looked colder and darker in that visionary hollow than in reality: and the strange little figure there gazing at me with a white face and arms specking the gloom, and glittering eyes of fear moving where all else was still, had the effect of a real spirit: I thought it like one of the tiny phantoms, half fairy, half imp, Bessie's evening stories represented as coming out of lone, ferny dells in moors, and appearing before the eyes of belated travellers" (11).

Jane's realization of herself as a character, as a being from a story, provokes her unconscious determination also to be the teller of her story and thereby to control the part she plays in that story. By resisting the phantom voice, she resists being the "tiny phantom" these narrative competitors try to make her. If Jane is to have any authentic identity of her own, she will have to escape the control and manipulation of the Reeds—and everyone else who tells her who she is—by defining herself. As Jane demonstrates in her treatment of the dream in the red room, to define oneself is not necessarily to reveal oneself; rather it is to have control over the information by which one presents oneself to the world.[11]

Jane tells us that her vision of herself in the mirror caused the "violent tyrannies" of the Reed family to roll through her "disturbed mind like a dark deposit in a turbid well" (11, 12). She resents Georgiana's deceptive beauty, which is able to "purchase indemnity for every fault," and John's cruel greed, which "spoiled" his own family without any cost to himself (12). Jane figures this "deposit" of resentful dream thoughts in economic terms, and she seems to convert them in her nightmare into psychological capital that she invests in her own self-assertion, first to the sympathetic doctor Mr. Lloyd and then to Brocklehurst and the Reeds themselves. "Poverty looks grim to grown people," Jane reflects to herself as she tells the doctor her story of abuse; "still more so to children: they have not much idea of industrious, working, respectable poverty; they think of the word only as connected with ragged clothes, scanty food, fireless grates, rude manners, and debasing vices: poverty for me was synonymous with degradation" (20). But Jane's poverty is a state of mind as well as a material condition. When she adds that she "was not heroic enough to purchase liberty at the price of caste," she equates her liberty with her psychological enrichment and continues to establish a sense of self that is construed in economic terms, as a series of purchases, deposits, and payments. Whereas Jane's self-assertion after her nightmare results in another banishment   this time to Lowood School—what seems like a defeat for her in the manifest plot is a victory in the hidden plot. Her strong statement enables Jane to escape the exploitative voices of the Reeds, educate herself, and gain a profession. When she returns to the Reeds she is earning a living. They are not only impoverished but dead or dying or confined. Jane stifles their voices in her nightmare and, as her subsequent dream accounts indicate, also converts her encounters with them into the material that allows her to speak for herself.[12]

The red-room scene in which Jane dreams of resisting an alien voice and subsequently deploys her own voice to preserve herself is played out in a more dramatic dream event at Lowood School, when Jane goes to sleep beside the dying Helen Burns and awakes alone. The account of this event, like the one that preceded it, is strategically presented by Jane. She reveals her strategy at the opening of the chapter in which she records the results of that event: "This is not to be a regular autobiography," she admits. "I am only bound to invoke memory where I know her responses will possess some degree of interest" (72). Jane recognizes that *she* will determine what accumulates interest in this account and that the privilege of representing or refusing to represent her past is *her* possession. Jane's account of the death of Helen is a case in point: it accomplishes the disempowerment of Brocklehurst in Lowood, Jane's assumption of professional authority in the institution, and her eventual independence from it as well. Helen Burns is a kind of dreamy double for Jane throughout her time at Lowood; her removal from the text at the moment of Jane's awakening is a sign of Jane's complete rejection of this oppressed voice. The image of Helen may remain with Jane and be resurrected in the form of her subsequent nightmares of infantile helplessness, but as quiet and harmless as Helen Burns appears, she must be stifled as firmly as Jane's other oppressive nightmare.

Helen, who has put her faith in a heavenly economy, has no investment in the earthly one. "Hush, Jane!" she says in response to Jane's criticism of Brocklehurst; "the sovereign that created your frame, and put life into it has provided you with other resources than your feeble self" (60). But Jane is convinced that her only resource is herself. When Helen adds that "besides this earth, and besides the race of men, there is an invisible world and a kingdom of spirits," Jane hears the ghostly voice of her red-room dream, a voice she knows she must resist and convert into a resource for her own voice. But Helen chooses to divest herself of her own resources. She accepts the "untidy" badge that defines her as a "Slattern," which Miss Scatcherd forces her to wear "like a phylactery" around her forehead (64). Helen merely repeats this one-word story of her life. She even urges Jane to take the same course. "Learn from me," she instructs Jane, "not to judge from appearances. I am, as Miss Scatcherd said, slatternly; I seldom put, and never keep, things in order; I am careless; I forget rules; I read when I should learn my lessons; I have no method; and sometimes I say, like you, I cannot bear to be subjected to systematic arrangements. This is all very provoking to Miss Scatcherd, who is naturally neat, punctual, and particular" (48). Helen adopts Miss Scatcherd's voice and vocabulary here in accounting for herself, sacrificing her own words in favor of those systematic arrangements that "the sovereign" has placed over her. As far as Helen is concerned, she is "as Miss Scatcherd said" she is. When she is falsely accused, she refuses to make any explanation to exonerate herself. No wonder the outspoken Jane "wondered at her silence" (46).

Even before she dies, Helen collaborates with her erasure from this world by withdrawing from it into a dream world. During her lessons, she tells Jane, "I fall into a sort of dream" (49). "When I should be listening to Miss Scatcherd, and collecting all she says with assiduity, often I lose the very sound of her voice." But the sound of Miss Scatcherd's voice and of the others that dominate Helen are the places in which she has lost herself. They have made Helen begin to speak of herself in the third person, writing herself out of her own life story. Helen is not only Jane's silenced dream-self, she is an example of something that Jane must not allow her dreams to become: mere escapist fantasies unconnected to her desires in this world. Appropriately, then, both Helen and Jane fall asleep in the same bed, but only Jane awakes. "I was asleep, and Helen was—dead," Jane says, seeming to draw a casual relation (72). Like Helen, Jane had been given a sign to wear at Lowood, a sign whose text had again questioned her authority over herself: it read "Liar." But unlike Helen, Jane resisted and transformed her sign of humiliation into a symbol of heroism. She retaliated on its author, Brocklehurst, by "telling all the story of my sad childhood" to Miss Temple, both vindicating her authority and exposing Brocklehurst as the liar (62). Jane retaliates once again when she awakens from the dream during which Helen dies; this time she helps provoke an inquiry that eventually costs Brocklehurst executive and financial control over the institution. Because of his "wealth and family connections," unfortunately, he remains treasurer of the school, but because Jane relies on the resources of her own story, he no longer exploits the school financially (72). In fact, he eventually puts Jane on the payroll.

The most severe potential threat Jane faces, however, is not Helen Burns but Bertha Mason. In an even more extreme way than Helen, Bertha is a silenced narrator, locked away, unable to tell her own story except in the occasional shrieks and cries that escape the attic at night. She is also a commodity, the "wealthy marriage" bargained for by Rochester's father to keep his son from being "a poor man" (268). The daughter of his father's business acquaintance, the beautiful but presumably insane Bertha Mason comes to Rochester with a fortune of thirty thousand pounds. For this sum she is sold to him, and the disinherited Rochester (who says he was "piqued" by his "competitors" to marry her) is bought off (269).[13] In Bertha Mason economic dependency and psychological incapacity are given their most literal equation. She is only Rochester's mad money, not the "partner" he had sought in marriage (268).

Like Helen, Bertha is a dream-self for Jane whose first view of her, like her last view of Helen, is in the bedroom—this time in the reflection of her own mirror. Bertha is seen putting on and then destroying the veil Jane was to wear as Rochester's bride. This visitation occurs directly after Jane has dreamed two foreboding dreams about her marriage to Rochester, and we learn of it when she tells those dreams to him. Rochester even tries to explain the vision of Bertha away as another dream of Jane's. He may, unwittingly, be close to the truth. Jane wakes from her dream to the dreamlike appearance of her silenced predecessor, warning her of the cost of marrying Rochester. This warning seems to act out the implications of the tapestry covering the doors that lead to Bertha Mason's cell, a depiction of Judas's betrayal of Christ for thirty pieces of silver. This silent narrative becomes Rochester's cover story for Bertha's life. Potentially, Jane is warned, it could also be hers. Like Jane's dreams, the tapestry signifies the reduction of the person who marries Rochester to a prisoner with a price on her head.

Even before her climactic dreams, Jane seems to be aware of this possibility. Immediately after his proposal, Jane notes that Rochester looks on her like a sultan viewing "a slave his gold and gems had enriched" (236). But Jane refuses to be commodified in this way as an object purchased by Rochester's wealth: "Don't consider me an equivalent for one; if you have a fancy for anything in that line, away with you sir, to the bazaars of Stamboul . . . and lay out in extensive slave-purchases some of that spare cash you seem at a loss to spend satisfactorily here" (236–37). The terms of Jane's and Rochester's cash relations have been strained from the start. As her employer, he seeks to control her by giving her less money than he owes her or to manipulate her by giving her more. He tries to get his money back when he learns she will use some of it to advertise for a new position after he marries. Unable to persuade her to surrender her wages, he tries to extort from her a promise that she will *not* advertise but allow him to find her a new place. But Jane maintains control of herself, refusing his gifts and insisting on her due. After offering to be her "banker" for some of the money he owes her, Rochester asks Jane at least to let him "look at the cash" he has just paid her. But she holds firm: "No sir," she says; "you are not to be trusted" (197–98).

The essential economic configuration of Jane and Rochester's relationship is given symbolic form by Rochester himself when he masquerades as a gypsy fortune-teller and charges Jane a shilling for the privilege of hearing her life story told for her. He proposes to "read" Jane's face and hands for a sum, to treat her as a "customer" with whom to make "deals" (172). At the same time, he refers to her as a mysterious text that tells a silent "tale" only he can narrate (176). In so doing, Rochester reveals his deep intentions. He desires to be the voice of Jane's experience, to represent her life before it is lived, and thereby to gain ownership of it. He admits as much when, in the voice of the gypsy, he anticipates Jane's resistance to the fortune he reads in her. Looking into her eyes, he articulates what she might be thinking when he affirms her need for a partner in love. "I need not sell my soul to buy bliss," he hears her saying. "I have an inward treasure, born with me, which can keep me alive if all extraneous delights should be withheld; or offered only at a price I cannot afford to give" (177). Rochester is on the mark. Jane does not resist thinking of her inner self as an economy; she only refuses to be sold short or overcharged. Jane herself describes this entire event as "a kind of dream" in which the gypsy's words sounded like "the speech of my own tongue." "Did I wake or sleep?" she asks herself. "Had I been dreaming? Did I dream still?" (175, 177). Thus far, all Jane's dreams and quasi dreams offer her either a silenced person (Helen or Bertha) who is a threatening model for herself and whom she must therefore resist or the opposite, a powerful voice (Mr. Reed's ghost or Rochester) that might speak for her and therefore must be suppressed if Jane is to be author of her own story. Jane's literal dreams throughout the novel increasingly enable her to realize what these earlier dreams and dreamlike events figure for her: she desires to dictate the terms of her psychological independence herself, to make her "inward treasure" her own "fortune."

This desire becomes explicit in the central dream events of the novel, narrated by Jane to Rochester on the night before they are to marry. Jane begins her account by telling Rochester her thoughts on the day before she dreams, explaining her resentment and anxiety over his attempts to manipulate her with his wealth. Jane tells him how when she opened his gift of an expensive wedding veil, she realized it was intended to "cheat me into accepting something as costly" as the previous gifts, which she had refused. "I smiled as I unfolded it, and devised how I would tease you about your aristocratic tastes, and your efforts to masque your plebeian bride in the attributes of a peeress" (247). Jane knows that the veil only masks the reality of an economic barrier between them and that the economic reality corresponds to a psychological barrier that divides them as well. Despite Rochester's attempts to interrupt and dismiss her narrative, Jane insists he let her "talk undisturbed," and she begins to tell the first of her dreams, in which she pictures this "barrier dividing us":

> On sleeping, I continued in dreams the idea of a dark and gusty night. I continued also the wish to be with you, and experienced a strange, regretful consciousness of some barrier dividing us. During all my first sleep, I was following the windings of an unknown road; total obscurity environed me; rain pelted me; I was burdened with the charge of a little child: a very small creature, too young and feeble to walk, and which shivered in my cold arms and wailed piteously in my ear. I thought, sir, that you were on the road a long way before me; and I strained every nerve to overtake you, and made effort on effort to utter your name and entreat you to stop—but my movements were fettered, and my voice died away inarticulate; while you, I felt, withdrew farther and farther every moment. (247–48)

The barrier, of course, is in one sense the fettered Bertha Mason, whose voice, once purchased, has also died away inarticulate (and, incidentally, whose financial victimization foreshadows Jane's). The child that Jane has charge of in the dream seems in its inarticulate wailing to warn Jane against following Rochester and suffering Bertha's fate. The child also connects this dream to the other Jane dreamed just before she returned to, and triumphed over, the Reeds. In addition to representing her desire to cease being an inarticulate and dependent child, this dream-child has a number of other resonances: it could represent the new self that Jane will become in marrying Rochester or Jane's own neglected childhood or even the silenced Helen Burns. According to Margaret Homans these multiple associations suggest that the threat the dream represents is tied not to any particular part of Jane's self the child represents, but to the general danger of Jane's self-fragmentation.[14] I concur, but wish to emphasize that Jane's fragmentation here is attributable, as it has been before, to the thing that Jane's dream-self and her dream-infant have in common: their inability to speak authoritatively and articulately.

Jane's second dream of the unknown child and her presentation of it to Rochester both emphasize this point. Before Jane is able to tell her second dream to Rochester, he interrupts her again by urging her to repeat his own teasing words of love; she meets this request with an assertion of her right to tell her own story first: "I will tease you and vex you to your heart's content, when I have finished my tale," she tells him, "but hear me to the end" (248). Jane knows that she must articulate her inner fears and desires, and the second dream she tells is really an elaboration of the first, an expression of her desire that her voice not die away without articulating her own independence, financial and psychological:

> I dreamt another dream, sir: that Thornfield Hall was a dreary ruin, the retreat of bats and owls. I thought that of all the stately front nothing remained but a shell-like wall, very high and very fragile-looking. I wandered, on a moonlight night, through the grass-grown enclosure within: here I stumbled over a marble hearth, and there over a fallen fragment of cornice. Wrapped up in a shawl, I still carried the unknown little child: I might not lay it down anywhere, however tired were my arms—however much its weight impeded my progress, I must retain it. I heard the gallop of a horse at a distance on the road; I was sure it was you; and you were departing for many years, and for a distant country. I climbed the thin wall with frantic, perilous haste, eager to catch one-glimpse of you from the top: the stones rolled from under my feet, the ivy branches I grasped gave way, the child clung round my neck in terror, and almost strangled me: at last I gained the summit. I saw you like a speck on a white track, lessening every moment. The blast blew so strong I could not stand. I sat down on the narrow ledge; I hushed the scared infant in my lap: you turned an

angle of the road: I bent forward to take a last look; the
wall crumbled; I was shaken; the child rolled from my knee,
I lost my balance, fell, and woke. (248–49)

The child that "wailed piteously" in Jane's ear, an emblem of her
own threatened narrative voice, is still cradled protectively by Jane
in this second dream. "However much its weight impeded my
progress," Jane tells Rochester, seeming to intuit the significance
of this unknown "charge," "I must retain it." This dream is more
than a symbolic representation of her present danger and her
determination to retain possession of her narrative voice. The
dream also expresses Jane's desire for the "ruin" of Rochester—
the very leveling of their economic differences that will later be
accomplished by Bertha Mason's rage. When Jane reaches the
summit in her dream, she sees Rochester "lessening" as she rises;
in this she seems both to desire and to predict Rochester's pay-
ment of the charges incurred by his veiled dealings with her. In
her dream, Jane sees what she will be told about later: Rochester
amidst "an immense quantity of valuable property destroyed"
(375).

The two desires appear inextricably linked in the dream. Jane
must be financially independent of Rochester in order to maintain her narrative control over her life. But the dream also figures
a conflict in Jane's desires. She remains tempted by his mastery
over her—she wants to follow him down the road he travels.[13]
Jane feels a perilous attraction to surrendering her life to his
authority. But to this seduction she does not yield. The cost of
giving in to such a desire would be the loss of the child and the
strangling of Jane's own voice. The child's destiny has consistently
been identified with Jane's, and in this dream she falls to the
ground as the child falls from her grasp. The more powerful
desire expressed in the dream is Jane's desire to retain possession
of this child and her own voice, superseding even her desire to
be with Rochester. This stronger desire was already expressed in
an earlier dream in which Jane sees Miss Ingram "closing the gates
of Thornfield against me and pointing me out another road"
(213). Eventually, Jane must take that other road—away from

Thornfield, the symbol of her economic and psychological servitude. And when she sees Rochester in this dream as "lessening every moment," she sees his power and fortune as diminished to precisely the degree they will be at the end of her story.

Rochester seeks to silence Jane as soon as she has narrated the two dreams, dismissing them first as "unreal" and then as, at best, confused notions, "half dream, half reality" (250–51). But Jane persists in valuing her dreams as integral aspects of her reality: the dreams have been, she says, "all the preface, sir; the tale is yet to come" (249). And as Jane tells of Bertha Mason's appearance in her looking glass (knowing, somehow, that the incident must follow her dreams as the text to which they were the preface), she recalls her nightmare in the red room and challenges Rochester to identify the strange visitor. Once he reassures (or warns) Jane by saying, "I must be careful of you, my treasure," Rochester tries to pass off the mysterious guest as the servant Grace Poole. But Jane is not satisfied, and will not be until she learns the true identity of her visitor the following day. Jane's attention to her dreams as *her own* psychic treasure helps protect her from becoming another treasure in the possession of Rochester. In this dream, she retains what Freud would call "the capital" of her "unconscious wishes" by asserting the power of her own voice in the place of the alien voice she had repressed in the red-room dream. She makes out of her own mind what she earlier had expressed a desire for in financial terms. "If I had ever so small an independency," she had wished to herself, "if I had but a prospect of one day bringing Mr. Rochester an accession of fortune, I could better endure to be kept by him now" (236). In her account of this dream, Jane asserts her independence and makes both a "treasure" and "fortune" of herself.

The next dream Jane recounts occurs immediately after she has discovered the truth about Bertha Mason's identity. Her marriage made impossible by the discovery of another Mrs. Rochester, Jane must decide whether to leave Thornfield and follow her own path or accept Rochester's latest offer—to keep her as his mistress. Now she dreams of herself in the presence not of an un-

known and "piteously wailing child" but of a radiant and articulate female form:

> I dreamt I lay in the red-room at Gateshead; that the night
> was dark, and my mind impressed with strange fears. The
> light that long ago had struck me into syncope, recalled in
> this vision, seemed glidingly to mount the wall, and trem-
> blingly to pause in the centre of the obscured ceiling. I lifted
> up my head to look: the roof resolved to clouds, high and
> dim; the gleam was such as the moon imparts to vapours
> she is about to sever. I watched her come—watched with
> the strangest anticipation; as though some word of doom
> were to be written on her disk. She broke forth as never
> moon yet burst from cloud; a hand first penetrated the sable
> folds and waved them away; then, not a moon, but a white
> human form shone in the azure, inclining a glorious brow
> earthward. It gazed and gazed and gazed on me. It spoke
> to my spirit: immeasurably distant was the tone, yet so near,
> it whispered in my heart—"My daughter, flee temptation!"
> "Mother, I will."
> So I answered after I had waked from the trance-like
> dream. (281)

The fear of the "word of doom" does indeed recall the patriarchal,
"preternatural voice" that Jane stifled in the red-room nightmare.
It also recalls the powerful, passionate voice with which Rochester
tried to persuade Jane to remain in Thornfield as his "best reward"
(281). But those male voices are transformed here and replaced
by a female voice. The two female figures in the dream—a
mother and a daughter—recall Jane's more recent dreams of a
woman and child. As an orphan, Jane has no mother; she is her
own "author." And this dream-mother whom Jane has dreamed
up is herself, the mother of her voice, the guardian of her power
to resist the voices that seek to own her. In this dream, as in the
others, Jane is both mother and daughter. But now she speaks
clearly as an independent adult; she is no longer the helpless,
sobbing infant. Now Jane is the resplendent self she has created

from the light that flickered on the wall in the red room; and the word of doom which had to be stifled there has now become a word of salvation which Jane speaks to herself—whispers, as she says, "in my heart."

The gradual formation of Jane's vision of herself in this dream was anticipated in the paintings of female figures which she had earlier shown and described to Rochester. The images of those paintings are as surreal and fantastic as her dream, and Rochester even speculates that they are things Jane "must have seen in a dream" (111). One of the paintings depicts a "woman's shape" that resembles the "white human form" of the dream in startling detail: "The dim forehead was crowned with a star; the lineaments below were seen as through the suffusion of vapour; the eyes shone dark and wild; the hair streamed shadowy, like a beamless cloud torn by storm or by electric travail. On the neck lay a pale reflection like moonlight; the same faint lustre touched the train of thin clouds from which rose and bowed this vision of the Evening Star" (110).

Jane paints as she dreams—in images of power. She shows these female figures "crowned" in one case "with a star" and in another "with a ring of white flame" in the "likeness of a Kingly crown" (110–11). Yet, like the images of a dream, they were not available as sources of self-understanding or power for Jane. "In each case," she laments," I had imagined something which I was quite powerless to realise" (111). But the voice spoken in the last dream seems to enable Jane to realize that power in her life. The continuities between the images articulated in Jane's dream accounts and those pictured in her paintings converge in the final verbal assertion that concludes this last dream, an assertion by which she assumes control of her own life: "I will." Jane's final dream account in the novel ends with the words that both awaken her and affirm her power to act independently. The same words that could have been spoken as a wedding vow to Rochester, declare her independence from him instead. Here, they literally reduce her to poverty, but psychologically they bring her into possession of herself.

Jane finds it almost impossible to recount the ensuing period of economic destitution which was the cost of her decision to leave Rochester. She attributes the difficulty of relating this part of her tale not so much to physical suffering as to the attendant "moral degradation" brought by her poverty. Once again, Jane translates her economic condition into a metaphor for her psychological condition. She explains that the old woman who refused her offer to exchange a handkerchief for a loaf of the woman's bread might be right—"if the offer appeared to her sinister, or the exchange unprofitable" (289). Jane has herself recently refused a sinister and, she knows, ultimately unprofitable offer from Rochester. But her refusal has been costly and has strained her stock of psychic capital. "I am sick of the subject," Jane says as she begins to recount this period of her poverty. "Let me condense now" (289). In her dream accounts, Jane has already provided a condensed narrative of her psychic economy. In the condensed narrative that follows those dreams, Jane realizes both her material and her psychological fortune.

When Jane is finally saved from destitution by the "charity" of the Rivers family, she makes it clear from the outset that she must be "independent" of it as soon as possible: "Show me how to work, or how to seek work: that is all I now ask" (306). Like the other figures Jane must resist in her journey toward self-possession, St. John Rivers endangers Jane on more than a merely economic level: he threatens her authority over herself. Indeed, his is a more radical threat than Rochester's because the plot in which he attempts to absorb Jane would not only change her name but deny her access to her own desires and invert the terms by which she has learned to define herself. The "religious plot" St. John espouses is the most fraudulent of all, a more sophisticated version of the divine economy of Brocklehurst and Helen Burns. "I can offer you but a service of poverty and obscurity," he tells Jane. "*You* may even think it degrading," he says, recognizing her equation of poverty with psychic degradation. He then proceeds simply to turn the equation around. For the "Christian labourer," he explains to her, "the scantier the meed his toil brings—the higher the honour" (311). But the hypocrisy of this inversion is exposed in St. John's rhetoric when, after Jane has become an heir, he urges her to leave her job as a teacher— "turning to profit the talents which God has committed to your keeping" (344). Then, when he argues against her dividing her inheritance with him and his sisters, he bases his appeal upon the "importance twenty thousand pounds would give" in attracting a husband.

Jane knows that more than her bank account would be stolen away under such circumstances and she sees that St. John is commodifying her with his remarks just as Rochester did to Bertha: "I will not be regarded in the light of a mere money speculation," she reproves him (341). Finally, when he proposes to Jane that she marry him and prudently invest her riches by joining his mission to India, St. John's deceptive masking of the discourse of capitalism with the sentiment of Christianity is made clear: "A part of me you must become," he tells her; "otherwise the whole bargain is void" (359). With this, Jane is able to see through this "bargain" and recognize its cost. It is an "offer" motivated by a "counterfeit sentiment," she tells him. "I scorn you when you offer it" (359). His spirituality is exposed as a counterfeit currency with which St. John seeks to purchase her authority over herself, and Jane will not be taken in by it.

Yet, despite her strong resistance to his offer, St. John almost prevails in getting Jane to agree to the bargain. She frees herself from his uncanny power only after she has another dream and makes another verbal assertion of her authority over that dream. Like her other narrative competitors, St. John expressed a linguistic threat. He begins by compelling her to learn Hindustani, the exotic language that only he speaks, so Jane may speak only to him. "He acquired a certain influence over me that took away my liberty of mind," Jane confesses as she begins to speak the new language. "I could no longer talk or laugh freely when he was by" (350). His voice clearly gains ascendancy over her own as Jane realizes that his "freezing spell" is produced by the words he speaks. "I trembled to hear some fatal words spoken which would at once declare and rivet the spell," Jane says when St. John almost persuades her to take up his offer (354). And when she responds to his coercion with the reply, "My heart is mute," his "deep relentless voice" claims, "Then I must speak for it" (354).

As in *Frankenstein* or *Wuthering Heights*, the religious language that would "speak for" an unarticulated self must be resisted and replaced by another explanatory vocabulary. Here, however, the cleric St. John even indicates what that other language might be—the language of the marketplace. This economic discourse is perhaps most dramatically demonstrated when he informs Jane of her inheritance. He reveals that he knows her true identity and offers her the legacy of twenty thousand pounds in the course of telling her own life story for her: "I find the matter will be better managed by my assuming the narrator's part, and converting you into a listener," he tells her (334). It is as if the family inheritance is being offered to Jane at the price of "converting" her from the author of her own story into a listener to it, and the conversion is "managed" by the clergyman-executor St. John. Jane seems to sense the danger in this arrangement, noting that the way she has learned this information is "a very strange piece of business" (337). Her decision to divide the inheritance with her cousins is not only a mark of her own generosity and gratitude but a strategy by which she can both accept the money and retain control over her business. Once again, she dictates the terms of the agreement. Later, when Jane is once again at the brink of succumbing to St. John's plan for her life, he repeats the same offer in a subtler and more powerful form, reading to her from Scripture the promise that those who follow Christ "shall inherit all things" if they acknowledge their names to be "already written in the Lamb's book of life" (367). This time, a *spiritual* inheritance is offered. But once again, it is offered in exchange for authority over Jane's self, for the privilege of writing her name.

Only Jane's voice stands between her and this final threat. And only the intervention of the powerful voice that calls her name enables Jane to avoid St. John's pressure. Strangely enough, Jane at first identifies the mysterious yet familiar voice as belonging to Rochester, miraculously summoning her across the miles that separate them. His inexplicable account of the same night seems to reinforce this uncanny interpretation. At this critical point in the narrative, the novel seems to be its most traditionally "gothic." But Jane manages to convert her supernatural hypothesis into a psychological one when she realizes that this voice that speaks only her name "seemed in *me*—not in the external world" (371). She finally theorizes that it must have been some "nervous impression" or "delusion" from her own mind which "opened the doors of the soul's cell" and "wakened it out of its sleep" in the form of this voice (371). Jane interprets the voice as the awakening and freeing of her inner self, then, the expression of her own unconscious desires, which instinctively spoke out of her dreams from the start. The voice articulates her demand that she be free to be herself—to be Jane and not Mrs. Rivers *or* Mrs. Rochester. Through the agency of Jane's dream plot, the "preternatural voice" of her first dream has been converted into *her* charge, *her* possession, *her* authority over herself.

Her interpretation of the mysterious inner voice that Jane had initially thought to be Rochester's is also a delayed dream account. The final dreams of her autobiography occur just a few pages earlier. In a series of "strange" and "agitated" dreams, Jane finds herself involved in "some exciting crisis," "amidst unusual scenes, charged with adventure, with agitating risk and romantic chance." Then she dreams that she meets Rochester, that in "hearing his voice . . . the hope of passing a lifetime at his side, would be renewed, with all its first force and fire" (323). In her climactic encounter with St. John, Jane projects the repressed desire expressed in her dream into her waking life. She hears Rochester's voice again and then converts it into an expression of her own identity. At this moment of crisis, Jane assumes the role of narrative voice in her own life, taking up all the voices that have sought to speak for her and making them aspects of her own hopes and desires.

Jane comes into her financial inheritance because she unconsciously writes her real name on the cover of her portrait pad, thus revealing her true identity to St. John. She comes into her narrative "inheritance" when she unconsciously speaks that name, simultaneously releasing herself from the bondage of St. John's voice, accounting for her dreams, and subsuming all other narrative voices to her own. In both cases, she has unconsciously "advertised" herself, as she had done intentionally in the newspaper advertisement that garnered her her first job. Jane's first written narrative of herself is in terms of a commodity in the marketplace. Her final verbal account in her autobiography is as a person in possession of herself. When Jane rejoins Rochester and announces to him, "I am independent, sir, as well as rich: I am my own mistress," her authority over her psychic and economic self is assured (383). Rochester acknowledges as much when he asks Jane to give him "the narrative of [her] experience" (387). Her "autobiography" is the account of her acquisition of the power to represent that experience as her own. Jane even describes her subsequent marriage to Rochester as an extended act of narration in which she manages his life as she has her own—by putting it into words: "For I was then his vision, as I am still his right hand. Literally, I was (what he often called me) the apple of his eye. He saw nature—he saw books through me; and never did I weary of gazing for his behalf, and of putting into words the effect of field, tree, town, river, cloud, sunbeam— of the landscape before us; of the weather round us—and impressing by sound on his ear what light could no longer stamp on his eye" (397). Here Jane essentially equates her marriage to Rochester with her writing of the book of his life together with her own. All their shared experience is mediated through her eyes and words. The story is entirely hers to tell, and Rochester is her character now. In completing this narrative, Jane has succeeded in fulfilling her long-held ambitions of being financially independent and telling her tale to the end. At the same time, Charlotte Brontë has managed to fulfill her dream of one day becoming an author by writing a book worthy of its advertisements.

But there is something unsettling about the product. The formulation of a self in terms of a competitive economic model incurs tremendous costs. The marriage of Jane (the wealthy narrator) to Rochester (the bankrupt and disabled listener) represents more a split than it does a union.[16] Jane has not really under-mined the pattern of economic and psychological monopoly which characterized her earlier life; she has simply gained control of the means of its production. The plot of the novel has been arranged in such a way that for Jane to win the position of nar-rative power, Rochester must either die (as Mrs. Reed, Helen Burns, and St. John Rivers must) or surrender that position of power to Jane—at the cost of his fortune, his eyesight, and his hand. "He cannot read or write much," Jane notes laconically at the end (397). So she does it for him, both literally and figura-tively. She may be a benevolent manager of Rochester's life, but benevolence, as Jane has already learned from St. John, may itself be a form of economic and psychological tyranny. The model of the unconscious mind as an entrepreneur seeking to earn and invest the capital of its own desires appears in *Jane Eyre* to be based upon a model of psychic scarcity in which self-interest necessarily destroys all competition and precludes anything like a just marital partnership. The world outside the self and all the individuals in it are thought of either as competitors that must be converted into suppliers or as consumers of the product the self manufac-tures and markets independently.

Jane Eyre may just as well be Charlotte Brontë's implicit critique of the social and economic oppression of women which charac-terized the patriarchal world in which she lived. It may even be a shout of radical protest against the more general injustice of the existing economic order in England in the period of the Chartist rebellions. But Brontë's novel may take part in a political act of another kind: the domestication and neutralization of po-litical and economic forces (like Chartism) by psychologizing them, by turning the materials of history into the materials of consciousness.[17] Regardless of the level of conscious control we can impute to Brontë and the political implications she may have intended for the novel, her deployment of the rhetoric of capi-talism to represent the inner self in *Jane Eyre* clearly attests to the increasing power of the nineteenth-century bourgeois conception of the psyche as a commodity in a marketplace, and to the trou-bling consequences of that conception as well. [Mikhail] Bakhtin would maintain that Freud's theory of the unconscious "very distinctly reflects the behavioral-ideological point of view of a petit bourgeois" and that the "inner speech" of the Freudian unconscious is "founded on the economic being" of the whole culture.[18] Brontë's novel of self-construction is a part of that cultural discourse, and the interpretation Brontë gives to the dreams of *Jane Eyre* anticipates those of the scientists in profound ways. . . .

Notes

1. Memoir of Ellis Bell prefixed to the Smith, Elder posthumous edition of Emily Brontë's *Works* (1850), quoted in Winifred Gérin, *Charlotte Brontë: The Evolution of Genius* (1967), p. 306.

2. See Gérin, *Charlotte Brontë*, p. 308. Charlotte wrote to Aylott and Jones 11 May [1846], urging them to spend more than the agreed £2 on advertising, "especially as the estimate is increased by nearly £5, in consequence, it appears of a mistake. If you do not object, the additional amount of the estimate can be remitted when you send in your account at the end of the first six months." The authors eventually agreed to contribute £31 10s. 0d. toward cost of publication (and later added another £5) and agreed to pay £2 for advertising in literary journals.

3. *The Brontës: Their Lives, Friendships, and Correspondence in Four Volumes*, ed. Thomas J. Wise and J. Alexander Symington (1933), 1:91. Quoted in Helene Moglen, *Charlotte Brontë: The Self Conceived* (1984), p. 23.

4. See Rosemarie Bodenheimer's valuable analysis of the way Jane places her story within a variety of fictional forms that are "partly to be used, partly to be exorcised and denied as limitations in the scope of Jane's character or Brontë's narrative powers" ("Jane Eyre in Search of Her Story," *Papers on Language and Literature* 16 [Fall 1980]: 387–402). See also Jerome Beaty, "*Jane Eyre* and Genre," *Genre* 10 (Winter 1977): 619–54.

5. See Terry Eagleton, *Myths of Power: A Marxist Study of the Brontës* (1975); Sadoff, *Monsters of Affection* (1982); Margaret Homans, "Dreaming of Children: Literalization in *Jane Eyre*," in her *Bearing the Word* (1986); Moglen, *Charlotte Brontë*; Gilbert and Gubar, *The Madwoman in the Attic* (1979); and Gayatri Chakrovorty Spivak, "Three Women's Texts and a Critique of Imperialism," *Critical Inquiry* 12 (Autumn 1985): 243–61. My reading employs the work of all these critics, shifting the emphasis to the rhetoric by which the self is "conceived" in the novel and the language and plot forms that embed an idea about how the psyche works.

6. Elizabeth Rigby, Review of *Jane Eyre, Quarterly Review* 84 (December 1848): 174.

7. Gertrude Himmelfarb, *The Idea of Poverty: England in the Early Industrial Age* (1985), p. 370.

8. Sigmund Freud, "Fixation to Traumas—the Unconscious," *Introductory Lectures on Psychoanalysis,* Standard Edition 16:275.

9. Robert Heilman's influential essay "Charlotte Brontë's 'New' Gothic" (reprinted in *The Brontës,* ed. Ian Gregor [1970]) maintains that the "new dimension of Gothic" that Charlotte Brontë discovered is at least partially evidenced in the use she makes of "strange, fearful symbolic dreams" in *Jane Eyre,* in which Brontë is "plumbing the psyche, not inventing a weird decor" (p. 99). Though I believe many gothic texts do the same thing, I agree that Brontë has extended this process considerably.

10. According to Herman Rapaport, in *"Jane Eyre* and the *Mot Tabou,"* *Modern Language Notes* 94 (December 1979): 1093–104, the ghostly voices in *Jane Eyre* can be traced to the absent "collective mother" of the text. "If one were to pursue a poetic of hauntedness," he claims, "of a text that disclosed disembodied voices, perhaps the voices of ancestors or departed lovers or of the damned, one might turn to Charlotte Brontë's *Jane Eyre"* (p. 1093). Rapaport sees the Reed ghost as "death re-inforced, at the same time that it is negated, revenged, mastered. And the ghost, that necessary accomplice, is acting here as signifier of desire, an imaginary agency facilitating the achievement of pleasure" (p. 1094). My reading is consistent with Rapaport's, except that I see Jane as making those disembodied voices her own through repression and rearticulation, and thereby essentially "mothering" herself.

11. In this regard, I agree with John Kucich's treatment of the role of repression in Charlotte Brontë's novels. "In fundamental ways," he says, "expression and repression cooperate and enhance each other by being identically opposed to direct self-revelation" (*Repression in Victorian Fiction* [1987], p. 47). As I show in this chapter, Jane's strategic use of dream accounts sometimes takes the form of expression and sometimes of repression.

12. Gilbert and Gubar assert that Charlotte Brontë intended the red-room incident as "paradigm of the larger drama that occupies the entire book," largely because Jane so often recalls the incident at crucial moments in her career (p. 341). I want to point out that its recollection is connected with dream experience in each case, and it is paradigmatic

in linking dream events with issues of authority (note both sets of dreams at Thornfield).

13. See Spivak, "Three Women's Texts."

14. Homans, *Bearing the Word*, p. 92.

15. In *Monsters of Affection*, Sadoff gives an elaborate and compelling psychoanalytic reading of the "dialectic of master and slave" in Brontë's work, which Sadoff connects with the persistent Brontëan figure of the punishing father whom the daughter wishes to please.

16. In "The Place of Love in *Jane Eyre* and *Wuthering Heights*," Mark Kinkead-Weekes links the limitation of the relationship between Jane and Rochester to the "remorseless concentration on the first-person creation of Jane," which denies Rochester a sense of being a "self in his own right" and reduces him to a "projection" or "focus" for Jane (p. 78). I believe that the essentially "capitalistic" psychic economy of the novel demands the same for all the other characters—that Jane either manages the capital of the story or is managed by someone else in it (see *The Brontës*, ed. Ian Gregor [1970]).

17. Nancy Armstrong argues this point effectively for the Victorian novel in general. She reads the novelistic creation of a language for the psychologically knowable self as a "feminization" of the subject, designed to "enclose certain cultural materials within a structure of consciousness that would further decontextualize and remove these materials from history" (*Desire and Domestic Fiction*, p. 225). Desire, she contends, becomes displaced in the novel from the political into the domestic, the sexual, and the psychological. But as we have seen in *Jane Eyre*, even these displacements can be encoded within a language that exposes the very political and economic conditions that are supposed to be suppressed.

18. Volosinov [Bakhtin], *Freudianism: A Marxist Critique*, pp. 89–90.

Excerpts from *Allegories of Empire*

JENNY SHARPE

◆　◆　◆

Slave as Emancipator

A slavish bondage to parents cramps every faculty of the
mind. . . . This strict hand may in some degree account for
the weakness of women . . . and thus taught slavishly to submit to their parents, they are prepared for the slavery of
marriage. (Mary Wollstonecraft, *A Vindication of the Rights of
Woman,* 1792)

Charlotte Brontë deploys the feminist metaphor of domestic slavery for staging one woman's rebellion against sexual and economic bondage. As an orphan and poor relation at Gateshead,
the young Jane has a social rank even lower than that of the
servants. When her cousin, John Reed, violently attacks her for
reading books that do not belong to her, she compares him to a
Roman slave driver: "You are like a murderer—you are like a
slavedriver—you are like the Roman emperors!" (*JE,* 8).[1] Her
triple denunciation makes public an analogy she had previously

kept to herself. Language assumes a force of its own, transforming her former passive resistance into active and open rebellion. The ten-year-old Jane, "like any other rebel slave . . . resisted all the way" (*JE*, 9). Subsequently punished for her unacceptable behavior, she is locked in the haunted red room where "the mood of the revolted slave" (*JE*, 11) keeps alive her sense of injustice. Unable to handle the unruly child any longer, Mrs. Reed decides to send her to the Lowood Institution for orphaned girls. Jane, increasingly compelled to voice her oppression, responds to her aunt's actions by accusing her of being a cruel and deceitful woman—an outburst that gives her "the strangest sense of freedom" (*JE*, 31). This opening scene, with its movement from bondage to freedom and from an imposed silence to speech, has been triumphantly claimed by feminist critics. Yet, if one reads the scene in terms of its slave references as I have, one notices that assertions of a rebellious feminism are enacted through the figure of a rebel slave.

Although Jane identifies the master/slave relation as Roman, the idea of a *revolted* slave had to have come from a more recent past. There were the slave uprisings of Jamaica in 1808 and 1831, Barbados in 1816, and Demerara in 1823. Brontë's novel clearly draws on the moral language of the abolitionists. And it is important to recognize the degree to which the active resistance and open rebellion of black slaves shaped the language of the British campaign to end slavery.[2] Abolitionists disseminated leaflets and pamphlets describing the suffering that provoked slaves to strike back at their masters in so violent a form. The scale of the 1831 Jamaican uprising and the severity with which it was suppressed gave the antislavery movement the impetus needed to pass an emancipation bill two years later. Jane may derive the proper name of slavery from the book she is reading (Goldsmith's *History of Rome*), but the analogy she makes between her own oppression and slavery relies on the historical memory of recent events in the West Indies.

Following the success of the antislavery movement, English women and workers harnessed its language for articulating their own struggles for equality.[3] The slave analogy was nothing new to the nineteenth century, but with the increased popularity of abolitionism in the 1820s, the oppression of European women was more explicitly compared to the West Indian system of slavery. "This state of the civilized wife," proclaims one defender of women's rights, "worse than that of the female West Indian slave, is termed a state of equality."[4] Women abolitionists also made the analogy between their own subordinate place in the antislavery movement and that of the slaves on whose behalf they spoke. And, members of the working class publicized the existence of "white slavery" in English factories. Yet, the social groups that identified themselves *as* slaves did not necessarily identify *with* black slaves. For instance, the working-class argument of "white slavery" was derived from the planter's defense of slavery— namely, that labor conditions in the West Indies were better than those in English factories. And, working-class organizations that lobbied for improving factory conditions were openly hostile to the predominantly middle-class abolitionists for their preferential treatment of black slaves.[5] If the analogy between race relations in the West Indies and class and gender relations in England did anything, it was to empty slavery of its racial signification. In this regard, the slave metaphor that Brontë deploys does not break with the discourse of her times. There is no character of a West Indian slave to be found in *Jane Eyre*; she remains inaccessible except through Jane's own acts of rebellion. Yet, the figure of slavery, coupled with the shadowy existence of Rochester's West Indian wife, points to the presence of a racial memory. A faint imprint of the "black slave" can be discerned in the narrative demand on Jane to disassociate herself from the anger that is so crucial in establishing her childhood resistance. In the last instance, the agency of the female as individualist cannot be enacted through the figure of a rebellious slave because slaves were not considered part of civilized society.

Abolitionist literature addresses the black slave as a human being who is less than human and as an incipient individual whose human potential is locked up in an unnatural system of slavery. Slaves are represented as the victims of cruel masters who have them fettered in body, mind, and soul *and* as a people who are active in obtaining their own freedom. The contradictory representation of the black slave as one who desires freedom but has no free will of his own (and I use the male pronoun advisedly) manifests itself in the demand made upon abolitionists to assume the voice of the black slave. The ambiguity in the famous slogan reproduced on boxes, ornaments, letterheads, and posters—"Am I not a man and a brother?"—with its iconic representation of a Negro in chains shows the double inscription of one who both is and is not a man. The rebellious slave, as one who acts but cannot cognize his actions, is a contradictory figure of resistance, as is evident in an 1824 tract entitled *The Rights of Man (Not Paines) but the Rights of Man, in the West Indies:*

> Nothing can be more evident than, that, if the slave-master will rule his slave by the law of power,—(which must ever be the case where slavery exists, for no man is a slave willingly,) the Slave has a right to make use of the law of power in return. When the master is strongest, the slave must submit; and when the slave is strongest, the master must suffer the effects of his contumacy. . . . Unprotected, then, as the Slave is by law;—upon the principles of natural right and justice, the allegiance he owes to the law, is *nothing*. He is out of its pale on every hand,—he is not a member of civilized society,—and, consequently, has a right to rid himself of the chains of his bondage, in whatever manner, at whatever time, and as soon as he can . . . as long as his present state continues, the Slave has a right to rebel;—no moral guilt whatever, that I see, can possibly attach to him, for attempting to assert what is the universal birthright of mankind, or for claiming to himself the *right and lordship of his own body.*[6]

According to this pamphleteer, the violence slaves commit during times of rebellion would be immoral without the prior violence of the master enslaving them against their wills. Slaves are spoken of as being active in obtaining their freedom, but it is an agency predicated on their exclusion from civilized society. In other words, they do not act as "free agents" in the sense of being able to assume a moral responsibility for their actions.

Missionaries were especially disturbed by the immorality of a system in which black slaves, having no control over disciplining their bodies, were not accountable for their souls. "Every slave being compelled, under pain of corporal punishment, to yield implicit obedience to the will of the master," writes one abolitionist, "the Negroes, as a people, are as destitute of correct morality as they are of liberty."[7] Since slave rebellions are perceived as a savage response to an even more barbaric system for extracting labor power, once blacks are free they no longer have the right to revolt.

Jane's development from a rebellious child into a self-assertive woman is represented by her movement from the instinctive rebellion of black slaves toward assuming the moral responsibility of a cognizing individual. The figure of the rebel slave, as I have already indicated, lacks the cognition on which moral agency is based. This is the mark of racial difference, a point of resistance for extending the meaning of the slave rebellions to a female agency predicated on speech. Unlike black slaves, Jane names herself as "a free human being with an independent will" (*JE*, 223). But more than that, the novel stages what constitutes an appropriate form of resistance for achieving self-autonomy within socialized space.

Since open revolt threatens the laws of civilized society, Jane's education into adulthood involves learning to control her anger and to channel her desires into a socially acceptable form of self-determination. Even though her childish explosions of anger are liberating, in retrospect, the adult Jane comments on these instances as improper conduct for a child. The rebellious female child is not quite human; she is a bad animal, a mad cat, a heathen, and a fiend. Unchecked rebellion is particularly identified as the savage response of uncivilized nations. Jane's friend at Lowood, Helen Burns, chastises her for wanting to "strike back" at those who are cruel and unjust, saying, "Heathens and savage tribes hold that doctrine; but Christians and civilised nations disown it" (*JE*, 50). The young Jane at first finds the concept of Christian endurance difficult to comprehend. She does, however, keep her humiliation to herself when Brocklehurst makes a public example of her. As she struggles to stifle her sentiments, Helen walks by and gives her the strength of self-control. "It was as if a martyr, a hero, had passed a slave or victim, and imparted strength in the transit" (*JE*, 58). For Jane, Christian endurance means being positioned as a victim to be saved; for Helen, it means suffering in this life to reap the rewards of heaven. The second stage of Jane's life ends with Helen dying of consumption, happy in the knowledge that she is going to her Maker. At this point in its narration, the novel confronts its reader with two equally undesirable alternatives for female socialization: the silent space of passive victimage or the tragic space of early death. And so the first stage of Jane's education draws to a close. Having established an irreconcilable conflict between her desire for self-assertion and her preassigned gender role of self-denial, the educational novel moves into a new phase that shows her negotiating a socialized space that does not negate a female self. And it is the civilizing mission that provides the grounds for her negotiations.

Jane Eyre charts the success of its heroine in resolving the conflict between self-determination and socialization that structures the *Bildungsroman*.[8] As a female *Bildungsroman*, however, it also stages the impossibility of such a resolution because the socialization of women means submitting to a male head of household. The difficulty the novel has in resolving this conflict should cause one to question Sandra M. Gilbert and Susan Gubar's approving description of "the astounding progress toward equality of plain Jane Eyre."[9] Brontë's novel of development is structured less as a woman's progress toward a final goal than as her negotiation of the narrow restraints of fixed gender roles. The same force of emotions that can be liberating for Jane also "masters" her good sense when she falls in love with her employer. This is why, despite the value placed on feelings, she stresses the need to subject them to a "wholesome discipline" (*JE,* 141). Jane's struggle for independence involves finding a socially acceptable form for rejecting the restrictions imposed upon poor relations, governesses, mistresses, and wives. In other words, she requires a domestic form of resistance, a language that can bring the force of political insurgency into the "woman's sphere" of the home. The doctrine of "feminine influence" and "woman's mission" provides one possible mode of articulation.[10]

The limited power available to middle-class women at the time Brontë was writing is expressed in the idea of their influential yet subordinate position vis-à-vis men. According to the doctrine of feminine influence, women do not exercise power directly in the public sphere but indirectly through their relationship to men as wives, mothers, and daughters. Sarah Lewis (who, like Brontë, was herself a governess) explains in her influential book, *Woman's Mission* (1839), the far-reaching effects of women's domestic role:

> Power is principally exerted in the shape of authority, and is limited in its sphere of action. Influence has its source in human sympathy, and is as boundless in its operation.
>
> If there were any doubt which of these principles most contributes to the formation of human character, we have only to look around us. We see that power, while it regulates men's actions, cannot reach their opinions. It cannot modify dispositions nor implant sentiments, nor alter character. All these things are the work of influence. Men frequently resist power, while they yield to influence an unconscious acquiescence.[11]

Since Lewis is a woman writing a tract for other women, her problem is one of explaining to her readers that their subordination to men can be a source of power. This is why she suggests that what women lack in political authority they make up for through moral influence in their homes. Since women's influence in the public world is limitless only if its scope is restricted to the private sphere, the idea of feminine influence suggests an inherent conflict between a woman's desire for personal advancement and a disinterested duty to her family. Lewis asks whether it is possible for women to conduct their lives according to a doctrine, the object of which is "to awaken the sense of power, and to require that the exercise of it be limited; to apply at once the spur and the rein."[12] She resolves the problem by advising her readers to value their training in denial, devotion, and sacrifice— in short, female self-renunciation:

> The one quality on which woman's value and influence depend is the renunciation of self, and the old prejudices respecting her, inculcated self-renunciation. Educated in obscurity, trained to consider the fulfillment of domestic duties as the aim and end of her existence, there was little to feed the appetite for fame, or the indulgence of self idolatry. Now here the principle fundamentally bears upon the very qualities most desirable to be cultivated, and those most desirable to be avoided.[13]

Lewis's tract, which locates female self-renunciation at the heart of women's power, is a paradigmatic text of the debate within which *Jane Eyre,* as a domestic novel, finds itself. Upon devaluing the domestic virtue of self-renunciation, Brontë breaks with the position that Lewis represents. Yet, if self-denial is what reins in women's power so that moral order can be maintained, how can Brontë reassure her readers that its devaluation will not lead to moral chaos? This is the question the novel addresses in Jane's negotiations for a language in which women's power will not threaten the moral order. And, nowhere is the horror of female self-indulgence more vividly imagined than in the inordinate passions and appetites of Bertha Mason.

Rochester's first wife is commonly read as a symbolic substitute for Jane Eyre and the monstrous embodiment of unchecked female rebelliousness and sexuality.[14] Gilbert and Gubar, for instance, characterize Bertha as "Jane's truest and darkest double" that represents the rebellious passions she has been trying to repress since childhood. Hence, they see the madwoman's opposition to the forthcoming wedding as a figurative and psychological manifestation of Jane's own desires for independence that her marriage to Rochester would negate.[15] Bertha Mason is a Calibanesque figure—a cannibalistic beast who chews her brother's flesh to the bone, a fiend who spews forth obscenities, and a monster who cannot control her sexual appetites. The resemblances between Bertha and Shakespeare's monstrous figuration of the Carib native have caused some readers to identify her as a member of the colonized. In a reading that is otherwise sensitive to history, Susan Meyer understands the racial ambiguity suggested by her creole heritage and swarthy complexion as sufficient evidence that the first Mrs. Rochester is black. This reading permits her to describe Bertha as a Maroon or runaway slave even though, as the daughter of a merchant-planter, she belongs to the class of slaveholders.[16]

In Jamaica, the term creole may have designated all native-born population (both of African and European origin), but in England it was a derogatory name for the West Indian sugar plantocracy. *Jane Eyre* is a novel of the 1840s, a time when slavery was so unpopular that only those who directly benefited from it continued to defend it. Bertha Mason is a female version of the "immoral West Indian planter," a literary stereotype that, following the abolition of the African slave trade, was commonly invoked as "a useful shorthand for depravity."[17] It is clear from Rochester's description of his first wife that it is not her madness he finds so intolerable as her debauchery.

> I lived with that woman upstairs four years, and before that
> time she had tried me indeed: her character ripened and
> developed with frightful rapidity; her vices sprang up fast
> and rank: they were so strong, only cruelty could check
> them; and I would not use cruelty. What a pigmy intellect
> she had—and what giant propensities! How fearful were the
> curses those propensities entailed on me! Bertha Mason,—
> the true daughter of an infamous mother,—dragged me
> through all the hideous and degrading agonies which must
> attend a man bound to a wife at once intemperate and
> unchaste. . . . a nature the most gross, impure, depraved, I
> ever saw, was associated with mine. . . . And I could not rid
> myself of it by any legal proceedings: for the doctors now
> discovered that my wife was mad—her excesses had pre-
> maturely developed the germs of insanity. (*JE*, 269–70)

The particular form of Bertha's insanity bears the signs of an idle plantocracy in the state of decline. Since the self-indulgence of the planter class was considered responsible for feeding its vices, it is not madness that is the cause of Bertha's moral degeneration but rather the other way around—her "excesses" have strained her minuscule mind to the point of unhinging it.

Jane often refers to her own state of mind, when consumed by her love for Rochester, as a condition of madness. Yet, it is her superior intellect as well as her recognition of the need for "laws and principles" (*JE*, 279) that separates her own excesses from Bertha's. Narratively speaking, the plantation woman is sacrificed so that an upwardly mobile English woman of an ambiguous class can replace her as Rochester's wife. The partnership in marriage that Jane achieves at the end is contingent upon the appearance of Rochester's first wife. But the narrative function of the creole stereotype is also to disassociate a pure English race from its corrupt West Indian line.

Due to the long history of racial mixing in Jamaica, the scandal the creole presented to the British was the possibility of a white person who was not racially pure. (In defense of the creole's racial purity, Edward Long outlines in his *History of Jamaica* [1774] an elaborate classification system, according to which Negro blood can be "bred out" over five generations.)[18] As a member of the white-identified planter class, Bertha is perhaps more threatening than a free person of color, for she shows that "whiteness" alone is not the sign of racial purity.

Rather than being equated with color, racial purity is identified with an English national culture. Rochester makes a point of distinguishing himself from the planters that punish their slaves when he says that he refused to control Bertha with cruelty. And, as a true English woman, Jane embodies the new honesty and national pride that will guide England in its overseas social mission. Rochester indicates that no other woman comes close to expressing what for all intents and purposes are the signs of an English national character, "cool native impudence, and pure innate pride" (*JE, 237*). Jane provides a lengthy account of the degradation and humiliation she suffers following her flight from

Thornfield when, poverty stricken and weak with hunger, she is reduced to common begging. The detailed description of her Christian endurance of these trials produces a narrative that shows her as having earned, through hard work and determination, the real source of her success—which is to say, an inheritance from a rich uncle in Madeira, a port of call on the trade route between the Guinea coast and the West Indies. An inheritance is necessary for narrowing the class difference between Jane and Rochester, while the hardships she suffers distance her from the idle class of the West Indian plantocracy. Her financial gain and his loss of Thornfield make them economically equal. But economic independence in and of itself is insufficient for female emancipation in marriage—that is, so long as the value of self-renunciation is attached to the woman's domestic role.

The famous passage from chapter 12 that extends the action of political rebellion to the "silent revolt" (*JE, 96*) of women is paradigmatic of a constant reworking of the domestic sphere in order to accommodate the social values of individualism. Since domestic women influence the public domain only in relationship to men (i.e., through their influence), they are not individuals in the sense of being moral agents. As Denise Riley explains, "If women are only to be thought *in relation,* then the status of being a woman while being a social-ethical subject is a logical impossibility."[19] It is my contention that the paradox of being an individual in the domestic sphere is resolved by defining the English woman in relation to other women instead of to men. In *Jane Eyre,* a domestic form of social agency is established through a national and racial splitting of femininity, with the creole woman serving as a figure of self-indulgence and the Oriental woman of self-immolation.

Sati as Feminine Ideal

To say that woman is an angel . . . is to imply that her specialty is self-effacement, resignation, and sacrifice; it is to suggest to her that woman's greatest glory, her greatest happiness, is to immolate herself for those she loves. . . . It is to say that she will respond to absolutism by submission, to brutality by meekness, to indifference by tenderness, to inconstancy by fidelity, to egotism by devotion. (Maria Deraismes, "La Femme et le droit"[20])

Jane's life story is based on a model of self-determination that derives from social action in the public sphere. Hence, despite the marriage of equality with which the novel ends, its narrative energy goes into demonstrating the impossibility for a domestic woman to be both an individual and a wife. So long as she is a wage earner, Jane has a certain degree of autonomy at Thornfield. The first time she meets Rochester, she refuses to speak at his command but instead scolds him for assuming an attitude of superiority. Yet, the novel also makes it clear that "governessing slavery" (*JE*, 238) is no model for female emancipation. Because they were educated, governesses were not considered part of the working class, even though they were wage earners. Yet, the lower-middle-class women who earned their living as private tutors were so dependent on their employers for their keep that many ended up in the poorhouse. The discrepancy between the governess's social status and her economic class manifests itself in the difficulty a book on education has in defining her place in the home: "The real discomfort of a governess's position in a private family arises from the fact that it is undefined. She is not a relation, not a guest, not a mistress, not a servant—but something made up of all. No one knows exactly how to treat her."[21] The uneasiness this writer expresses has to do with the ambiguous position of the governess as one who both embodies the domestic ideal and threatens it. As an educator, she is a role model for middle-class children; as a domestic woman who is also a wage earner, she transgresses the separation of spheres that ensures Victorian morality.[22]

Jane especially threatens middle-class morality when she breaks with social norms by agreeing to become Rochester's wife. Drawing attention to the discrepancy in their age, wealth, and social status, Mrs. Fairfax, the housekeeper, warns her that "gentlemen in his station are not accustomed to marry their governesses" (*JE*, 233). Jane soon discovers that, despite the legitimacy of her forthcoming marriage, she is positioned as mistress rather than wife. In this regard, her ambiguous class status reveals a certain truth about the domestic woman. Rochester may think that dressing his future wife in rich silks and expensive jewelry is an expression of his love, but in her eyes he is claiming ownership over her body. Jane's suspicions are confirmed when he playfully compares her worth to the purchase price of "the grand Turk's whole seraglio" (*JE*, 236). At this moment there is a strategic shift in the slave analogy. To begin with, the master/slave relation is both gendered and Orientalized, which means that it is now a direct statement about gender hierarchies. But more important, Jane explicitly rejects the role of slave as the sign of Rochester's mastery over her. In response to his inquiry as to what she will do while he is "bargaining for so many tons of flesh," she proclaims: "I'll be preparing myself to go out as a missionary to preach liberty to them that are enslaved—your harem inmates amongst the rest" (*JE*, 237). Jane does not identify herself as a slave in order to express her desire for liberation, as she did when she was a child. Rather, she assumes the position of a missionary who will free others that are enslaved. Slavery cannot figure female rebellion because the slave in this instance is an Oriental woman who is passive and agentless. By positioning herself as a missionary, Jane empowers herself with the moral superiority of British civilizers at the precise moment that her own morality is undermined. In other words, an assertion of *racial* superiority discursively resolves Jane's class and gender inferiority in relationship to Rochester.

The Eastern references are sustained throughout the scene of their courtship, which ends with a historical figuration of the Hindu woman. After a reverie on the devotion he expects from his future wife, Rochester sings a love song in which the woman promises to live and die with her man. Jane responds with the following outburst: "I had as good a right to die when my time came as he had: but I should bide that time, and not be hurried away in a suttee" (*JE*, 240). Here, Hindu widow-sacrifice refers to the self-sacrifice that the doctrine of woman's mission requires of English women. As a proper name for a woman's submissiveness, meekness, and devotion to her husband, sati locates female passivity in Hindu women. The Eastern analogy of gender hierarchies exposes the barbarism of English marriage laws, but only inasmuch as Oriental despotism is a paradigm for such barbarism. In this regard, the metaphors of harem women and sati in *Jane Eyre* belong to a civilizing discourse that produces its own object of negation.

The moral imperative of modern colonialism to bring the colonized into civil society meant that natives had to be "made" savage before they could be civilized. The signs of this requirement are visible in W. W. Hunter's lecture entitled "England's Work in India" (1879–80), given during a more self-conscious time of imperialism than the 1840s. The force of his words does not go into describing England's civilizing work but the cruel and bloody practices of the Indians:

> The rising generation in India have been freed from superstitious terrors, they have been led to give up cruel practices, they have learned to detest and despise their forefathers' bloody rites. Widow burning, infanticide, hook-swinging, self-mutilation, and human sacrifice—these are the few familiar relics of the old bondage under which the Indian intellect cowered and the Indian heart bled. Great as has been the material progress of India during the past century, its emancipation from ignorance and priestcraft forms is, to my mind, a far more splendid memorial of British rule. Truly the people that walked in darkness have seen a great light.[23]

"Barbarism" is the truth-effect of a selective description of Indian culture as the negative pole of a civilizing influence. And, the native male appears especially barbaric in the colonial reforms intended to alleviate the condition of women. The modalities of this discourse can be discerned in the redefinition of sati as a crime during the years leading up to the Abolition Act of 1829.

In her careful reading of the official records, Lata Mani argues that the Hindu widow was neither the subject nor the object of a discourse on the abolition of sati but the grounds for colonial intervention in Indian society.[24] The British may have desired to end what they considered to be a savage practice, but not at the risk of jeopardizing their relationship with Hindus. By demonstrating that they were defending the widow's rights, they could circumvent the label of interventionists. The early legislating of widow-sacrifice was thus predicated on finding a precedent in ancient Sanskrit texts and on distinguishing "good" (voluntary) from "bad" (coerced) satis. In other words, the British effectively sanctioned widow-sacrifice so that they might abolish it. Since the *religious* sanctioning of sati was open to debate, a regulating of the practice hinged on the place of the woman's will. Magistrates carefully monitored the burnings in order to determine whether Hindu widows went willingly to their death or were coerced.

What is significant to Mani is the process by which the widow's subjectivity is effaced so that others might speak for her. The woman who speaks in the official records does so at the command of the civil servant entrusted with introducing a new moral order. And, her speech is framed in a manner that positions the civilizer as the agent of change and the native woman as an object to be saved. The magistrate mediating the widow's speech addresses her as the victim of religion if she gives her consent and of pundits and relatives if she resists. The legislative prohibition of sati thus hinges on a construction of the widow that requires men (both British and Hindu) to speak on her behalf. Mani counters this effacement of female agency by making the widow the subject of a feminist discourse. The feminist critic, however, is faced with a double bind: to address the widow as a victim is to risk representing her as an object to be saved; to introduce her agency is to open up the possibility of a voluntary suicide.[25] This is why Mani insists that we entertain "the possibility of a female subjectivity that is shifting, contradictory, inconsistent."[26] By this she means that we should refuse a discourse that reduces agency to the singular moment of a "decision" and be attentive to the contradictions between speech and action in the widow's active negotiations of death. By focusing on what eyewitness reports marginalize—the violence of being burned alive, the widow's suffering and her resistance—Mani loosens the bind between victim and passivity. She shows that in cases of so-called voluntary satis, some widows were drugged or weighed down with wood. Others, who were persuaded to commit sati for familial or economic reasons, sometimes attempted last-minute efforts to escape by jumping from the flaming funeral pyre. Since widows who declared their intention to become satis often changed their minds, a reading of their agency in terms of "voice" can only produce a narrative of female acquiescence.

An attention to the widow's shifting subjectivity is all the more necessary in view of the force of colonial explanations that freeze her image into a *tableau vivant* of death. The following description of a sati by a British magistrate is emblematic, for Mani, of how the meaning of a highly interpretable text is fixed:

> If it were desired to portray a scene which should thrill with horror every heart, not entirely dead to the touch of human sympathy, it would suffice to describe a father, regardless of the affection of his tender child, in having already suffered one of the severest miseries which flesh is heir to, with tearless eye leading forth a spectacle to the assembled multitude, who with barbarous cries demand the sacrifice; and unrelentingly delivering up the unconscious and unresisting victim to an untimely death, accompanied by the most cruel tortures.[27]

Mani explains that what the magistrate "sees" is based on unexamined presuppositions about the actors in question: the relatives are cruel and cold-blooded; the crowd is barbaric and bloodthirsty; and the widow is an unresisting victim. I would add to the cast of characters that the European is a moral agent. The magistrate positions the horrified onlooker who is sympathetic to the widow's plight as one who is morally superior to the cruel and unfeeling crowd enjoying the spectacle. In this manner, any sympathy a Westerner might feel for the widow is expressed through the colonial construction of her as a victim to be saved.

The trope of "human sympathy" does not establish a common

identity between colonizer and colonized so much as it identifies the racial superiority of the English. This same structure is visible in *Jane Eyre*. Although Jane expresses a sympathy for harem women, she does not identify herself as one but positions herself as a missionary woman who will save them. But more than that she distinguishes herself from Hindu women by declaring her refusal to burn on her husband's pyre. Rather than establishing a shared identity between the English and Hindu woman, the novel's reference to sati ranks Hindu women low on the feminist scale of emancipation. This distancing of the English woman from her Eastern sisters enables the problem of female emancipation in marriage to be resolved in what constitutes the final stage of Jane's development.

After fleeing from Thornfield following her discovery of Bertha Mason's existence, Jane enters into a relationship with a new "despotic" master. Under the tutelage of St. John Rivers, she finds herself an obedient student who is increasingly fettered to his will. He wants her to join the Indian missions, work for which she feels she has no vocation. Missionary work is guided by the spirit of self-sacrifice rather than the mutual reinforcement of self-interest and progress that characterizes the colonialism of the first half of the nineteenth century. The overseas missions, strongly evangelical in character, have a curiously feminine form. "Evangelical manhood, with its stress on self-sacrifice and influence, came dangerously close to embracing 'feminine' qualities," explain Leonore Davidoff and Catherine Hall, and for this reason manliness was reinforced through a control of emotions, the religious duty of work, and, above all else, the separation of a "woman's sphere."[28] The enforced masculinity of evangelicalism is evident in the coldhearted, duty-bound St. John, who considers his labor for God to be above the petty concerns of humankind.

Unlike colonial civilizers, the missionary was willing to sacrifice his life for the greater good of humanity, an act of martyrdom that placed him squarely within a Christian allegory.[29] St. John expresses his "hopes of being numbered in the band who have merged all ambition into the glorious one of bettering their race—of carrying knowledge into the realms of ignorance—of substituting peace for war—freedom for bondage—religion for superstition—the hope of heaven for the fear of hell" (*JE*, 329). Missionary wives, however, did not have the same access to the heroic discourse of self-sacrifice as their husbands. An English woman who joined the Christian missions was obliged to efface herself on two counts, one religious and the other sexual. Living and working with Indian women, they ranked low in a rigidly hierarchical Anglo-Indian society that disapproved of religious conversion and European contact with poor and low-caste natives (the primary group that converted to Christianity). The thought of working with Indian women appeals to Jane, for it is only when St. John raises this possibility that she agrees to become his helpmate. But she also does not want to be a missionary wife, saying: "I am ready to go to India, if I may go free" (*JE*, 356). This option is not available to her because, as St. John informs her, single women are not allowed to join the Christian missions.

Even though Jane cannot be the missionary that she once declared she would become, that does not mean she is in the same position as Indian women. St. John's desire makes no lesser demand on her than her life because she knows she lacks the stamina to work under the hot Indian sun. Yet, her premature death is also spoken of as voluntary on her part, for she understands her obedience to be an act that is "almost equivalent to committing suicide" (*JE*, 364). The unspoken text of Jane's being "grilled alive in Calcutta" (*JE*, 366) is a colonial discourse on Hindu women who were burned alive on their husbands' pyres.[30] Unlike the Hindu women who are "hurried away in a suttee," Jane exercises her free will and voice-agency. Prying her own desires away from the hypnotic power of St. John's, she reverses her former passivity and, upon doing so, names him as the agent of her death. She enunciates the oppressiveness of marriage customs that demand a wife's devotion to her husband when she declares that the sacrifice St. John demands of her is nothing short of murder: "If I were to marry you, you would kill me. You are killing me now" (*JE*, 363). He, in return, calls her words "violent, unfeminine, and untrue." With this act of resistance Jane finally comes into her own, thereby proving her passionate outburst to be both feminine and true.

What often passes unnoticed in feminist readings of Jane's final ascendancy into power is that her agency is underwritten by a male voice. She is able to refuse St. John only after hearing Rochester call out her name; her future husband, in effect, names the new assertive female. The male voice behind Jane's assertion of her power means that she is not an individuated self in the sense of being autonomous from her husband. Instead of defining Jane as a social agent, the novel reorders the doctrine of "female influence" so as to grant women agency in the domestic sphere. Yet, the domestic individual is a condition of possibility for women's entry into public life. In the decades following the publication of *Jane Eyre*, middle-class English women interpreted the domestic ideal in a manner that permitted them to take their duties outside the home. By redefining prostitution, alcoholism, and child-labor laws as domestic issues, moral crusaders were able to win control over certain sectors of the public sphere. *Jane Eyre* is a novel that hovers on the horizon of middle-class English women's bid for social power.

Yet, the domestic individual creates a conflict for the novel's romantic plot, which works toward its own utopian vision of female emancipation in marriage. The conflict between marriage and passionate love, a woman's duty to her family and her self-determination cannot be resolved so long as the separation of spheres is left intact. In terms of its final reconciliation, the novel does not alter the domestic sphere so much as it asserts that a woman can find self-fulfillment in devotion to her family. As Carol Ohmann observes, Brontë's "radicalism was always in tension with conservative tendencies, and she was better, even in *Jane Eyre* and *Shirley*, at posing social problems than at sighting ways to solve them."[31] The problem of self-determination for the domestic woman is resolved through a linguistic power capable of making the feminine virtue of self-sacrifice represent self-fulfillment. "Sacrifice! What do I sacrifice?" Jane declares in anticipation of her marriage to Rochester as her story draws to a close;

"famine for food, expectation for content. . . . is that to make a sacrifice? If so, then certainly I delight in sacrifice" (*JE*, 392).

The almost magical metamorphosis of feminine self-sacrifice into its polar opposite is impossible within the constraints of a marriage plot; it requires the burning body of the Hindu widow as an icon for the angel in the house. In this regard, it is not simply a case of the "native female" being excluded from a discourse of feminist individualism, as Spivak suggests.[32] Rather, Jane's appeal to the moral mission of colonialism for asserting her own autonomy indicates a triangular relationship whereby English women's bid for domestic power passes through the racial hierarchy of colonialism. In short, the silent passivity of the Hindu woman is the grounds for the speaking subject of feminist individualism.

Brontë's first novel gives us the faint glimmer of a discursive relationship between the domestic virtue of self-renunciation and Hindu widow-immolation that becomes more explicitly articulated during the post-Mutiny period. Following the trajectory of Jane's narration that ends with St. John sacrificing his life for the Christian missions, I take the English woman's story overseas to India. Barred from the noble work of the civilizing project, the English woman enters a colonial iconography of martyrdom only in the capacity of victim. Unlike her male counterpart, it is her brutalized corpse rather than her body of good deeds that is of significance to the moral mission of colonialism.

Notes

[1. Charlotte Brontë. *Jane Eyre* (New York: Norton, 1971). All further references to this work, abbreviated *JE*, will be included in the text.]

2. In *Moral Imperium: Afro-Caribbeans and the Transformation of British Rule, 1776–1838* (Westport, Conn.: Greenwood Press, 1987), Ronald Kent Richardson explains abolitionism as a selective humanitarianism that emerged in response to slave rebellions, because they threatened Christianity and a Western system of values. The standard histories of West Indian slave rebellions are Eugene D. Genovese, *From Rebellion to Revolution: Afro-American Slave Revolts in the Making of the New World* (New York: Vintage,

1981), and Michael Craton, *Testing the Chains: Resistance to Slavery in the British West Indies* (Ithaca, N.Y.: Cornell University Press, 1982). For slave women's resistance, see Barbara Bush, *Slave Women in Caribbean Society, 1650–1838* (London: James Curry, 1990), 51–82, and Stella Dadzie, "Searching for the Invisible Woman: Slavery and Resistance in Jamaica," *Race and Class* 32, no. 2 (October–December 1990): 21 38. I have not had a chance to look at Moira Ferguson's *Subject to Others: British Women Writers and Colonial Slavery, 1670–1834* (New York: Routledge, 1992), which was published after I completed this manuscript.

3. For the popularity of the antislavery position in England, see Seymour Drescher, "Public Opinion and the Destruction of British Colonial Slavery," in *Slavery and British Society: 1776–1846*, ed. James Walvin (Baton Rouge: Louisiana State University Press, 1982), 22–48, and James Walvin, "The Public Campaign in England against Slavery, 1787–1834," in *The Abolition of the Atlantic Slave Trade: Origins and Effects in Europe, Africa, and the Americas*, ed. David Eltis and James Walvin (Madison: University of Wisconsin Press, 1981), 63–79. The antislavery issue was still current in the 1840s, as emancipation had not yet been achieved in the United States.

4. William Thompson, *Appeal of One-Half the Human Race, Women, against the Pretensions of the Other Half, Men, to Retain Them in Political and Thence in Civil and Domestic Slavery; in Reply to a Paragraph of Mr Mill's Celebrated "Article on Government"* (1825), 86, cited by Barbara Taylor, *Eve and the New Jerusalem: Socialism and Feminism in the Nineteenth Century* (New York: Pantheon, 1983), 35.

5. For a discussion of working-class hostility to abolitionism, see Patricia Hollis, "Anti-Slavery and British Working-Class Radicalism in the Years of Reform," in *Anti-Slavery, Religion, and Reform*, ed. Christine Bolt and Seymour Drescher (Hamden, Conn.: Archon, 1980), 294 315. By focusing on the post- rather than the pre-Emancipation period, Betty Fladeland makes the counterargument that the working class forged alliances with abolitionists. See " 'Our Cause Being One and the Same': Abolitionists and Chartism," in *Slavery and British Society, 1776–1846*, ed. Walvin, 69 99. For a reading of the worker/slave metaphor in the English industrial novel, see Catherine Gallagher, *The Industrial Reformation of English Fiction: Social Discourse and Narrative Form, 1832–1867* (Chicago: University of Chicago Press, 1985), ch. 1.

6. Anthropos, *The Rights of Man (Not Paines) but the Rights of Man, in the West Indies* (London: Knight & Lacey, 1824), 14, 16.

7. Thomas Cooper, *Facts Illustrative of the Condition of the Negro Slaves in Jamaica* (London, 1824), 13, 14.

8. Franco Moretti, *The Way of the World: The Bildungsroman in European Culture* (London: Verso, 1987).

9. Gilbert and Gubar, *The Madwoman in the Attic* (New Haven, Ct: Yale University Press, 1979), 370.

10. For a discussion of women's negotiations within the doctrine of "woman's mission," see Barbara Taylor, *Eve and the New Jerusalem* (New York: Pantheon Books, 1983), 123–30, and Leonore Davidoff and Catherine Hall, *Family Fortunes: Men and Women of the English Middle Class, 1780–1850* (Chicago: University of Chicago Press, 1987), 114–18, 180–88.

11. Sarah Lewis, *Woman's Mission* (New York: Wiley & Putnam, 1839), 14.

12. Ibid., 47.

13. Ibid., 49. Sarah Ellis makes a similar argument in *The Women of England, Their Social Duties, and Domestic Habits* (London: Fisher, 1838), 52–81.

14. The following list is by no means exhaustive: Showalter, *A Literature of Their Own*, (Princeton, N.J.: Princeton University Press, 1977), 118–22; Maurianne Adams, "*Jane Eyre*: Woman's Estate," in *The Authority of Experience: Essays in Feminist Criticism*, ed. Arlyn Diamond and Lee Edwards (Amherst: University of Massachusetts Press, 1977), 146; Barbara Hill Rigney, *Madness and Sexual Politics in the Feminist Novel: Studies in Brontë, Woolf, Lessing, and Atwood* (Madison: University of Wisconsin Press, 1978), 20–29; Marxist-Feminist Literary Collective, "Women's Writing: *Jane Eyre, Shirley, Villette, Aurora Leigh,*" *Ideology and Consciousness*, 3 (Spring 1978): 34–35; Cora Kaplan, *Sea Changes: Culture and Feminism* (London: Verso, 1986), 171–74; Pat Macpherson, *Reflecting on Jane Eyre* (London: Routledge, 1989), 10–58.

15. Gilbert and Gubar, *The Madwoman in the Attic*, 359–60.

16. Susan L. Meyer, "Colonialism and the Figurative Strategy of *Jane Eyre*," *Victorian Studies* 3, no. 2 (Winter 1990):252–59. With the exception of this important difference, my reading of West Indian slavery overlaps with that of Meyer. An earlier version of my conclusions, which I arrived at independently of her essay, appears in [Jenny Sharpe,] "Scenes of an Encounter: A Double Discourse of Colonialism and Nationalism" (Ph.D. diss., University of Texas at Austin, 1987), 94–127.

17. C. Duncan Rice, "Literary Sources and British Attitudes to Slavery," in *Anti-Slavery, Religion, and Reform*, ed. Bolt and Drescher, 328–29. Wylie Sypher quotes extensively from I. B. Moreton's *Manners and Customs in the West India Islands* (1790) for outlining the characteristic qualities of the creole "type": "The men, he says, are 'of a sickly, pale, yellowish complexion, meager, weak, and emaciated as to appearance'; yet they are 'open-hearted, generous, kind and hospitable to excess; proud, vain,

high-spirited and flighty to an extreme; lazy, dull, and indolent . . . ; and volatile as air where drinking, whoring, gaming, or any kind of dissipation invites; so that their hearts and fortunes seldom agree.' Moreton declares that the creole gentleman keeps wenches until 'a day or two before . . . marriage,' and that one may see his 'white, mestee, quadroon, and mulatto children, all brothers and sisters, playing together.' He also disapproves of the creole girl; though many are 'prudent, chaste, and fine women,' they are generally lascivious and overdressed" ("The West-Indian as a 'Character' in the Eighteenth Century," *Studies in Philology* 36, no. 3 [July 1939]: 503–20). As a member of the Jamaican plantocracy, Edward Long describes "the native white men, or Creoles, of Jamaica" in decidedly more noble terms, as "lovers of freedom, fond of social enjoyments, tender fathers, humane and indulgent masters" (*The History of Jamaica*, 3 vols. [London, 1774], 2: 261). For an etymology of *creole* in Jamaica, see Edward Brathwaite, *The Development of Creole Society in Jamaica, 1770–1820* (Oxford: Clarendon Press, 1971), xiv–xvi, and in the Americas, José Juan Arrom, *Certidumbre de América* (Madrid: Gredos, 1971), 11–26. Sir Walter Scott's characterization of George Staunton in *The Heart of Midlothian* (1818) ([London: Collins Classics, 1963], 313–14), is a good example of the Creole stereotype in nineteenth-century British literature: "The father of George Staunton had been bred a soldier, and, during service in the West Indies, had married the heiress of a wealthy planter. By this lady he had an only child, George Staunton, the unhappy young man who has been so often mentioned in this narrative. He passed the first part of his early youth under the charge of a doting mother, and in the society of negro slaves, whose study it was to gratify his every caprice. . . . When he was about ten years old, and when his mind had received all the seeds of those evil weeds which afterwards grew apace, his mother died, and his father, half-heart-broken, returned to England. . . . He took his son to reside with him at the rectory; but he soon found that his disorders rendered him an intolerable inmate. And as the young men of his own rank would not endure the purse-proud insolence of the Creole, he fell into that taste for low society, which is worse than 'pressing to death, whipping, or hanging.' " When read alongside Brontë's representation of the creole woman as the source of Bertha's madness, Scott's characterization of Staunton's mother as indulgent shows the emergent duty of English mothers to raise a superior race for nation and Empire.

18. Long, *The History of Jamaica*, 2: 321.

19. Denise Riley, *"Am I That Name?" Feminism and the Category of "Women"*

in History (Minneapolis: University of Minnesota Press, 1988), 41. I. B. Schneewind describes how the ethical agency of the individual is contingent upon social and political structures; see "The Use of Autonomy in Ethical Theory," in *Reconstructing Individualism: Autonomy, Individuality, and the Self in Western Thought*, ed. Thomas Heller et al. (Stanford, Calif.: Stanford University Press, 1986), 64–75.

20. A public address given in the 1860s.

21. Elizabeth Missing Sewell, *Principles of Education, Drawn from Nature and Revelation, and Applied to Female Education in the Upper Classes* (London, 1865), II: 240, cited by M. Jeanne Peterson, "The Victorian Governess: Status, Incongruence in Family and Society," in *Suffer and Be Still: Women in the Victorian Age*, ed. Martha Vicinus (Bloomington: Indiana University Press, 1972), 9–10.

22. Mary Poovey, *Uneven Developments: The Ideological Work of Gender in Mid-Victorian England* (Chicago: University of Chicago Press, 1988), 126–63.

23. William Wilson Hunter, "England's Work in India," in *The India of the Queen and Other Essays* (London: Longmans, Green, 1903), 127.

24. The following discussion of sati is based on Lata Mani's important essay, "The Production of an Official Discourse on Sati," in *Europe and Its Others*, 2 vols., ed. Francis Barker et al. (Colchester: University of Essex Press, 1985), 1:107–27.

25. As Mani points out, an attention to agency is imperative for displacing a colonial construction of the widow as an object to be saved. She also issues the warning, however, that we treat First World and Third World feminist discourses as discontinuous. An insistence on the widow's agency could have detrimental effects in India, where "current legislation of sati, by making women attempting sati liable to punishment, implicitly conceives of them as 'free agents' " ("Multiple Mediations: Feminist Scholarship in the Age of Multinational Reception," *Feminist Review* 35 [July 1990]: 37–38).

26. Lata Mani, "Cultural Theory, Colonial Texts: Reading Eyewitness Accounts of Widow Burning," in *Cultural Studies*, ed. Lawrence Grossberg, Cary Nelson, and Paula Treicher (New York: Routledge, 1992), 397.

27. Parliamentary Papers on Hindu Widows (1825, xxiv, 243), cited by Mani, "The Production of an Official Discourse," 122.

28. Davidoff and Hall, *Family Fortunes*, 111–12.

29. C. Duncan Rice explains the emblematic value of Christian martyrdom to the overseas missions: "Much of the tension created by commitment [to the missions] could be resolved by exposure to violence and suffering. . . . To risk martyrdom, real or imagined, was a fruitful

means of releasing such tensions. . . . Livingstone's demise came to provide one of the most celebrated scenes in the Victorian iconography of death" ("The Missionary Context of the British Anti-Slavery Movement," in *Slavery and British Society*, 158).

30. Interestingly enough, a collector's wife, Fanny Parks, describes sati as the "grilling" of widows in her travel journal, *Wanderings of a Pilgrim in Search of the Picturesque*, 2 vols., reprint edition (1836; Karachi: Oxford University Press, 1975), 1:162.

31. Carol Ohmann, "Historical Reality and 'Divine Appointment' in Charlotte Brontë's Fiction," *Signs* 2, no. 4 (1977): 757.

32. Gayatri Chakravorty Spivak, "Three Women's Texts and a Critique of Imperialism," in *"Race," Writing, and Difference*, ed. Henry Louis Gates, Jr. (Chicago: University of Chicago Press, 1986), 264.

Jane Eyre

"Lurid Hieroglyphics"

SALLY SHUTTLEWORTH

◆ ◆ ◆

I N *JANE EYRE* BRONTË extends her analysis of the ways in which ideological pressures of class, gender, and economics are played out in the domain of subjectivity. Traditional readings of the novel which regard it primarily as a drama of the psyche, where society is consigned to the role of backdrop, fail to register the ways in which the language of psychology in the novel is itself politically defined and charged. Similarly feminist celebrations of Brontë's depictions of sexual rebellion fail to take into account the ways in which the novel is framed by the discourses of Victorian psychology.[1] Medical texts of the era foregrounded the same three concerns which dominate Brontë's novel: the mechanics of self-control, the female body and sexuality, and the insurgence of insanity.

Psychology however, has never been an innocent discipline: in the Victorian period, as today, the writing of the self is a political act. In this conflict-ridden tale of upward female mobility, and flagrant female rebellion, Brontë's own political ambivalences are recorded in the ways in which she mobilizes contemporary psychological discourse. Cutting across the overarching narrative of self-improvement through self-control, one finds depictions of internal struggle cast in terms of both racial and class conflict. Although Brontë does not, as in *Shirley*, foreground the political dimensions of class and gender polarities in this novel, the realm of psychic struggle is clearly associated in her mind with the dynamics of social struggle and insurrection. The drama of social interaction is played out, however, on the terrain of the female body, which is treated, by Jane's antagonists and lovers alike, as an object to be regulated, controlled, and decoded.

Jane Eyre follows a similar social trajectory to *The Professor*. Each text records the transition of an outcast figure from a position of social marginality to confirmed membership of the gentry. Both Jane and Crimsworth make their way by hard work, thus avoiding the taint of upper-class idleness, and the overt money-grubbing of trade. The relationship between this plot and the analysis of surges of energy within Jane's inner emotional life, and the depiction of Bertha's madness is not tangential, I will argue, but fundamental. The issue of "madness" or female sexuality cannot be isolated out from this wider social and economic context which actively defines them.[2]

The drama of social ascent and erotic exchange is once more focused on the activities of reading and surveillance. Jane's courtships with both Rochester and St. John, for example, are competitive exercises in interpretative penetration. A preoccupation with unveiling is not restricted to the thematics of the text, however. In the preface to the second edition of *Jane Eyre*, Brontë, responding to those who had criticized the religious tendency of the book, significantly aligns her own authorial stance with the act of unmasking: "To pluck the mask from the face of the Pharisee, is not to lift an impious hand to the Crown of Thorns."[3] Invoking the authority of the Bible for her own stance, Brontë warns that her work will constitute a radical, political act of unveiling. The world, "may hate him who dares to scrutinize and expose—to rase the gilding, and show base metal under it—to penetrate the sepulchre, and reveal charnel relics: but, hate as it will, it is indebted to him" (p. xxxi).[4] The connections of this sexualized rhetoric of unveiling to the overt political sphere are made explicit in Brontë's own comments on the preface, which she had concluded with a eulogy of Thackeray as the "first social regenerator of the day." In a letter to W. S. Williams, Brontë makes clear that she had associated Thackeray's role as regenerator, mastering and rectifying a warped social body, with the contemporary revolution in France. The letter passes from praise of Thackeray as the high priest of the goddess of truth to the observation that "I read my preface over with some pain—I did not like it. I wrote it when I was a little enthusiastic, like you, about the French Revolution."[5]

For Brontë, the connection between the rhetoric of unveiling the truth and an overt political movement of insurrection is painfully evident. Writing again two weeks later, Brontë returns once more to the topic of the French Revolution, contrasting her skepticism about the end results with her faith in the Germans' "rational and justifiable efforts for liberty." Using the language of earthquakes and tremors, which occurs throughout *Jane Eyre* to describe upheavals in the psychological domain, she makes clear that she perceives England to lie under similar threat of social insurrection:

> It seems, as you say, as if change drew near England too. She is divided by the sea from the lands where it is making thrones rock, but earthquakes roll lower than the ocean, and we know neither the day nor the hour when the tremor and heat, passing beneath our island, may unsettle and dissolve its foundations.

Like the forces of female violence and insanity in *Jane Eyre*, that "crime . . . that lived incarnate in this sequestered mansion, and could neither be expelled nor subdued by the owner . . . [but] broke out, now in fire and and now in blood, at the deadest hours of night" (p. 264) the forces of political rebellion are figured as latent, secretive, and beyond control. England might be "sequestered" by the sea but is nonetheless liable to find her foundations shaken and her mansion razed by fire to the ground. The implicit associative connections in this letter between the psychological and political domains are confirmed in the ensuing praise of Thackeray whose power stems from his calm "self-control": "*he* borrows nothing from fever, his is never the energy of delirium—his energy is sane energy, deliberate energy, thoughtful energy ... Thackeray is never borne away by his own ardour—he has it under control."[6] Thackeray's activities as social unveiler are thus aligned not with the delirium of revolution but with the Germans' "rational and justifiable efforts for liberty," not with female excess but masculine control. The text of *Jane Eyre* itself, however, is by no means so clear-cut with reference either to social and gender politics or authorial stance, as these subsequent reflections might imply. The firm distinctions Brontë is proposing here are themselves the subject of interrogation in the novel.

Brontë's observations on the different forms of energy reveal the ideological hegemony established in nineteenth-century discourse by ideas of the controlled circulation of energy: the same model could be applied to the economy, the social body and the psyche, or the production of writing; to working-class riots in England, political revolutions in France, or slave rebellions in the colonies; to the processes of the female body and the eruptions of insanity; or to the novels of Thackeray. The dividing line between the forceful, useful channeling of energy, the full utilization of all resources, and the overspill into revolution or insanity was a thin one. The problem was particularly acute because the nineteenth century had witnessed the dissolution of binary divisions between health and sickness, both social and physiological. The new paradigm emerging in physiological and social discourse was one in which the old "Manichean" divide between health and sickness, good and ill, had been supplanted by a sliding scale of the normal and pathological.[7] The differentiation between activities which would lead to health or disease was now only one of degree; depending on the state of the organism, the same activity could lead to perfect health or dangerous excess. Central to this new discursive regime was the elusive concept of the "normal": the power to determine and define the normative state hence became crucial.

In the discourses of both political economy and psychiatry one can see the same preoccupation with the normal, the same attempt to define when control modulates into hysteria. Political economy concerned itself with that indefinable line which marked the transition from a healthy, expanding economy producing useful goods, to a sick system characterized by gluts, overstocked markets, and financial panic. Psychiatry employed a similar economic model of the psyche, exploring the ways in which healthy attempts to develop all the faculties to the full could quickly shade over into monomania, delirium, insanity; the only demarcating factors would be those of balance and control. Insanity and ill-health were not absolutes but rather states of health pushed to extremes. The discourses of political economy, medicine, and psychology all converged in their preoccupation with the balanced channeling of energy within the individual body.

Brontë's depiction of Thackeray's "sane," "deliberate energy" contrasts the useless waste of energy in the delirious movements of insanity, with the social power and productivity deriving from self-control. In *Jane Eyre* she brings a similar model of interpretation to bear. The incipient parallel which runs throughout the novel between Jane and the "mad" Bertha turns on the issue of the flow of energy: at what point does productive forcefulness turn into self-destructive anarchy? For a Victorian woman the question was peculiarly fraught since women were biologically defined as creatures of excess, throbbing with reproductive energy which had to be sluiced away each month, and yet could not be dammed up or controlled without real threat to the balance of the psyche. In constructing the parallel histories of Jane and Bertha, Brontë constantly negotiates between these different models of womanhood, trying to find an image of female empowerment and control which would not also be a negation of femininity.

Although the question of energy control is played out primarily on the terrain of the female body, its ramifications in the text concern all social groups who seek to overturn the established lines of demarcation between "normal" and "pathological" behavior; between praiseworthy exertion and self-help, and destabilizing "revolutionary" activity. The famous passage in *Jane Eyre* where Jane compares the plight of women, condemned to lives of inactivity, to that of workers who are forced by the social paralysis imposed on their faculties into revolutionary action, is not merely an isolated allusion but rather raises to the level of explicit statement the implied parallels which run through the text.

At a linguistic level, the narrative of *Jane Eyre* enacts the novel's central thematic: order and structure are imposed on disruptive, inchoate material. Jane's claims to have achieved social success, to have moved out of her initial state of social and psychological marginality, are vindicated by her ability to tell a "credible" tale and thus win from readers a conviction of her probity and sanity. The measure of her success is the degree to which we as readers believe we are listening to the workings of "sane energy" rather than the ravings of delirium. Syntactically, Jane's prose gives the impression of surges of energy which are yet restrained within legitimate social bounds. As Margot Peters has pointed out, Brontë's style is characterized by a practice of syntactic inversion, which creates a sense of pervasive tension.[8] The novel replicates linguistically Jane's attempts to transgress social boundaries while remaining within an accepted social framework; to maintain energy at the highest level of excitation without bursting through into pathology.

Like its predecessor, the history of "Jane Eyre" describes an arc through a whole series of problematic social boundaries. As a child Jane occupies the difficult terrain between servant and kin: kept at a distance from the family she is also "less than a servant, for you do nothing for your keep" (p. 9). Her life as an adult repeats this pattern: as a governess, she is again neither servant nor kin. Fulfilling the role of wife or mother for monetary gain, she is aligned with the members of that other "anathematized race," prostitutes, who similarly substitute an economic relation for a familial one, and who together with that other marginal female figure, the madwoman, haunted the Victorian imagination.[9] With her flight from Thornfield, Jane transgresses the social demarcations of class, occupying simultaneously the positions of lady and beggar; the Rivers' servant, Hannah, immediately places her once more in recognized categories of social liminality, prostitution and criminality: "You are not what you ought to be" (p. 428).

In traversing the domains of social and psychological marginality, *Jane Eyre* explores the intersection of models of the psyche and of social order. Jane's problematic status in the social and economic sphere is replicated in the psychological domain where she is aligned with the two figures from the discourse of Victorian psychiatry who demarcated the sphere of excess: the passionate child and madwoman. Following her eruption of childhood temper she comes to reside, in the household's eyes, within the borderland of insanity, and on the cusp between humanity and animality, thus preparing for her later association with Bertha. In both the social and psychological domains, wasteful, polluting excess is set against productive, healthy regulation. Jane depicts her history as a battle on two fronts: the internal struggle to regulate her own flow of energy, and the external, social fight to wrest control of the power of social definition. Her battle with the Reeds concerns the issue of denomination: where the boundary demarcating the normal and "natural" should be drawn. As in *The Professor*, the site of struggle rests in the dual sphere of control and penetration: regulating the self and unveiling the other.

From the opening paragraphs of the novel, where a defiant note of self-assertion is quickly introduced, it becomes clear that the narrator of *Jane Eyre* is a figure involved in the processes of self-legitimation. Jane's reference to her sense of being "humbled by the consciousness of my physical inferiority" to her cousins actually suggests an opposing sense of *mental* superiority. Her account of her alienation from the family circle reveals a curious blend of envy and disdain. Jane is writing as an outsider who longs to be included, but yet whose self-definition and sense of self-worth stems precisely from her position of exclusion and sense of difference. Like the upwardly-mobile middle classes, Jane is fighting a battle for definitional control. Her relatives, the Reeds, have usurped the categories of both society and nature: Jane is to be excluded, Mrs. Reed declares, until she learns, paradoxically, to acquire a "more natural" disposition. At issue is the clash between two models of mind and the "natural." Against Mrs. Reed's identification of the "natural" with her own social expectations, Jane, by contrast, identifies herself with an independent realm of physiological energy and innate capacity: a "natural" endowment which cannot, without violence, be constrained within the gentry's normative rules for social behavior. Her physiological model of the self thus aligns her with the phrenologists and the social economists who sought to analyze social dynamics entirely in terms of energy circulation.

Brontë's representation of Jane's adolescence draws on two fundamental strands in nineteenth-century psychology: the phrenological depiction of the mind as the site of warring faculties, conceived not as abstract intellectual powers but as distinct sources of physiological energy; and a separate tradition which focused on the female reproductive system as the source of destabilizing energies. Whereas the phrenologists emphasized the goals of self-control, and the hierarchical ordering and directing of mental energies, medical theories of the uterine economy suggested that female mental energy would always be overwhelmed by the forces of the reproductive system. Although in practice the two strands often overlapped, it is important, for analytic purposes, to maintain a distinction in order to explain why, in *Jane Eyre*, the rhetoric of liberating energy is also allied to the language of self-defeat and disgust. In dramatizing the ebbs and flows of Jane's internal conflicts, Brontë explores in depth the complex forms of female subjectivity engendered by contradictory formulations within Victorian discourse.

Jane's strategy of response to oppression is concealment, a retreat to a physiologically suggestive interiority, "enshrined" behind the red curtain. In dragging her out of her shrine and exposing her to public view, John Reed enacts a gross physical parody of the more subtle forms of female unveiling in psychiatric discourse. His literal unveiling is matched, however, by Jane's own figurative unveiling in her sudden eruption into passion, thus confirming Victorian fears of the latent fires within the female body. In the class and gender war in which she is engaged Jane is bound to lose. Her attempts to pit her ideational wealth against his material power prove futile. To John Reed she becomes a "rat," a term which demotes her from humanity to the animality reserved in contemporary rhetoric for the violence of the lower classes. As a dweller in the sewers, she is, furthermore, associated with both class and sexual contamination.[10]

The red room in which Jane is subsequently imprisoned functions, like the third story of Thornfield, as a spatialized configuration of Victorian notions of female interiority.[11] The flow of blood which had marked Jane's entrance, associates her confinement with both the onset of puberty and the polluting effects of suppression within the female frame. Jane's responses capture the bewildering, contradictory formulations of femininity in Victorian discourse. Catching sight of herself in the mirror, she is not reassured by a comforting specular identification with the physical coherence of her image but rather precipitated into spirals of increasing terror.[12] That "visionary hollow" confirms only her own insubstantiality, an endlessly retreating center of self (p. 12). The fears of spirits and phantoms it engenders set in motion the extended network of imagery which draws Jane and Bertha together within an associative nexus of the "non-human."

Jane's own language for herself in childhood repeatedly stresses her lack of a sense of coherence. She is a "heterogeneous thing," an "uncongenial alien" distinguished from her cousins by her innate endowment of "propensities" (pp. 13–14). Her oscillation between defiant self-assertion and a sense of internal fragmentation can be traced not simply to contradictory constructions of femininity but also to contradictions within the dominant Victorian theories of self-control. According to Combe, "Man is confessedly an assemblage of contradictions," a conflict-ridden association of "heterogeneous elements."[13] His fierce advocacy of the doctrines of self-improvement and advancement is based, paradoxically, on a physiological model of the psyche which undercuts earlier theories of a unified psychological principal. Combe's domain of selfhood is not the originating source of emotion, thought, or action but rather the shifting balance or product of internal conflicts: a battleground of warring, autonomous energies, where conflict is inscribed not as an occasional lapse but as a necessary principle of existence. As a model of mind it takes to an extreme the principles of laissez-faire economics.

Whereas in *The Professor* Brontë had been content to chart the difficulties attending Crimsworth's ascent to an achieved state of repressive self-control, in *Jane Eyre* she explores the contradictions at the heart of theories of unified selfhood. Jane dwells repeatedly on her internal divisions, her lack of a unifying, controlling centre of self. In her conversations with Mrs. Reed, "something spoke out of me over which I had no control" (p. 28). Although constrained grammatically to the use of "I," Brontë draws attention to the illusory fiction of unified control connoted by that term. The language of Jane's self-representation at this time emphasizes the implied political parallel between the upsurge of psychic energies and the swell of revolutionary fervor both in England and and Europe and in the slave revolts in the West Indies. Jane's mood is that of a "revolted slave"—her brain in "tumult" and her "heart in insurrection" (pp. 12–13). Taking the contemporary Tory rhetoric of social revolt as the eruption of animal energies, the convulsive thrashings of insanity, Brontë reverses its import to suggest a necessary, though equally unstoppable, outflow of constrained psychological force, whose release is essential for the health of the organism.

Brontë's analysis of the shifts and turns in Jane's emotions traces the material, physiological flow of her energies. The figure "Jane" exists not as controlling agent but rather as the site of violent, contradictory charges of material energy. Following the "gathering" and "launching" of her energies in a verbal assault on Mrs. Reed, Jane depicts her sensation of expansion and exultation: "It seemed as if an invisible bond had burst, and that I had struggled out into unhoped-for liberty" (p. 39). This notion of an emergence into selfhood occurring with an unleashing of physiological powers is reiterated later by St. John Rivers in describing the impact of his decision to become a missionary: "my cramped existence all at once spread out to a plain without bounds . . . the fetters dissolved and dropped from every faculty" (p. 462). In each case, responsibility for social rebellion is displaced onto a material sphere; it is not the individual but rather the physiological faculties which act to overthrow the fetters of social constraint.

The phrenological theory of innate, unrealized capacity lies behind this dual image of justified revolt and of the psychological exhilaration to be obtained from faculty exertion. Each faculty, Combe argued, "has a legitimate sphere of action, and, when properly gratified, is a fountain of pleasure."[14] Moving beyond the instrumentalist basis of Bentham's "felicific calculus" with its integrated, associationist model of selfhood, Combe offers the alluring notion of buried treasure within the self, multiple sources of gratification, only waiting to be released. Brontë's novel reveals the seductive attractions of this philosophy which simultaneously privileged ideas of a private, interiorized domain of authenticity and authorized movements of social revolt—the challenging of entrenched systems of social interest and power. Yet Combe's theories were no more divorced from the sphere of economic interest than those of Bentham. Behind the rhetoric of pleasure and social liberation lies the dominant economic principle of Victorian industrial expansionism: full maximization, full utilization, and free circulation of all resources.

At the end of *The Professor* Brontë had offered a tantalizing portrait of female self-development in the image of Lucia. *Jane Eyre* looks more chillingly at the difficulties faced by a Victorian woman in fulfilling this goal. In Jane's case the rhetoric of liberation conflicts with her internalized fears of the disruptive forces of female energy. Searching for a fit "emblem" to depict the processes of her mind she turns to the image of fire, which recurs so frequently in mid-Victorian medical representations of the dangerous, destabilizing energies of the uterine economy: "A ridge of lighted heath, alive, glancing, devouring, would have been a meet emblem of my mind when I accused and menaced Mrs. Reed: the same ridge, black and blasted after the flames are dead, would have represented as meetly my subsequent condition" (pp. 40–41). In Brontë's hands, the common rhetorical image of female sexuality is transformed into an analytic tool to suggest the ways in which the internalization of conflicting models of the psyche creates a sensation of self-defeat, of self-consuming energy. Jane is left once more in fear of herself and of the seemingly unrestrainable force of her own faculties. She dreads offering an apology to Mrs. Reed lest she re-excite, "every turbulent impulse of my nature. I would fain exercise some better faculty than that of fierce speaking; fain find nourishment for some less fiendish feeling than that of sombre indignation" (p. 41). The language of the passage encapsulates Victorian social hopes and fears: doctrines of self-improvement through the "nourishment" and "exercise" of the faculties are set against more deep-rooted fears of social turbulence and "fiendish" female behavior.

Images of turbulence and fire permeate Victorian discussions of working-class life and political organization.[15] Sir James Kay Shuttleworth's work, *The Moral and Physical Condition of the Working Classes*, warns of the dangers of "the turbulent riots of the people—of machine breaking—of the secret and sullen organization which has suddenly lit the torch of incendiarism."[16] Similar rhetoric occurred in psychiatric texts. The physician Georget gave a more sympathetic warning of the consequences of women's social situation; prohibited from outward expression of their sexual feelings, they are forced "to feign a calmness and indifference when an inward fire devours them and their whole organization is in tumult."[17] The association between fire and femininity is not solely metaphorical, however. There were also abundant medical accounts of the "insane cunning" of women which could be seen in "the perpetration of *secret* murders by wholesale poisoning, or in secret incendiarism."[18] The working classes and women alike are accused of secrecy, of suddenly erupting after years of quiescence into turbulence and both literal and figural incendiarism.

Jane's primary crime, in her aunt's eyes, is her sudden flaring into violence which suggests a history of secrecy and concealment. On her deathbed, Mrs. Reed recurs once more to her bewilderment as to "how for nine years you could be patient and quiescent under any treatment, and in the tenth break out all fire and violence" (p. 300). At the time of Jane's outbreak the servants had scrutinized her face "as credulous of my sanity," wondering how a girl of her age could have "so much cover" (p. 10). Mrs Reed similarly gazed at her "as if she really did not

know whether I were child or fiend" (p. 28). Jane defies her op-
pressors' theories of physiognomical correspondence, secretly
nursing within her, in a hideous parody of motherhood, the hidden germs or "minute embryos" of insanity and social disruption.[19] As passionate child, Jane Eyre is one of the first literary
embodiments of that new object of fear in Victorian social and
medical discourse. Together with the hysterical woman, the passionate child was perceived as a being dominated by the processes
of the body, outside rational control; both were therefore viewed
as disruptive, marginal groups, on the borders of "real" humanity.[20] This simultaneously lowly, yet threatening, status was further reinforced by writings within political economy and anthro-
pology which linked women and children together with savages
and operatives as figures on the bottom rungs of civilization.[21]

In its focus on passion, *Jane Eyre* has been seen as a very un-
Victorian text; its organizing psychological assumptions, as I have
suggested, however, are drawn directly from the energy dynamics
of nineteenth-century economic and psychological discourse. The
problems of an industrial culture, of simultaneously maximizing
and restraining energy resources, are replicated in the psychological sphere. According to Combe's Malthusian economy of the
psyche, "All the faculties, when in excess, are insatiable, and, from
the constitution of the world, never can be satisfied."[22] In the
mind, as in society, the economics of scarcity and competition
are in operation. Development must work hand in hand with
control. Jane desires to starve her "fiendish" feelings and to find
"nourishment" for her more socially acceptable faculties. Her
mingled exultation in, and fear of, her new-found powers is mirrored in the social realm where pride in the seemingly endless
potentiality of the industrial economy, with its liberation of previously unutilized and imprisoned energies, was indissolubly
linked with fear of the monster they had created, whose powers
might turn out to be unstoppable.

The psychological correlative of this position is complex. Passion could not, in itself, be dismissed as fiendish. Indeed in
Combe's work this preoccupation with energy flow gives rise,
significantly, to a validation of passion. "PASSION," he observes, "is

the highest degree of activity of any faculty. . . . Hence there can be no such thing as *factitious* passion."[23] His model of the mind is of a constant, competitive struggle between different forms of passion. Against the rationalist philosophers who had insisted on the illusory nature of strong emotions, Combe proclaims the psychological and material validity of all passionate sensations. His stance also has significant ramifications with regard to childhood. Whereas Locke had argued that passion could only be the outcome of extensive experience, and thus was an attribute solely of adult life, Combe suggests that it could be experienced with equal force by children.[24] The Victorians' fears of the passionate child, and the enthusiasm with which they policed the borders of childhood, establishing it as an explicit social and psychological category, can be linked to this shattering of the developmental continuum.[25] The sacred ideas of hierarchy and linear progression were under threat: children had now been granted the same unruly energies as undisciplined adults.

The narrative structure of *Jane Eyre* mirrors this challenge to developmental hierarchy. Like that other mid-Victorian portrait of a passionate child, *The Mill on the Floss*, it seems to follow the developmental pattern of a *Bildungsroman*, while in actuality offering the very reverse of a progressive, linear history.[26] Jane, as child, presents the same psychological formation as Jane in adulthood. The history she offers is that of a series of moments of conflict, a series, moreover, which does not display the characteristics of progression; but rather the endless reiteration of the same. This non-progressive format is demonstrated most clearly in her comments on her response to the loss of Miss Temple. On the day of Miss Temple's marriage, Jane recounts, "I altered": "I tired of the routine of eight years in one afternoon" (pp. 99–101). Jane represents her mind as a microcosm of the asylum in which she had been placed; while it had seemed that "better regulated feelings had become the inmates of my mind," her mind now "put[s] off all it had borrowed of Miss Temple . . . I was left in my natural element; and beginning to feel the stirring of old emotions" (pp. 99–100). Jane's life is a history of eternal recurrence, offering a challenge to the forces of institutional order; no matter how firmly the "inmates" might be subject to external direction and regulation, they remain essentially unchanged, ready at any moment to "break bounds." The Freudian model of the mind and the "scandalous" notion of infant sexuality find their roots in mid-Victorian economies of the psyche.

The Victorian preoccupation with simultaneously maximizing and restraining energy, which underlies the repetitive cycle of Jane's history, reverberates throughout contemporary discourse: in debates on the "machinery question" and the problems of labor or in medical and social discussions of the female role.[27] As with the productive working-class body, the reproductive energies of the female body had to be fully utilized, without transgressing the fine line of regulatory social control. The problem was particularly fraught with regard to women since the very energies which fueled their essential role of reproduction were also deemed to be dangerously at odds with their required domestic role. Brontë explores in *Jane Eyre* two alternate institutional models for the disciplining and controlling of female energy, two forms of "asylum": Lowood and the third floor of Thornfield.

The system at Thornfield represents the vestiges of a prior era, when the "animal" insane were kept hidden and mechanically restrained (as Bertha is after each outbreak) and no attempt was made at cure or recuperation. "Nature" was given free rein, but the inmates were in consequence cast out from the ranks of humanity. Lowood, by contrast, conforms more to the system of moral management (with a leaven of physical violence); individuals are to be "saved" for society by the careful regulation of their inner impulses. As Brocklehurst declares, "we are not to conform to nature" (p. 73). Discipline is achieved both by mortification of the flesh and by constant inspection and surveillance. Jane's punishment for being a liar is to stand on a stool and be displayed to the public gaze.

In depicting events at Lowood, Brontë explores the consequences of restraining female energy. Two models are offered, both associated with death. Whereas the other girls die of the contagious disease of typhus, Helen is granted a more dignified death from consumption, which as I noted earlier, was consistently linked in Victorian medical texts with a repression of sexuality. In physiological terms, her internal productive forces, turned inward upon themselves, become self-consuming. Helen achieves her wish to become a "disembodied soul," burning in purifying fire the forces of sexual desire (p. 298). The other girls, however, are brought to a death which reeks of putrid animality. Whereas Helen is permitted a form of transcendence, the other girls in the asylum are driven inwards into their own materiality which, once restrained, obstructed in its flow, becomes a source of pollution. The two forms of death prefigure that of Bertha who is not allowed to be consumed, like Helen, by purifying fire, but smashes down to her native earth in an apotheosis of her intrinsic animality: "dead as the stones on which her brains and blood were scattered" (p. 548).

Surviving the fires of self-consumption, and the diseases of obstruction, Jane depicts her escape from Lowood in terms of the upsurge of clamorous, independent energies. Her initial responses to Thornfield are framed outside any personal sense of agency: "My faculties . . . seemed all astir. I cannot precisely define what they expected, but it was something pleasant" (p. 118). The "I" who speaks is differentiated both from the source and experience of emotion. This famous novel of defiant self-assertion persistently undercuts notions of an originating, unified self. Jane's restlessness, which translates into social discontent, is defended on the grounds of physiology: "Who blames me? Many no doubt; and I shall be called discontented. I could not help it. The restlessness was in my nature; it agitated me to pain sometimes" (p. 132). Seemingly aware of the accusations which might be leveled at her text, Brontë permits her heroine to draw on the discourse of internal, competing energies in order to absolve herself of responsibility for her rebellious thoughts. It was precisely such passages, however, which caused Elizabeth Rigby to attack the novel as a "proud and perpetual assertion of the rights of man": "We do not hesitate to say that the tone of the mind and thought which has overthrown authority and violated every code human and divine abroad, and fostered Chartism and rebellion at home, is the same which has also written *Jane Eyre*."[28]

Rigby's indignant review picks up on the implied parallels between female and working-class revolt which run through the narrative and are later to be foregrounded in *Shirley*. Jane's famous assertion of female rights makes these parallels quite explicit:

It is in vain to say human beings ought to be satisfied with tranquillity: they must have action; and they will make it if they cannot find it. Millions are condemned to a stiller doom than mine, and millions are in silent revolt against their lot. Nobody knows how many rebellions besides political rebellions ferment in the masses of life which people earth. Women are supposed to be very calm generally: but women feel just as men feel; they need exercise for their faculties, and a field for their efforts as much as their brothers do; they suffer from too rigid a restraint, too absolute a stagnation, precisely as men would suffer; and it is narrow-minded in their more privileged fellow-creatures to say that they ought to confine themselves to making pudding and knitting stockings, to playing on the piano and embroidering bags. (p. 133)

Ostensibly the passage articulates support for the reformist position adopted by by Combe, that women, as well as men, should be allowed to exercise their faculties to the full. The demand is not for radical change but rather that women should be allowed to participate in the given social order in more decisive fashion. But against this reformist reading we must place the explosive energy of the passage, and the explicit linking of the position of women and workers. The vision is that of a silent but seething revolt, merely waiting to erupt.

Writing in the era of Chartism, and at a time when political revolution was about to explode throughout Europe, Bronte was not employing her terms loosely. Her letters of 1847 and 1848 show a recurrent preoccupation with the phenomenon of political rebellion, though her shifting responses reveal a significant ambivalence. In April 1848 she speaks of Chartism as an "ill-advised movement . . . judiciously repressed": collective political action should be replaced by "mutual kindliness" and the "just estimate of individual character."[29] Two months later, when the focus of her letter is the more personally implicative issue of the plight of governesses, this individualist perspective and emphasis on restraint is ultimately overthrown. After insisting initially that what governesses most require is "self-control" and "the art of self-possession," Brontë reverses her position in the postscript:

> I conceive that when patience has done its utmost and industry its best, whether in the case of women or operatives, and when both are baffled, and pain and want triumph, the sufferer is free, is entitled, at last to send up to Heaven any piercing cry for relief, if by that cry he can hope to obtain succour.[30]

This same ambivalent shifting between the politics of control, and the inescapability of rebellion, underlies the passage in *Jane Eyre*.

The ideological power of Combe's phrenological social platform and the whole self-help movement lay in its ability to defuse the political challenge of working-class insurgency: in its individualist focus on self-improvement, it directed attention away from class-based action and facilitated the internalization of social controls. Yet the reformist implications of this position are only operative if emphasis is placed firmly on the processes of regulation and control. Jane's strident utterance, by contrast, seems to focus rather on the impossibility of restraint and the inevitability of rebellion. Combining ruling-class fears of the animal masses with the reformist platform of self-development, Brontë articulates a political position which extends beyond, and undercuts, the bourgeois ideology of the dominant narrative. Rebellion is figured as an irresistible physiological process which "ferments" not in the masses (understood as human subjects) but in "the masses of life which people earth." Social and political rebellion is conceived as an inevitable upswelling of a homogeneous animal life-force.

Brontë is drawing here jointly on the rhetoric of the medical obsession with the disruptive potentiality of female reproductive energies and on depictions of working-class animality. Sir James Kay Shuttleworth, for example, traced many of the problems of society to the working-class body. There was, he maintained, "a licentiousness capable of corrupting the whole body of society, like an insidious disease, which eludes observation, yet is equally fatal in its effects." Unlike criminal acts, this disease was so insidious and secretive as to escape even the controlling, classificatory powers of statistics: "Sensuality has no record, and the relaxation of social obligations may coexist with a half dormant, half restless impulse to rebel against all the preservative principles of society; yet these chaotic elements may long smoulder, accompanied only by partial eruptions of turbulence or crime."[31] Working-class sensuality stands as a figure of political rebellion; like the workings of latent insanity, and the hidden processes of the female body, it smoulders in secret, gathering its forces of disruption beyond the control of social regulation.

In Brontë's text, the associative connections lying behind Jane's vehement defense of female faculty development are made clear in the continuation of the passage where Jane suggests that it is thoughtless of men to laugh at women,

> if they seek to do more or learn more than custom has pronounced necessary for their sex.
>
> When thus alone, I not unfrequently heard Grace Poole's laugh: the same peal, the same low, slow ha! ha! which, when first heard, had thrilled me: I heard, too, her eccentric murmurs; stranger than her laugh. (p. 133)

From men's laughter at women, Jane moves to the uncanny laughter of female response, which she initially locates in a member of the servant class. Her own bodily "thrill" of response directly implicates her within this disruptive domain.[32] Brontë's attitudes to the sexual and social challenge offered by the figure of Bertha/Grace are, however, far more ambivalent than Rigby's review might lead one to believe.

Notes

1. See Sandra Gilbert and Susan Gubar, *The Madwoman in the Attic: The Woman Writer and the Nineteenth-Century Literary Imagination* (New Haven:

Yale University Press, 1979), and Barbara Hill Rigney, *Madness and Sexual Politics in the Feminist Novel* (Madison: University of Wisconsin Press, 1978).

2. It is on this point that I would like to differentiate my work from Elaine Showalter's excellent study, *The Female Malady: Women, Madness, and English Culture, 1830–1980* (New York: Pantheon, 1985), which considers the notion of female madness within a narrower framework of social explanation.

3. Charlotte Brontë, *Jane Eyre*, ed. Jane Jack and Margaret Smith (Oxford: Clarendon Press, 1969), p. xxxi. All references to this edition will be given in future in the text.

4. See Matthew 23: 27.

5. T. J. Wise and J. A. Symington, *The Brontës: Their Lives, Friendships and Correspondence*, 4 vols. (Oxford: Basil Blackwell, 1933), vol 2, p. 198. Hereafter cited as *Letters*. To W. S. Williams, 11 March 1848.

6. *Letters*, vol. 2, p. 201. To W. S. Williams, 29 March 1848.

7. See Georges Canguilhem, *Essai sur quelques problèmes concernant le normal et le pathologique*, (Publications de la Faculté des Lettres de l'Université de Strasbourg) (Paris: 1950), p. 18.

8. Margot Peters, *Charlotte Brontë: Style in the Novel* (Madison: University of Wisconsin Press, 1973), p. 57.

9. See Mary Poovey, *Uneven Developments: The Ideological Work of Gender in Mid-Victorian England* (London: Virago, 1989), ch. 5, and M. Jeanne Peterson, "The Victorian Governess: Status Incongruence in Family and Society," in Martha Vicinus, ed., *Suffer and Be Still: Women in the Victorian Age* (Bloomington: Indiana University Press, 1972), pp. 3–19.

10. See Peter Stallybrass and Allon White, *The Politics and Poetics of Transgression* (Ithaca, NY: Cornell University Press, 1986), ch. 3.

11. For a further reading of this inferiority see Elaine Showalter, *A Literature of Their Own: British Women Novelists from Brontë to Lessing* (Princeton: Princeton University Press, 1977), and Karen Chase, *Eros and Psyche: The Representation of Personality in Charlotte Brontë, Charles Dickens, and George Eliot* (London: Methuen, 1984), chs. 3 and 4.

12. Brontë's text points to the inadequacies of forms of Lacanian analysis which do not take full account of the contradictory subject positions offered within a given culture.

13. George Combe, *Elements of Phrenology*, 3rd ed. (Edinburgh: John Anderson, 1828), p. 60.

14. George Combe, *The Constitution of Man Considered in Relation to External Objects*, 7th ed. (Boston: Marsh, Capen and Lyon, 1836), p. 104.

15. As Susan Meyer has pointed out in her excellent article. "Colonialism and the Figurative Strategy of *Jane Eyre,*" *Victorian Studies* 33 (1990), 247–68, the language of fire was also employed in representations of the revolt of that other oppressed group whose presence informs the text of *Jane Eyre,* the West Indian Slaves (p. 254).

16. James Kay Shuttleworth, *The Moral and Physical Condition of the Working Classes Employed in the Cotton Manufacture in Manchester* (London, 1832; repr. Shannon: Irish University Press, 1971), p. 47.

17. Quoted by John Conolly in "Hysteria," in J. Forbes, A. Tweedie, and J. Conolly, eds., *The Cyclopaedia of Practical Medicine,* 4 vols. (London: Sherwood et al., 1833), vol. 2, p. 572.

18. "Woman in her Psychological Relations," *Journal of Psychological Medicine and Mental Pathology,* 4 (1851), p. 33. The writer here is echoing the work of Thomas Laycock. See for example, the section on "Insane Cunning" in *A Treatise on the Nervous Diseases of Women; Comprising an Inquiry into the Nature, Causes, and Treatment of Spinal and Hysterical Disorders* (London: Longman, 1840), p. 353.

19. John Reid, *Essays on Hypochondriasis and Other Nervous Afflictions,* 2nd ed. (London: Longman, 1821), p. 314.

20. See Thomas Laycock, *An Essay on Hysteria* (Philadelphia: Haswell, Barrington and Haswell, 1840), p. 107.

21. See Nancy Stepan, "Race and Gender: the Role of Analogy in Science," *Isis* 77 (1986), p. 264.

22. Combe, *Constitution of Man,* p. 72.

23. Combe, *A System of Phrenology,* 3rd ed. (Edinburgh: John Anderson, 1830), p. 540.

24. Ibid.

25. For an examination of the fears aroused by the passionate child, see Michel Foucault, *The History of Sexuality,* Vol. 1, trans. R. Hurley (Harmondsworth: Penguin, 1981).

26. See Penny Boumelha, "George Eliot and the End of Realism," in Sue Roe, ed., *Women Reading Women's Writing* (Brighton: Harvester Press, 1987), pp. 15–35; George Eliot, *The Mill on the Floss,* ed. S. Shuttleworth (London: Routledge, 1991), p. 495; and Susan Fraiman, *Unbecoming Women: British Women Writers and the Novel of Development* (New York: Columbia University Press, 1993), chs. 4 and 5.

27. For a discussion of the economic side of this debate, see Maxine Berg, *The Machinery Question and the Making of Political Economy, 1815–48* (Cambridge: Cambridge University Press, 1980).

28. Elizabeth Rigby, Review of *Jane Eyre, Quarterly Review,* 15 (April 1848); repr. in Miriam Allott, *The Brontës: The Critical Heritage* (London: Routledge and Kegan Paul, 1974), pp. 109–10.

29. *Letters,* vol. 2, p. 203. To W. S. Williams, 20 April 1848.

30. *Letters,* vol. 2, p. 216. To W. S. Williams, 12 May 1848.

31. Kay Shuttleworth, *The Moral and Physical Condition,* p. 38.

32. Susan Fraiman in chapter 4 of *Unbecoming Women* offers a very insightful reading of the centrality of Grace, the servant figure, in the text, highlighting the importance of Jane's concern with her relations to the working class.

"Dreadful to Me"

Jane Eyre and History

HEATHER GLEN

◆　　◆　　◆

"IT HAS NO LEARNING, no research, it discusses no subject of public interest," wrote Charlotte Brontë shortly after the publication of *Jane Eyre*.[1] Even the novel's admirers have been inclined to echo this view. "Of the novels included here," Kathleen Tillotson announces categorically, in her *Novels of the Eighteen-Forties,* "*Jane Eyre* has the least relation to its time."

> Such social commentary as it may offer is oblique, limited, incidental. It is both in purpose and effect primarily a novel of the inner life, not of man in his social relations, it maps a private world . . . a love-story, a Cinderella fable, a Bluebeard mystery, an autobiography from forlorn childhood to happy marriage: this novel makes its appeal first and last to "the unchanging human heart."[2]

For *Jane Eyre*'s fairy-tale shapings, its archetypal themes of search for love and escape from danger, above all, perhaps, its representation of childhood suffering, do seem to point away from its specific historical moment, and towards areas of experience which all can readily understand. "Who that remembers early child-hood, can read without emotion the little Jane Eyre's night jour-ney to Lowood?" asked Sydney Dobell, in an early review.[3] "Pas-sages read like a page out of one's own life," G. H. Lewes declared.[4] And generations of girls have thrilled, with similar empathy, to Jane's story of passionate love.[5] The meanings its critics have traced in it may have changed with changing *mores,* but in its evocation of vulnerable childhood, its representation of desire, *Jane Eyre* has seemed to speak less of historical difference than of its readers' most intimate concerns.

Yet it was with regard to its handling of those universal themes of childhood suffering and passionate love that the question of the novel's historicity was first most sharply posed. In 1857, when Elizabeth Gaskell's *Life of Charlotte Bronte* had familiarized readers with the real-life "originals" of Mr. Brocklehurst and Lowood school, a review in the *Christian Observer* attacked Charlotte Brontë for her depiction of them: "her picture is that of a morbid fancy, mixing up fiction with fact, and traducing, with a random pen, an Institution to which she and her family were wholesale debt-ors."[6] From June to August of the same year, a controversy raged in the correspondence columns of the *Halifax Guardian* as to the accuracy of the novel's "picture" of the Clergy Daughters' School.[7] Ex-pupils wrote in defending its diet and discipline; Char-lotte Brontë's widower replied with counterexamples. Neither side seems to have doubted that here, at least, Charlotte Brontë was addressing herself to a subject of considerable "public interest." Similarly, and no less confidently, the novel's unprecedented em-phasis on a woman's passionate desire was explicitly measured against its first critics' views of "real life." "It is not thus that generous men make their advances, or that women worthy of the name are won," wrote William C. Roscoe, of Brontë's depic-tion of courtship.[8] "Passion occupies too prominent a place in her pictures of life," Harriet Martineau complained, in her otherwise admiring obituary; in representing "love" as women's "whole and sole concern," the author of *Jane Eyre* had given a quite false view of their lives.[9] "The author has struck only one chord of the human heart . . . and has set it vibrating alone, to the exclusion of all the rest," echoed Émile Montégut in 1857. *"Jane Eyre* is a passionate dream, a perfect castle in Spain."[10] To some, at least, of its earliest readers, it seems, this "Cinderella fable" spoke controversially of contemporary actualities rather than of universal truth.

The correspondents who disputed the details of the regime at Cowan Bridge school in the *Halifax Guardian* may have had rather naïve notions of the relation between fact and fiction. But their argument over *Jane Eyre*'s "truthfulness" does point toward that which its author's apologetic sense that "it discusses no subject of public interest" obscures. In her representation of Jane's childhood—to which a third of the novel is devoted—Charlotte Brontë is dealing with a set of power relations no less socially significant than those issues of class and gender and race with which recent critics have been concerned. Here, that which appeared so disquietingly as a coda to Crimsworth's story—the figure of the subjugated child—occupies the center of the stage. It is not here distanced into the third person, as it was in *The Professor,* or as it had been in Dickens' *Oliver Twist,* first published in serial form ten years before. Jane tells of her childhood sufferings with an intimacy and a directness hitherto unparalleled in fiction; and the shape they assume in the telling is a quite distinctive one.

"There was no possibility . . . ," Jane begins; and in the novel's very first paragraph, before the reader learns her name, she records that of one whose authority prescribes the limits of her world. If hers is an urgent, first-person voice, it is not exactly a freely expressive one. In face of this forbidding other, the narrating "I" is not a subject but an object, awkwardly prominent, as Jane is in her exclusion: "Me, she had dispensed from joining the group." The direct voice of the child, "saddened," "humbled," excluded, gives way to the speech of one whose pronouncements have the force of general laws:

> Saying, "She regretted to be under the necessity of keeping me at a distance; but that until she heard from Bessie, and could discover from her own observation that I was endeavouring in good earnest to acquire a more sociable and

child-like disposition, a more attractive and sprightly manner,—something lighter, franker, more natural as it were—
she really must exclude me from privileges intended only
for contented, happy, little children." (7)

Like the text-bearing tablet that Jane is later to confront at Lowood, Mrs. Reed's words are mystifyingly incontestable: apparently impersonal, yet violent in their alienation from the child.
The [quotation marks], the formality, the use of the third person
all draw attention to this discourse, so different from that of the
opening sentences: it is objectified, placed on display. Jane's reply
to this speech—"What does Bessie say I have done?"—punctures
with its childish directness the balloon of this other's pomposity;
but the power of the discourse that places her by no means ends
there. Instead of an answer to her question there is a refusal of
dialogue: "Jane, I don't like cavillers or questioners." The urgent
first-person voice of the opening is met by condemnatory judgment—a configuration that is to recur throughout *Jane Eyre.*

This opening opposition between Jane's baffled subjectivity—
suffering, fearful, desperate, longing—and the disciplinary injunctions, the condemnatory judgments, of others soon becomes
actual violence: hands holding her down, bonds being prepared,
darkness and imprisonment. The sense, powerfully conveyed
through all the resources of a preternaturally suggestive prose, is
of a world that poses a threat to the protagonist's very being. Of
course, the young Jane's story is also one of rebellion, "fierce
speaking" and "fiendish feeling" (47). Her angry outburst against
her bullying cousin is the originating moment of that narrative
of self-assertion which is one way of reading *Jane Eyre.* But that
sense of a self in jeopardy and a persecutory reality which informs
the novel's opening portrait of the "dependent," threatened child
is not transcended as Jane matures, but articulated throughout,
a powerful undertow to its "Cinderella-fable" of survival, happiness, success. The world through which this heroine moves is not
merely repressive and disheartening but a murderous place in
which her survival is at stake.

It is a sense that seems to exceed even the bleakest construction of the material conditions of life in early Victorian England. Yet it is one that the novel from its opening locates within the discourses and the practices of a sharply seen actual world. For if Mrs. Reed is a monstrous figure, her speech is of a kind that would have been quite familiar to the novel's first readers. Thus, for example, Mrs Chapone's much-reprinted *Letters on the Improvement of the Mind* (1773), on which the relatively liberal curriculum of Roe Head School, where Charlotte Brontë was both pupil and teacher, was based: "To make you the delight and darling of your family, something more is required than barely to be exempt from ill-temper and troublesome humours. The sincere and gentle smiles of complacency and love must adorn your countenance. ... Conversation ... must be cultivated with the frankness and openness of friendship."[11] In the face of such discourse as this, the child is not a thinking, feeling subject but a creature to be disciplined and trained. This is the characteristic language of much early nineteenth-century English pedagogy. But *Jane Eyre* traces a darker logic in that pedagogy than many of its more well-meaning practitioners might have been prepared to admit.

Even as Jane is scolded and bullied, unjustly accused and punished, excluded and "kept at a distance," her tormentors portray themselves, mysteriously, as her "benefactors." "What we tell you is for your good," says Bessie, as she enjoins the child to "try to be useful and pleasant." "If you become passionate and rude, Missis will send you away, I am sure." "Besides," said Miss Abbot, "God will punish her: he might strike her dead in the midst of her tantrums, and then where would she go?" (13). Miss Abbot's is no general threat but the quite distinctive discourse of a specific ideology. As the Reeds, with their punishments and humiliations, are succeeded by that "pillar" of society, Mr. Brocklehurst, and by the institutionalized violence of his "evangelical, charitable establishment" (63), it becomes evident that in her depiction of Jane's traumatic childhood Charlotte Brontë is responding to a major social and cultural fact of early nineteenth-century England, which she herself had known in an especially extreme manifestation: that distinctive pedagogy which had developed out of the evangelical revival of the eighteenth century and which by

the nineteenth was enshrined in schools such as those at Kingswood and at Cowan Bridge and promulgated in hundreds of
tracts and articles, sermons and stories—which had become, indeed, in more or less modified form, probably the most powerful
ideology of child-rearing in early Victorian England.[12] When one
contemplates the surviving records of that pedagogy, the "strange,
startling and harrowing" configurations of Jane's story begin to
appear less as the work of a "morbid fancy" than as an emphatic
invocation of some of the key terms and concepts of a well-
known contemporary discourse; as familiar to the author of *Jane
Eyre* as the teapot in the Brontë household, with its sombre, gilt-
lettered text: "For to me to live is Christ, and to die is gain."

In evangelical thinking,[13] the child was a being very different
from the innocent child of Romanticism: not a unique individual,
whose potentialities should be allowed to unfold in as unob-
structed a way as possible, but a creature of "inbred corruption,"[14]
destined for hell. "You are a sinner, and without a gracious Saviour you must perish!": such is the tenor of the great evangelical
Legh Richmond's letters to his children, reprinted in a book that
"strongly attracted and strangely fascinated" Charlotte Brontë
when she read it at the age of 21.[15] It is this constellation of feeling
that *Jane Eyre* invokes, in describing her childish resistance to
John Reed as "roused by the same sentiment of deep ire and
desperate revolt which had stirred *my corruption* before" or her de-
parture from Gateshead as marked by "a sense of outlawry and
almost of *reprobation*" (27, 227; my italics):[16] it is to this that Brocklehurst appeals, when he declares "we are not to conform to
nature: I wish these girls to be the children of Grace" (64). From
the perspective of such thinking, the child was less a being to be
respected, or even acknowledged, than one whose "self-will"
needed, for his or her own sake, to be "broken" by rigorous
discipline, whose "passions" had to be curbed. The authority of
parent or teacher was absolute and unquestionable. In Mrs. Sherwood's best-selling evangelical novel for children, *The Fairchild Family*, the paterfamilias reminds his son, "I stand in place of God to
you, whilst you are a child."[17] "A wise parent . . . should begin to
break [his child's] will the first moment it appears," wrote John

Wesley. "In the whole art of Christian education there is nothing more important than this. The will of a parent is to a little child in place of the will of God."[18]

Evangelical beliefs were not merely articulated as doctrine: they found expression and reinforcement in a range of child-rearing practices. The evangelical child was the object of constant surveillance: that officious supervision which Mr. Brocklehurst enjoins the Lowood teachers to practice—"Teachers, you must watch her: keep your eyes on her movements, weigh well her words, scrutinize her actions, punish her body to save her soul" (66)—and of which Mr. Brocklehurst's prototype, Carus Wilson, had been especially proud. "It was often said of me," he is reported as saying, "that I had eyes in every part of me: and . . . I have no hesitation in saying that herein consisted one of the chief services I rendered to the School."[19] Legh Richmond advocated education at home, in small groups, to facilitate closer observation—"two or three may be watched every hour—evil checked as it arises—every occurrence improved—religion infused into every pursuit and instruction"; "I see more and more, daily," he wrote to his wife, "how desirable my own presence is, and that continually." "Such was his vigilance," his biographer reports, "that if a friend introduced his son under circumstances of common courtesy, he appeared restless and uneasy if the young people were left together without superintendence for a few moments."[20] "Vigilance" such as this was to the evangelicals merely an earthly reminder of the unceasing scrutiny of the all-seeing eye of God. Thus Carus Wilson's *The Friendly Visitor*, "published in monthly Tracts during the Year 1821" and designed for very young children, contains a chilling little dialogue, in which Mr. S. tells his godson Charles of a book that God keeps, in which all the child's sins are set down:

C.—Then God remembers the lie I told you before, when I was quite a little boy; and how I fell into a passion, and pushed my little cousin Margaret off the bank, and had nearly killed her.

Mr S.—Yes, God remembers all this.

C.—O dear! I shall be sadly frightened when the day of judgment comes. I was in hopes that everybody had forgot about my being naughty, since you and Mr Wilson never say anything about it now.

Mr S.—God forgets nothing, my dear.

THE END

"Our mother," wrote the novelist Charlotte Elizabeth Tonna of her childhood, "had taken infinite pains to assure us of one great truth—the omniscience of an Omnipresent God—and this I never could for a moment shake off."[21] "Remember! the eye of God is upon you in every place," Legh Richmond instructed his son. "Be where you will, do what you will, you may always say with Hagar in the wilderness—'Thou God seest me'."[22]

A similar vigilance was expected of the child himself. He or she was trained in the art of self-examination: a kind of spiritual account-keeping, in which every motive, every action, every moment, was monitored with care:[23]

> Every morning must begin
> With resolutions not to sin;
> And every evening recollect
> How much you've failed in this respect.[24]

"Teach [children] to render an account of all their thoughts to God," M. A. Stodart advised in *Principles of Education* (1844). "They will not then shrink from the piercing eye, the close observation of their fellow creatures."[25] "I am . . . slatternly; I seldom put, and never keep, things in order; I am careless; I forget rules; I read when I should learn my lessons; I have no method; and sometimes I say, like you, I cannot *bear* to be subjected to systematic arrangements": thus Helen Burns presents her spiritual account to Jane Eyre (56). The fictional Lucy Fairchild, in *The Fairchild Family*, is given a diary and told to keep "an account of what passed in her heart, that she might learn more and more to know and hate her own sinful nature."[26] The diary of Margaret Gray, 17-year-old daughter of an evangelical family in York, tells how, on 1 January 1826, she began to use the Biometer, a chart in which

the thoughts and employments of every day were to be recorded
with "extreme minuteness." Twelve days later, she was suffering
from "giddiness": this was succeeded by "inflammation of the
brain," "extreme restlessness," and—on the last day of the
month—by death.[27]

Evangelical condemnation was directed most particularly at
the sins of vanity and of lying—seen as perhaps the two worst
examples of that "self-will" which had to be broken in the child.
The "worldly sentiment of pride" that Mr. Brocklehurst seeks to
"mortify" in the pupils at Lowood (34) is attacked again and again
in evangelical writings. In Carus Wilson's *Friendly Visitor* for 1821
there is a report of an inquest on a servant who hanged herself
after getting into debt through love of dress, and girl readers are
warned:

> We are hurt to see your love of dress, and we reprove you
> for your smart clothes and fine curls.... We have lived a
> little longer in the world than you; and we have seen the
> end of many a poor girl who was fond of dress; and in pity
> to your souls we warn you. We wish to nip the evil in the
> bud. Bad habits, if not checked, will be sure to grow. You
> will covet finery which you see others have. In order to
> purchase it, you are tempted to steal. The next step perhaps
> is the gallows.

"Each of the young persons before us has a string of hair twisted
in plaits which vanity might have woven," splutters Brocklehurst
"My mission is to ... teach them to clothe themselves with
shame-facedness and sobriety, not with braided hair and costly
apparel" (64). If Jane, at Lowood school, is forced to display herself
as "a liar!" on a "pedestal of infamy" (66–7) such punishment was
not, in evangelical circles, unusual, or even unusually extreme.
The novelist Elizabeth Missing Sewell tells in her *Autobiography* how,
at the school she attended in the 1820s,

> ... if a child told a lie, she was not allowed any reward for
> three months, and was obliged to stand up in the school-
> room for several hours with a long black gown on, and a

piece of red cloth—cut in the shape of a tongue, and on which the word "Liar" was worked in white letters—fastened round the neck so as to hang down in front. The awe which fell upon the school when Miss Crooke in a solemn voice said, "Put on the Gown and the Liar's tongue," was indescribable.[28]

The issue of Carus Wilson's *Children's Friend* that appeared in June 1847, a few months before *Jane Eyre*, contains a story whose title tells all—"The Liar's Mouth Sewn Up": it is illustrated by a graphic woodcut. And the tract on the Liar that Mr. Brocklehurst gives to Jane has its prototype in dozens of such stories, by Carus Wilson and by others, in which liars meet dreadful earthly punishments or go to everlasting perdition. The message was driven home with singular ferocity. "All Liars shall have their part in the lake which burneth with fire and brimstone," Rowland Hill warns his infant readers; "and how grievously they are tormented you will see in the picture."[29] "Then let me always watch my Lips," resolves the child speaker of Isaac Watts' "Against Lying":

> Lest I be struck to Death and Hell
> Since God a Book of Reckoning keeps
> For every Lye that Children tell.[30]

"I was thunderstruck and almost distracted," declared one early nineteenth-century father, of his discovery that his 3-year-old son had told a lie, "for the information seemed to blast my most cherished hopes. This might, I thought, be the commencement of a series of evils for ever ruinous to our peace. . . . I am not sure that my agony, on hearing of his death, was much more intense than that which I endured, from an apprehension of his guilt."[31]

Evangelical children were not simply watched and warned. They were subjected also to a rigorous discipline, aimed at subduing the desires of the flesh, instilling humility and obedience, and fitting them for eternity. This was most famously institutionalized, of course, in schools school such as Kingswood and Cowan Bridge, with their monotonous, exacting routines—like the "rules . . . lessons . . . method . . . systematic arrangements"

(56) of the Lowood regime—in which every moment of the day had its allotted task, and children were uniformly attired, given the plainest food, and severely punished for their faults. Yet schools such as these merely provided spectacular, public examples of a discipline that was practiced to greater or lesser extent in hundreds of thousands of early Victorian homes. Daily life was closely regulated, Sabbath observance rigidly enforced, and even on weekdays prohibitions and restrictions were plentiful. The child's friendships and reading-matter were censored and controlled; and he or she was made to learn hymns and large portions of Scripture by heart. (A prominent item in Mr. Brocklehurst's cautionary repertoire is the paragon of "infant piety" who receives gingerbread-nuts in return for learning psalms). Catechizing, which had begun to be outmoded, was revived in the early years of the century. Evangelical catechisms were advertised in Hannah More's *Cheap Repository Tracts* and praised in the *Evangelical Magazine*[32] Such catechisms recur in *Jane Eyre*. At Jane's first meeting with the black marble Brocklehurst she is subjected to a form of catechizing; Sunday evenings at Lowood are spent "in repeating, by heart, the Church Catechism" (60); later, St. John Rivers is reported to have gone to Morton school to give a daily catechizing class.

Formal catechizing was, however, but the public, ritual face of much more intimately intrusive inquisitorial practices. The evangelical child was constantly questioned as to the state of his or her soul: parental letters to their children are filled with urgent interrogations. "It is time you seriously reflected on eternity, and the value of your soul," Legh Richmond urged one son after another's death. "You are a sinner; and without a gracious Saviour you must perish. Do you pray in Christ's name? and that earnestly, for the pardon of your sins?...Do you think of [your brother's] last words to you...? Have you written down his dying words, as I desired you?"[33] For evangelical discipline was not merely an external regime: it extended like rapine into the most private areas of the psyche. Richmond's lengthy description of his son Wilberforce's death today makes harrowing reading, not least because of the evidence it provides of the boy's desperate attempts to preserve an area of privacy in face of his father's equally desperate questioning. Indeed, the entire volume in which that account appears offers an (unintentionally) chilling picture of what the psychodynamics of a family life motivated by evangelical ideology might be. Richmond was not merely "very attentive to [his children's] regularity, neatness and good manners": "when he perceived youthful spirits rising to excess, he would throw in a remark to check the exuberance."[34] "While at home as well as when abroad," his biographer writes of him, "he kept up a correspondence with his family, which he used to call his *Home Mission*"— a correspondence motivated largely by his confessed inability to initiate "close personal conversation" with them. "When I begin, they are silent," he admits; "and it is not long before I also feel tongue-tied; yet I cannot be easy without ascertaining the effect of my instructions, and hence I have been driven to use my pen, because I could not open my lips." Richmond never used "corporal chastisement." Like Mrs. Reed, though no doubt from higher spiritual motives, he "kept the offender at a distance, or separated him from the society of his family, as one unworthy to share in their privileges and affections"—his "countenance" meanwhile expressing "the deepest anguish" at the sense of himself as "the author of a corrupt being." The result appears to have been acquiescence: or, as his admiring biographer puts it, "Perhaps there never was a family where the reign of love suffered less interruption."[35]

"Love" was certainly often invoked as the mainspring of evangelical pedagogy. The claim—very often sincere—was that those who thus watched and punished their little one were acting for their "own good," striving to ensure their salvation from a terrible doom. "Remember that your parents are commanded by God to correct your faults," enjoined John Angell James; "that they are actuated by love in performing this self-denying duty, and that it costs them more pain to inflict it, than it does you to endure it."[36] "I wished every stroke had been a stab," says Charlotte Elizabeth Tonna, describing the whipping her father gave her for telling a lie. "I wept because the pain was not great enough; and I loved my father at that moment better than even I, who almost idolized him, had ever loved him before."[37] "A poor little girl who had been taken into a school was whipped," tells Carus Wilson, in *The Children's Friend,* apparently of a child at Cowan Bridge school. "She asked, 'If they love us, why do they whip us?' A little girl of six replied, 'It is because they love us, and it is to make us remember what a sad thing sin is. God would be angry with them if they did not whip us.' "[38] ("Cruel? Not at all! She is severe: she dislikes my faults," says Helen Burns [55], of the terrible Miss Scatcherd.) "Precious, no doubt, are these little ones in your eyes; but if you love them, think often of their souls," exhorted J. C. Ryle, in a sermon preached a year before the publication of *Jane Eyre*:

> No interest should weigh with you so much as their eternal interests. No part of them should be so dear to you as that part which will never die. . . . To pet and pamper, and indulge your child, as if this world was all he had to look to, and this life the only season for happiness; to do this is not true love but cruelty.[39]

Yet if evangelical teaching was often sincerely motivated by a desperate desire to save the "little ones" at whom it was directed, its God was less a God of love than a God of vengeance·

> Two sinners God's just vengeance felt
> For telling one presumptuous lie·
> Dear children, learn to dread his wrath,
> Lest you should also sin and die.[40]

And it was enforced by a program of coercion and punishment, intimidation and humiliation, which—however it might be softened by affection or (as it was for the young Brontës) countered by other influences—was expressly designed to break the "spirit" of the child.

For evangelical discipline was aimed, above all, at the subjugation of self: not merely that denial of the flesh which might, in extreme cases, lead to actual death (as at Lowood), but also, and most centrally, the "mortification" of worldly impulses and desires (*JE* 76). The child's will had to be broken, lest he or she be damned: the successfully reared evangelical child was one who—like Helen Burns—had internalized the self-suppression thus imposed. This was a project far more extreme than that character-building "self-control" seen as essential to success in early nineteenth-century England which Brontë had portrayed in Crimsworth.[41] For its explicit aim was self-annihilation; and it was both motivated and mirrored by the evangelical emphasis on death.

"God has spared you," declares Carus Wilson, in a New Year address to a child whose "little companion" has died: "Why? That you may get ready to die. He has let you see a new year. Why? Because he wants you to seek a new heart and so be prepared for heaven."[42] To the evangelicals, life on earth was a mere preparation for the hereafter: death, therefore, was its climactic point—the moment of entry into bliss or perdition. When the 10-year-old Maria Brontë was questioned by her father as to "what was the best mode of spending time," hers was the orthodox response of the ideal evangelical child: "By laying it out in preparation for a happy eternity."[43] Long before she embarked on the use of the Biometer, the youthful Margaret Gray had recorded her grand aim in life: "to be deeply impressed with the vanity and unsatisfactory nature of all earthly things; to have realizing views of eternity; to look steadily to the near approach of death; to hold converse with heaven."[44] In 1797 the *Evangelical Magazine* printed a Spiritual Barometer, an aid to self-examination, by the use of which the child could monitor the state of his soul: its point of highest spiritual excellence was "Desiring to depart, to be with Christ."[45] Just such a "point of spiritual excellence" is prominently figured in the letter Jane quotes from St. John Rivers at the ending of *Jane Eyre*.

Death, indeed, was the central theme of evangelical pedagogy. The aim of the myriads of tracts and stories directed in these years at little children was to convince the child of the inevitability of death and of the dreadfulness of the punishment awaiting sinners. One such tract, "containing 'an account of the awfully sudden death of Martha G—, a naughty child addicted to falsehood and deceit' " (35) is presented by Brocklehurst to Jane: later, she tells how the pupils at Lowood were subjected to "evening readings from books of his own inditing, about sudden deaths and judgments, which made us afraid to go to bed" (123). Carus Wilson's actual output certainly conforms to this description. *The Child's Magazine, and Sunday-School Companion* for July 1824, which appeared the month before the 8-year-old Charlotte Brontë entered Cowan Bridge school, and is likely to have formed part of her reading there, contains an article entitled "On Man's Mortality," which instructs its young readers that "of nothing can we be more certain, than of this, however we may strive to forget it, we must die," and calculates the numbers of people dying throughout the world:

Each year Thirty-three millions three hundred thousand
Each day Eighty-three thousand
Each hour Three thousand four hundred and fifty
Each minute Fifty-seven
Which amounts almost to One each second.

"If the mortality be so great each year, and even each day," it concludes, "is it not more than probable that some one of our fellow-creatures is this moment departing from the world? And before an hour has elapsed, more than three thousand souls who are still inhabitants of time will have passed into eternity! What a motive to induce us to think frequently and seriously upon death, and to live in a state of continual preparation for our solemn change!" Each issue of this journal—as of *The Children's Friend*—contains at least one account of an early death. Some describe the edifying deaths of pious children—those who have internalized evangelical strictures so effectively that all desire for self-preservation (at any rate in this world) has been obliterated in them. One such anecdote, which appears in *The Children's Friend* for 1826, is of particular interest, in that it concerns a girl who was a contemporary of Charlotte Brontë's at Cowan Bridge, entering the school in February 1824 at the age of 9 (the 8-year-old Charlotte was to join her in August of the same year) and dying at the age of 11 in 1826:

On the 28th of last September died in the Clergy School at
Cowen Bridge [*sic*] Sarah Bicker, aged 11 years. . . . Her com-
plaint was inflammation in the bowels, and her sufferings
were very great. . . . I had heard from her teachers that she
had expressed a desire to depart and to be with Christ and
I was anxious to assure myself that her hopes were well
founded. . . . I bless God that he has taken from us the child
of whose salvation we have the best hope and may her
death be the means of rousing many of her school-fellows
to seek the Lord while he may be found.

Before her holy death, Sarah Bicker had (it is reported) urged a
naughty companion to "humble her pride and pray to God, and
he would be sure to take away her heart of stone and give her
a heart of flesh": her words are echoed in Mr. Brocklehurst's
injunction to Jane Eyre: "You have a wicked heart; and you must
pray to God to change it: to give you a new and clean one: to
take away your heart of stone and give you a heart of flesh" (33).
(The allusion, in both cases, is to Ezekiel 11:19). Other stories—
like that of "the sudden death of the Liar," which Brocklehurst
gives to Jane (67)—recount the dreadful deaths of the unrepen-
tant. One such, in *The Child's First Tales,* describes that of a boy
who skated on the sabbath, fell through the ice, and was
drowned: "He left his school. He took his play on the Sunday.
And he thought he should go to hell for this. I fear he would
go there. How sad it is to think of!"[46] Another, recounted in
monosyllables for infant readers, tells of a little girl of 3, who
flew into a violent "pet" with her mother:

She was in such a rage, that all at once God struck her
dead. . . . No time to pray. No time to call on God to save
her poor soul. . . . And oh! where do you think she is now?
. . . We know that bad girls go to hell. . . . I do not think
that this poor girl's rage is now at an end, though she is in
hell. She is in a rage with her-self.[47]

For if for the regenerate death was the gateway to eternal bliss,
no evangelical child could be safe from fear of the terrible alter-

native. Even the saintly Wilberforce Richmond was tormented by doubts on his deathbed. "I often think how shocking it would be to go to hell," confided the 11-year-old Margaret Gray to the diary of self-castigation she kept for her mother's perusal, in 1820. "I can't bear the thought of it; and I think sometimes, suppose I was to die, where should I go to?"[48] To the child Jane, locked in the red-room at Thornfield, a dreadful question presents itself: "Was I fit to die?" (48). Sophisticated theologians might differ on the subject,[49] but the notion of everlasting punishment was prominent in evangelical writings for children in the first half of the nineteenth century. Thus, the evangelical catechism "For Children of Tender Years":

Q. What sort of a place is Hell?
A. A dark and bottomless pit, full of fire and brimstone.
Q. How will the wicked be punished there?
A. Their bodies will be tormented by fire.[50]

Thus Legh Richmond, to his 11-year-old son: "You have need to flee from the wrath to come. Repent, for the kingdom of heaven is at hand. The wicked and all the people that forget God, shall be turned into hell. Dear Willy, if you forget him, what will be your portion?"[51]

And thus Carus Wilson, in a memorable formulation:

'Tis dangerous to provoke a God
Whose power and vengeance none can tell;
One stroke of his almighty rod
Can send young sinners quick to hell.[52]

Jane's "ready and orthodox answer" to Mr. Brocklehurst's query, "Do you know where the wicked go after death?" could have come from any one of hundreds of evangelical tracts, with their graphic depictions of that fearful "pit full of fire." Her progress through the novel is attended by threats of Hell and damnation, from Miss Abbot's awful question (reminiscent of Carus Wilson)— "God . . . might strike her dead in the midst of her tantrums, and then where would she go?" (13)—to Brocklehurst's—"And should you like to fall into that pit and to be burning there for ever?" (32); from the terrible temptation of Rochester's "flaming glance," before which she is "powerless as stubble exposed to the draught and glow of a furnace" (317) to St. John Rivers's pointed reading of "the lake which burneth with fire and brimstone, which is the second death" (417).

If Jane's is an extreme example of a "universal" experience of childish vulnerability and humiliation, it has, then, a quite particular cultural inflection. Indeed, much in these early chapters of *Jane Eyre*—the injunctions and warnings directed at Jane; the discipline institutionalized at Lowood school, with its surveillance, its regimentation, its punishments and privations; the caricature-portrait of Mr. Brocklehurst and his publications; Helen Burns's pious (if slightly unorthodox) death—seems designed to offer less a peculiar, private nightmare-vision than a hostile but realistic portrayal of the ethos of evangelicalism. Brocklehurst's words virtually echo the published writings of his real-life prototype:[53] the punishments inflicted on Helen and Jane can be paralleled by the (often far worse) punishments suffered by disobedient children in hundreds of evangelical tracts. And if, as Carus Wilson's supporters indignantly noted, the depiction of the Lowood regime amounts to a "wholesale" attack on the methods of evangelical pedagogy, more subtly, but just as trenchantly, Jane's narrative challenges the values it sought to inculcate. The "restraint" and "chastisement" to which she is subjected are opposed by the "liberty" for which she strains, the "praise" she longs for; the acceptance and forbearance preached to her by those about her by the "rebellion and rage" that impels her on. Unmoved by threats of hellfire, and with remarkably little inner struggle, she makes her choice of earthly happiness: a choice whose difference from the path of evangelicalism is emphasized in her narrative's closing contrast between the mutuality of her life with Rochester and St. John Rivers's "undaunted" aspiration toward death.

Usually, *Jane Eyre*'s relation to the religious discourses on which it draws has been seen in a more positive light. Jane's refusal to depart from paths of virtue, the echoes from *Pilgrim's Progress* she repeatedly invokes, have seemed, to many, to signal a reworking of that Bunyanesque narrative of a journey through perils to "blessedness" which was evangelicalism's message of hope to the child. If Brocklehurst's religiosity, Helen Burns's self-immolation, the icy sternness of St. John Rivers are all rejected as paths to salvation, *Jane Eyre*, it is argued, does not reject that narrative: rather, it reinflects it, to suggest that the claims of nature and of Grace, of this world and the next, can finally be reconciled.[54] And much in the novel itself appears to support this view. Certainly, Jane's account of her progress toward happiness seems to be shaped and underwritten by conformations prominent in evangelical writings. Like theirs, her moral universe is one without nuance or ambiguity: a place of black-and-white judgment, where the good and the bad, respectively, receive their just deserts. John Reed, with his "shocking" end, Helen Burns, with her pious resignation, could be exemplary figures from evangelical tracts; so could the libertine Rochester, restless and unhappy in his search for worldly satisfaction, and condemned to a biblical punishment for his "offense" against God's law.[55] The nodal, epiphanic moments in which it is revealed to Jane what she must do— to "flee temptation" (319) or to "advertise" for a situation (86), the magical solutions that appear to her dilemmas (her discovery of her family, her uncle's legacy, Bertha's convenient death, even her "call" to return to Rochester) likewise have their parallel in evangelical writings: the *Methodist Magazines* Brontë knew as a child recorded dozens of examples of such Special Providences, or minor miracles performed for his chosen by God.[56] Here, as in puritan autobiography or evangelical tract, the social world appears as a place of solitary pilgrimage, and the self as a radical isolate, pursuing its own separate path to its own peculiar end. If this is most obviously true of those more or less orthodox Christians, Helen Burns and St. John Rivers—characters whose "ends" are figured prominently as images of solitary transcendence[57]—it may also be seen as in some respects true of Jane. "I still possessed my soul," she asserts, as she describes her flight from Rochester, "and with it the certainty of ultimate safety" (317). Like Bunyan's Christian, she struggles against temptation and defends her integrity:

and like an exemplary figure in an evangelical tract, she is re-warded with perfect happiness—though in this world, rather than the next.

Yet the configurations of evangelicalism appear in *Jane Eyre* not merely, or even mainly, thus, but distinctively, disconcertingly, to quite opposite effect. Jane's, as we have seen, is a story not merely of survival and triumph but of constant, imminent jeopardy. As a child, she is subjected to others' authority—inquisitorial, judg-mental, punitive; she is beaten, starved, frozen; warned both of death—"Children younger than you die daily" (32)—and of the dangers of hellfire. And that which at first appears as a realistic, if negative, representation of evangelical doctrines and practices is inscribed surrealistically throughout: in a plot in which, again and again, the other appears as dreadful in potency and the teller is threatened with extinction, and in a prose that repeatedly rep-resents self as impotent, endangered, and persecuted, not merely from without but from within. Feelings, in this narrative, have something of the autonomous energy of the figures who populate Bunyan's allegory. "As to my own will or conscience, impassioned grief had trampled one and stifled the other: I was weeping wildly as I walked along my solitary way; fast, fast I went like one de-lirious" (321). Self appears less as the agent of its own destiny, developing, acting, choosing, than as having its fate appointed for it—a sense that is reinforced by the premonitions and portents that punctuate Jane's narrative of ostensible self-making and choice.[58] If that "Providentialist" narrative of temptations with-stood and salvation arrived at owes its conformations to the dis-course of evangelicalism, so too does this other story, of ultimate powerlessness and irresolvable threat. That confrontation between the defenseless child and the persecutory other which is portrayed in the novel's opening pages resonates throughout—through its figures, its images, through the very syntax in which that story is framed.

These features of the novel were seen, by early readers, as "the work of a morbid fancy," "most extravagantly improbable."[59] Yet that "morbidity" is inscribed in the surviving documents of the period. The records of those who subjected little children to a

regime designed to break their wills and terrify them into submission testify to the actual, substantial existence in early Victorian England of a reality that might well appear "extravagantly
improbable." Of course, not all came under the sway of a Carus
Wilson. But, as *Jane Eyre's* echo of Mrs. Chapone indicates, even
more benign pedagogies partook of his methods.[60] The "context
of living fear" engendered by that lurid, familiar, intimidating
world of early nineteenth-century evangelicalism must for many
have been a paramount subjective fact.[61] For its pedagogy was one
of the most extreme forms imaginable of that regulatory system
of control by which, it is argued, bourgeois order was established
in nineteenth-century England: a stringent form of disciplinary
power, exercised upon those least able to resist or even question
it; one that seems to have operated in more or less extreme form
throughout large sections of the society,[62] and reached into the
deepest layers of the individual psyche.[63] It surveillance extended
to the most intimate recesses of the personality, its discipline to
the regimentation of every moment, its sanctions to the threat
not merely of death but of eternal perdition. Within the context
of its writings, that sense of ever-present existential threat which
attends Brontë's heroine's progress seems the stuff less of timeless
fantasy than of historical actuality: not a remote fairy tale, but
the texture of life as it was actually presented to and experienced
by hundreds of thousands of children in the England of its time.

"Crowds and crowds of little children are strangely missing
from the written record," writes Peter Laslett in *The World We Have
Lost*; "nearly half the whole community living in a condition of
semi-obliteration."[64] *Jane Eyre* portrays early nineteenth-century
England from the perspective of one such oppressed and "semi-
obliterated" child. Its concern is not with the psychological costs
of evangelical pedagogy, like such other mid-century fictions as
Dickens' *Bleak House* and *Little Dorrit* or Kingsley's *Alton Locke*. If Jane
speaks of the "morbid suffering" to which she is "a prey" (22),
and attributes her habitual childhood mood of "humiliation, self-
doubt, forlorn depression" (23) to her "life of ceaseless reprimand
and thankless fagging" (20), the ease with which she leaves each
stage of her life behind seems indeed to point away from any

such concern. The child is not here treated as a psychological case, or seen from the point of view of a later, more "realistic" maturity. Rather, as Doreen Roberts suggests, the young Jane's "magnified vision . . . establishe[s] the dominant viewpoint and prepare[s] the reader for the persistent distortion which is the essence of the book's method."⁶⁵ For with its opening emphasis on the repressive, death-directed practices and doctrines of early nineteenth-century evangelicalism and its closing image of the missionary St. John Rivers, dying to this world, ambitious for the next, the novel draws attention to the reality in which its "melodrama" is based: not merely the manifest reality of privation and punishment epitomized by "Lowood Institution," but the more insidious reality of that self-subjugating discipline, that ideology of death and judgment, promulgated in the writings of Carus Wilson and his like. This "mere domestic novel" is not, it would appear, simply a striking rendition of an individual subjectivity. In its distinctive representation of the world as experienced by and presented to the child, it offers a powerful realization of some of the most fundamental processes whereby a whole society conceived of and constructed itself.

Notes

1. Charlotte Brontë to W. S. Williams, 28 October 1847. Margaret Smith (ed.), *The Letters of Charlotte Brontë* (3 vols.; Oxford: Clarendon Press, 1995–), vd. 1, p. 554.

2. Kathleen Tillotson, *Novels of the Eighteen-Forties* (Oxford: Clarendon Press, 1954), 257–8.

3. [Sydney Dobell], *The Palladium,* 1 (1850), 171.

4. G. H. Lewes, "Recent Novels: French and English," *Fraser's Magazine,* 36 (1847), 691–2.

5. For a suggestive account of the history of such response, see Patsy Stoneman, *Brontë Transformations* (Hemel Hempstead: Harvester Wheatsheaf/Prentice Hall, 1996).

6. *Christian Observer* n.s. 234 (June 1857), 428.

7. T. J. Wise and J. A. Symington (eds.), *The Brontës: Their Lives, Friend-*

ships, and Correspondence (4 vols.; Oxford: Basil Blackwell, Shakespeare Head Press, 1933), vol. 4, app. 1.

8. William C. Roscoe, "The Miss Brontës," in *Poems and Essays*, ed. R. H. Hutton (2 vols.; London: Chapman and Hall, 1860), 2: 350.

9. Miriam Allot (ed.), *The Brontës: The Critical Heritage* (London: Routledge, 1974), 302.

10. Ibid., 372.

11. Hester Chapone, *Letters on the Improvement of the Mind. Addressed to a Lady*, new ed. (London: Harvey and Darnton, 1820), 117. The Parsonage Museum at Haworth possesses a copy of this pedagogical guide and advice book for young ladies, presented to Charlotte Brontë's friend Ellen Nussey as a "prize for good and ladylike conduct" at Roe Head School.

12. On the nature and importance of evangelical pedagogy, see Paul Sangster, *Pity My Simplicity* (London: Epworth Press, 1963); David Grylls, *Guardians and Angels: Parents and Children in Nineteenth-Century Literature* (London: Faber, 1978); Margaret Nancy Cutt, *Ministering Angels: A Study of Nineteenth-Century Evangelical Writing for Children* (Broxbourne: Five Owls Press, 1979); Doreen M. Rosman, *Evangelicals and Culture* (London: Croom Helm, 1984). Other late eighteenth- and early nineteenth-century systems of child-rearing, even "liberal" ones, seem to have shared many of the characteristics of this pedagogy. On Rousseau, for example, see Alice Miller, *For Your Own Good. The Roots of Violence in Child-Rearing* (London: Virago, 1983), 97: or, for a contemporary view, Mrs. Gaskell's account of her aunt's upbringing by a disciple of the "enlightened" Thomas Day (Elizabeth Gaskell, *The Life of Charlotte Brontë*, ed. Alan Shelston [London: Penguin, 1975], 87–8).

13. As Boyd Hilton notes, evangelicalism was "not a precise phenomenon," and "Evangelical attitudes" may be "attributed to many who would not have been regarded as 'Evangelicals' with a capital 'E' " (*The Age of Atonement: The Influence of Evangelicalism on Social and Economic Thought, 1795–1865* (Oxford: Clarendon Press, 1988), 7, 29); for this reason I shall not in this chapter capitalize the word. In essence, evangelicalism was a world-denying theology, distinguished by its emphasis on the need for redemption and on original sin. The evangelical Christian was not at home in this world and was not expected to look for temporal happiness. The only lasting joys were heavenly joys, and the main purpose of the Christian's sojourn in this world was to prepare for death. Such beliefs were not, Michael Wheeler suggests, confined to any single group,

but "exploited by preachers and teachers of many different persuasions": "God's wrath and the possibility of imminent judgment were central to orthodox Christian teaching, and were widely accepted commonplaces of popular belief" (*Death and the Future Life in Victorian Literature and Theology* [Cambridge: Cambridge University Press, 1990], 117).

14. *Christian Observer* (1806), quoted in Grylls, *Guardian Angels*, 48.

15. Legh Richmond, *Domestic Portraiture; or, The Successful Application of Religious Principle in the Education of a Family Exemplified in the Memoirs of Three of the Deceased Children of the Rev. Legh Richmond* (London: R. B. Seeley and W. Burnside, 1833), 76. For Charlotte Brontë's reading of this work, see Smith, *Letters*, vol. 1, 171.

16. "Corruption" was the "original Adam," the sinful nature of man; "reprobation" the state of being rejected by God and condemned to eternal perdition.

17. Mrs. Sherwood, *The History of the Fairchild Family, or The Child's Manual*, 14th ed. (London: J. Hatchard and Son, 1841), pt. I; 260.

18. Quoted in Philip Greven, *The Protestant Temperament: Patterns of Child-Rearing, Religious Experience, and the Self in Early America* (New York: Alfred A. Knopf, 1977), 37. Wesley's own mother, Susannah, had brought him up according to this system.

19. Clement Carus-Wilson Shepheard-Walwyn, *Henry and Margaret Jane Shepheard: Memorials of a Father and Mother* (London: Elliot Stock, 1882), 113.

20. Richmond, *Domestic Portraiture*, 15, 62.

21. Charlotte Elizabeth Tonna, *Personal Recollections* (London: R. B. Seeley and W. Burnside, 1841), 17.

22. Richmond, *Domestic Portraiture*, 55.

23. See Lenore Davidoff and Catherine Hall, *Family Fortunes: Men and Women of the English Middle Class 1750–1850* (London: Hutchinson, 1987), 88.

24. "The Way to Cure Pride," Ann and Jane Taylor, *Hymns for Infant Minds* (1808), in *The Poetical Works of Ann and Jane Taylor* (London: Ward, Lock, and Tyler, 1877), 25.

25. M. A. Stodart, *Principles of Education Practically Considered; with an Especial Reference to the Present State of Female Education in England* (London: R. B. Seeley and W. Burnside, 1844), 130.

26. Sherwood, *The Fairchild Family*, pt. I, 82–9.

27. Mrs. Edwin Gray, *Papers and Diaries of a York Family 1764–1839* (London: Sheldon Press, 1927), 256–9. The work in question was entitled,

"Biomètre ou Mémorial Horaire, servant à indiquer le nombre des heures données par jour à chacune des divisions. Par M. A. Jullien, de Paris, Auteur de l'Essai sur l'emploi du Temps." For a less extreme, but still tormented, example of such a diary, kept in the late 1830s, see Anthony Kenny (ed.), *The Oxford Diaries of Arthur Hugh Clough* (Oxford: Clarendon Press, 1990).

28. *The Autobiography of Elizabeth Missing Sewell,* edited by her niece, Eleanor L. Sewell (London: Longmans, Green., 1907), 13–14. On such punishments as "standard practices" see Juliet Barker, *The Brontës* (London: Weidenfeld & Nicolson, 1994), 125.

29. Quoted in Sangster, *Pity My Simplicity,* 139.

30. Isaac Watts, *Divine Songs, Attempted in Easy Language for the Use of Children,* facs. reproduction of 1st ed. of 1715 (London: Oxford University Press, 1971), 23.

31. *Eclectic Review,* 2nd ser. 18 (1822), 71.

32. Sangster, *Pity My Simplicity,* 40. See, e.g., Mr. Sherwood, *Stories Explanatory of the Church Catechism* (Wellington, Salop: F. Houlston and Son, 1821), and [Eliza Smith], *Chapters on the Shorter Catechism, a Tale for the Instruction of Youth,* 2nd ed. (Edinburgh: Paton and Ritchie, 1850).

33. Richmond, *Domestic Portraiture,* 76.

34. Ibid. 70.

35. Richmond, *Domestic Portraiture,* 73, 81.

36. John Angell James, *The Family Monitor, or A Help to Domestic Happiness* Birmingham, 1828), 179.

37. Tonna, *Personal Recollections,* 18–19.

38. Quoted in Wise and Symington (eds.), *The Brontës,* vol. 1, 72.

39. J. C. Ryle, "Train up a Child in the Way He Should Go," *A Sermon for Parents Preached in Helmingham Church* (1846), quoted in Elisabeth Jay, *The Religion of the Heart: Anglican Evangelicalism* (Oxford: Clarendon Press, 1979), 137.

40. Rowland Hill, quoted in Sangster, *Pity My Simplicity,* 134.

41. See Sally Shuttleworth, *Charlotte Brontë and Victorian Psychology* (Cambridge: Cambridge University Press, 1996), ch. 7, for an illuminating discussion of *The Professor* and "the art of self-control."

42. *The Children's Friend,* January 1845.

43. Gaskell, *Life,* 94.

44. Gray, *Papers and Diaries of a York Family,* 249.

45. Reproduced in Sangster, *Pity My Simplicity,* 147. Near the bottom of the scale, among the activities leading to perdition, is listed "love of novels."

46. William Carus Wilson, *The Child's First Tales* (Kirkby Lonsdale: A. Foster, 1836).

47. Ibid., 47.

48. Gray, *Papers and Diaries of a York Family*, 250.

49. See Geoffrey Rowell, *Hell and the Victorians: A Study of the Nineteenth-Century Theological Controversies Concerning Eternal Punishment and the Future Life* (Oxford: Oxford University Press, 1974).

50. Quoted in Sangster, *Pity My Simplicity*, 139.

51. Richmond, *Domestic Portraiture*, 210.

52. *The Children's Friend*, quoted in Wise and Symington (eds.), *The Brontës*, vol. 1, 71.

53. See, for examples, Rev. Angus Mackay, "The Brontes at Cowan Bridge," *The Bookman*, October 1894, reprinted in Wise and Symington (eds.), *The Brontës*, vol. 1, 71–75.

54. For examples of this kind of reading, see Barry V. Qualls, *The Secular Pilgrims of Victorian Fiction: The Novel as Book of Life* (Cambridge: Cambridge University Press, 1982), 51–69, and Thomas Vargish, *The Providential Aesthetic in Victorian Fiction* (Charlottesville: University Press of Virginia, 1985), 58–67.

55. Matthew 5:28–30.

56. Jay, in *Religion of the Heart*, 97 ff., traces the considerable controversy over this doctrine in the first half of the nineteenth century.

57. St. John "aims to fill a place in the first rank of those who are redeemed from the earth" (452); Helen's grave is marked "Resurgam" (82).

58. For a suggestive discussion of signs and portents in *Jane Eyre*, and their relation to the "essentially theological and pre-novelistic" allegory of the emblem books, see Hermione Lee, "Emblems and Enigmas in *Jane Eyre*," *English*, 30 (1981), 233–55.

59. *Christian Observer* n.s. 234 (June 1857), 428; unsigned review in *Christian Remembrancer*, quoted in Allott (ed.), *Critical Heritage*, 90.

60. If Carus Wilson seems an extreme figure, it is noteworthy that his school had the support of most of the progressive educationists of the day; and that the initial list of subscribers included not merely such prominent Evangelicals as William Wilberforce, Hannah More, and Charles Simeon, but local Members of Parliament and neighboring clergy; its regime, according to Juliet Barker, "was no worse, and in some respects more lenient, than at other comparable schools" (Barker, *Brontës*, 119–27). The Brontës, of course, not least through their experi-

ence as governesses, were familiar with quite other modes of child-rearing: thus Charlotte Brontë writes to Ellen Nussey in 1840 of the "unruly, violent family of Modern children" with whom her sister Anne has had to contend (Smith, *Letters*, vol. 1, 210). A recurring figure in their fiction is the indulged, usually upper-class child, like "Eliza, John, and Georgiana Reed." Less repressive attitudes—such as Brontë was to observe in the family of Mrs. Gaskell—are represented in *Jane Eyre* by Miss Temple and by Jane's treatment of Adèle. But the concern in *Jane Eyre* is not with presenting a "fair" or balanced picture of life in early nineteenth-century England, but with tracing the logic of the ideology that the narrating Jane confronts.

61. The *Dictionary of National Biography*'s claim that "most children of the English middle classes, born in the first quarter of the nineteenth century, were brought up on *The Fairchild Family*" is borne out by F. J. Harvey Darton. In the introduction to his *Life and Times of Mrs. Sherwood* (London: Wells Gardner, Darton, 1910), he records that "a prominent literary journal" had ten years earlier, asked "prominent men of the day" to name the two books of their childhood that they "remembered most vividly, or which had in one way or another impressed [them] most strongly": "Much divergence was discovered as regards the second of the two books named in each instance; but respecting the first there was agreement little short of unanimity. Practically all those who voted had been brought up, in the fifties of the nineteenth century, and earlier, on *The Fairchild Family*. They did not all like the book, but they had read it, and, it appeared, had read it thoroughly."

62. On the extraordinarily widespread circulation of evangelical tracts, and the manner in which they were distributed (through just one of the many agencies devoted to such purposes), see William Jones, *The Jubilee Memorial of the Religious Tract Society* (London: Religious Tract Society, 1850), and Samuel Green, *The Story of the Religious Tract Society* (London: Religious Tract Society, 1899). Carus Wilson's *The Friendly Visitor* was first issued in 1819, *The Children's Friend* in 1824. The latter ran for forty years, and even achieved an Arabic edition in 1870. According to Sheila A. Egoff, "over 50,000 copies of [*The Children's Friend*] and his adult publications, *The Friendly Visitor* and *The Christian Guardian*, were sold each month" (*Children's Periodicals of the Nineteenth Century: A Survey and Bibliography*, Library Association Pamphlet No. 8 [London, 1951], 9).

63. For a detailed account of the lifelong effects of evangelical pedagogy, see e.g. Elizabeth Missing Sewell's *Autobiography*, cited above.

64. Peter Laslett, *The World We Have Lost: England before the Industrial Age* (New York: Charles Scribner's Sons, 1965), 104.

65. Roberts, "*Jane Eyre* and the Warped System of Things," in Heather Glen (ed.), *Jane Eyre: New Casebook* (London: Macmillan, 1997), 147.

Excerpts from *Subjects on Display*

BETH NEWMAN

◆　◆　◆

Acquisition of legitimate culture by insensible
familiarization within the family circle tends to favour
an enchanted experience of culture which implies
forgetting acquisition.
—PIERRE BOURDIEU, *Distinction*

WHETHER JANE'S DISPOSITION against display is a matter
of nature or nurture, it determines that when she finds
herself among the Eshtons and Ingrams in Rochester's drawing
room—that is, when the novel places her there in order to establish Jane's superiority as an object of desire over the showy
Blanche— she again cultivates invisibilty. She retreats even
further from notice when Blanche, looking for the anonymous
"person" minding Adèle, asks with majestic insouciance, "Is she
gone? Oh, no! there she is still" (205). At this, Jane "feared—or
should I say, hoped?—the allusion to me would make Mr. Rochester glance my way; and I involuntarily shrank further into the
shade." Her desire for his attention is nearly vanquished by her
characteristic dread of being more generally noticed—and by the
sense of propriety that would make any effort to stand out a
violation of her social position as a governess, or even as someone
not a "fine lady" like the women of Blanche's set.

Here again, a pattern with a powerful psychical motivation
coincides with a model of social propriety: Jane's desire to avoid

being seen seems peculiarly fitted to the social norms of interclass protocol, as well as to an ideal that is setting itself up against the spectacle of aristocratic display. But in making Jane desire as much as fear that Rochester might glance her way, *Jane Eyre* complicates this happy conjunction of psychical and social determinations. Even while establishing Jane as the woman fitted for the idealized domesticity of the novel's conclusion, Brontë requires us to read the domestic woman's place in relations of seeing in terms that go beyond surveillance, and to acknowledge that scopophilic desire exceeds what can be satisfied in acts of moral supervision. Jane seizes the moment in Rochester's drawing room to become, in her own words, the "gazer," but when she does so her looking takes on a compulsive and therefore distinctly undisciplined and undisciplinary voyeuristic quality. Despite her responsibility for supervising Adèle, she relates, "my eyes were drawn involuntarily to [Rochester's] face; I could not keep their lids under control: they would rise, and the irids would fix on him. I looked, and had an acute pleasure in looking—a precious yet poignant pleasure" (203). The libidinal aspects of looking do not simply go away when the domestic woman (domestic by disposition and propensities) enters on the scene. As Brontë frankly acknowledges, an "acute pleasure in looking" belongs to feminine as well as to masculine Victorian subjectivity. The assertion of this kind of troubled pleasure suggests that the psychical is always already implicated in the social, and not always in ways that are complicit with the dominant ideology—for Jane's "acute pleasure in looking" indicates her wayward, undisciplined, libidinally active, class-crossing desire.[1]

Jane Eyre further suggests that the scopic drive, like all manifestations of the drive, works both ways, taking both the active form of looking and the "passive" form of exhibitionism, the pleasure in being looked at.[2] Despite her recoiling from the limelight, Brontë's display-renouncing heroine embodies the paradox suggested by Jane Taylor's novel: an exhibitionism that masquerades as inconspicuousness. It works smoothly because Jane finds a suitable way of sublimating and satisfying her exhibitionist impulses—or perhaps, rather, the novel finds one for her that does *not* announce itself as a form of display, and that in fact represents itself in terms more consonant with the domestic feminine ideal. That way is her art—the sketching and painting she engages in and exhibits here and there throughout the novel.[3] This is represented as a private, solitary pastime. We learn only incidentally that her work is displayed over the chimneypiece at Lowood (123); she agrees to show her portfolio to Rochester only when, tipped off by Adèle, he imperiously demands it of her (156); and Rosamond Oliver discovers her sketches while "rummaging" in Jane's drawers and cupboards (394), much as Charlotte Brontë, according to her own account, stumbled across Emily's carefully guarded poems.[4] As such, Jane's art presumably differs in its satisfactions from the "dashing and daring" performance of Blanche at the piano, which seemed "intended to excite not only the admiration, but the amazement of her auditors" (208). Yet Jane's art likewise excites admiration, impressing Rochester with its "peculiar" power (158) and "electri[fying]" Rosamond with surprise and delight (395). Jane's painting and sketching quietly satisfy an impulse toward a kind of display that is itself subordinated to pleasure in looking, as when she happily agrees to sketch a portrait of Rosamond, who wants to "show . . . papa": "I felt a thrill of artist-delight at the idea of copying from so perfect and radiant a model. She had then on a dark-blue silk dress; her arms and neck were bare" (395). Jane's artistic activities nicely illustrate the link between the scopic drive in both its active and passive forms and individual creativity, which, according to one study, "depends upon strong cathexes of scopophilia and exhibitionism."[5]

My point is not that we need to think of Jane's scopophilia in reductively sexual terms I do think we need to place it in the context of desire as psychoanalysis conceives of it—that is, as a potentially disruptive *libido* that draws its energy from the drive, and not only as what is produced in accordance with social and institutional requirements, as the panoptic model suggests. My point is rather that we can better understand Brontë's intervention in the ongoing Victorian exploration of ideal femininity by considering both the intrapsychical and social-historical forces that incubate Jane's subjectivity. The psychical mechanisms on which I have been focusing, therefore, cannot tell the whole story. What is striking in the novel's treatment of Jane's artistry (as well as of her character overall) is how it is made to signify in *social* terms. In other words, her painting and sketching, while avoiding direct display of her *person*, function as signs by which Jane displays her social status.

Jane's ability to draw and paint is simultaneously evidence of talent and an "acquirement" or "attainment," and therefore a credential by which even the portionless middle-class girls educated at Lowood can announce their genteel birth. In other words, it participates in the social semiotics by which class membership is asserted. Bessie Leaven makes this explicit when she admires, as the crown of Jane's years in school and the various skills she has acquired there, the painting displayed above the Lowood chimneypiece: "Oh, you are quite a lady, Miss Jane!" (123). Furthermore, Jane's painting and drawing indicate that her virtues lie not only in these ladylike artistic accomplishments, but also in what they reveal about her character. She paints cormorants and corpses, arctic wastes and ocean billows, unworldly beings inspired by *Paradise Lost* and landscapes she first encountered in Bewick's *History of British Birds:* in short, she seeks to paint the sublime. These subjects seem odd choices in their nondomestic, even antidomestic, impulses, but Brontë harnesses these impulses for her project of revising the feminine ideal. Her paintings tell that the little, poor, plain governess, despite the unprepossessing exterior that was an explicit part of Brontë's intention, contains interior depths of which neither the dazzling Blanche nor the sweet but shallow foundry heiress Rosamond Oliver could ever dream.[6]

This meaning of her painting emerges in the scene in which she obediently exhibits her portfolio to Rochester. He first insults her by questioning whether her sketches benefited from the aid of a master, thereby impugning her skill to a degree that, as he astutely observes, "pricks pride" (156). Nor does her originality escape his skepticism, for she next finds herself having to assure him that the ideas for her compositions have come out of her own head. This prompts him to ask, "The head I see now on your shoulders? . . . Has it other furniture of the same kind *within?*" (156; emphasis added). His question does not merely inquire about the breadth of her imagination. It also invokes the interiority by which Jane is distinguished from every other female figure in the novel except Helen Burns, Miss Temple, and the Rivers sisters— that is, other women who occupy a middling status between the servant class (like Bessie) and the rich.[7] Furthermore, Rochester's question explicitly links Jane's rich interiority, through the over- determination of the peculiar metaphor of "furniture," to the *domestic* interior(ity) for which Jane is apparently destined. Again, it is open to question whether this genteel domesticity is her desert by nature, as her claiming originality might suggest, or by achievement, measured by her acquisition of skill.

Rochester makes this ambiguity explicit when he evaluates Jane's portfolio as a drawing master might, assessing both her skill and her "thought" or originality. Though at first he seems in- clined to give her higher marks for originality, in the end he is less certain. "You had not enough of the artist's skill and science to give it [her "thought"] full being: yet the drawings are, for a schoolgirl, peculiar. . . . These eyes in the Evening Star you must have seen in a dream. . . . And what meaning is that in their sol- emn depth? And who taught you to paint the wind?" (158). With such a peculiar knack for painting things not strictly visible, like the wind, the suggestive depths in the evening star's eyes, and "the shape which shape which shape had none," no wonder Jane and her paintings seem "elfish" to him, denizens of some invisible other realm. His vacillation over whether her "thought" outstrips her skill, like her bristling at the suggestion that she was aided by a master, returns us to the question of origins. Is her artistry an expression of the charity-school education that includes les- sons in "French and drawing" (surely with the aid of a master of some kind), or is it innate, an endowment, part of her essence? This is no small question, for as a ladylike accomplishment Jane's art serves the task of making the social distinctions that compel Bessie, formerly a servant in the Reed household, to call her "*Miss Jane*" in pronouncing her a lady. And yet in order to perform the mystifications and naturalizations on which such social distinctions ultimately rest, this accomplishment must present itself as an aspect of Jane's essence that is independent of her material circumstances. Which of these accounts—the essential or the material—is more accurate the novel cannot conclusively say.

This equivocation is no accident. It circles around the question of whether Jane's artistry, itself an index of her character, arises from innate propensities and worth, or whether it represents a kind of pulling herself up by her bonnet strings. Brontë smooths over the question of whether Jane's artistic ability points to knowledge and skill insensibly acquired at the domestic hearth, and thus in some way almost innate, or at least a kind of birthright. By situating the hearth in question under Lowood's chimneypiece, she suggests both the subtle pedagogy of being to the manner born *and* merit achieved through effort and hard work, in accordance with middle-class ideology. This question has particular relevance in the sphere of art. In *Distinction: A Social Critique of the Judgment of Taste*, Pierre Bourdieu seeks to demystify the degree to which "art and cultural consumption are predisposed, consciously and deliberately or not, to fulfill a social function of legitimating social differences." He asserts that they do so in part by purporting to signal a "radical difference" between "the common herd" and those who can demonstrate the right kind of aesthetic appreciation—a difference "which seems to be inscribed in 'persons' ": "the ideology of charisma regards taste in legitimate culture as a gift of nature."[8] Though Bourdieu is discussing cultural consumption in late twentieth-century France, this argument lends itself, mutatis mutandis, to that straddling of artistic consumption and production marked by the cultivation of "accomplishments" in nineteenth-century English society. In terms of the novel's ideological project, Jane cannot seem to come by her artistry automatically, for that would class her with Blanche, who can brilliantly but effortlessly "rattl[e]" away at the keyboard while she prattles on about the weakness of men (208). At the same time, her worth must seem a product of nature at least in part, for that is what gives it its legitimizing power. Her artistry signifies her radical difference not only from those socially beneath her, like Bessie, but also, and especially, from those con-

ventionally placed above her, like Blanche, whose purely perfor-
mative (and therefore more unabashedly exhibitionistic) art seems
distinctly soulless and brittle. By equivocating over the sources of
Jane's artistic abilities and over the origins of Jane's other attributes, *Jane Eyre* can assert that its heroine naturally embodies the
character traits of the ideal domestic woman while still representing these traits as ideals to which one can aspire.

The semiotic function of Jane's painting and drawing points to
the fact that certain oblique kinds of feminine display accumu-
lated and communicated positive social meanings in the nineteenth century, despite the pietistic and moralizing rhetoric
against display at the beginning of the period. An increasing sec-
ularization loosened the grasp of the evangelical fervor of the
1780s and 1790s that had insisted on the subordination of worldly
interests to spiritual ones.[9] Indeed, as the middle classes gained
culturally and economically, it became not only convenient to
accommodate worldly interests, but even necessary to do so; for
credit depended on reputation, and middle-class enterprise, on
which so much depended, in turn depended on credit. What
better way of indicating creditworthiness than by manipulating
various conspicuous signs of dress, consumption, speech, etiquette, and the like, in order to display the family wealth? And
who better to do it than the woman, on whom the crucial task
of forging and consolidating social ties fell, as men busied themselves with the civic and economic pursuits that might be fur-
thered by these ties?[10]

But here's where the shoe pinches. the Christian ideals decry-
ing worldliness and display retained some of their force at least
ideally, despite changing social practices. *Jane Eyre* makes this clear
in its heroine's refusal to allow Rochester to dress her in brilliant
clothes and glittering jewels, and by deprecating little Adèle's
damnably French (read: Catholic and morally suspect) fascination
with "frocks." Clear too in Brontë's novel are the contradictions
between the negative and positive social meanings of display, as
when the pious Mr. Brocklehurst's "splendidly attired" and elab-
orately coiffured wife and daughters arrive at the school just in

time to miss the lecture delivered by their paterfamilias against luxuriant curls, plaited hair, and costly apparel (96–97). If the contradiction seems to escape Brocklehurst, it is because his wife and daughters dress, as the Lowood students are being trained, "in conformity to [their] social prospects" and positions (67)— and these differ considerably for the two sets of "ladies."

The Brocklehurst women seem to have reconciled themselves very smugly to what [Leonore] Davidoff has named a "divided ideal of social duty." According to Davidoff, the woman's responsibility for maintaining a family's social position, a responsibility motivated by economic self-interest, could conflict with the ideal of Christian duty. (She offers as a typical example that of a young woman required to choose between charitable and social activities, both of which involved expenditures of time and money.) Davidoff's insistence that it was young women's "*duty* to appear at balls and carry off gracefully their social role" suggests that the Brocklehurst ladies, being connected to an important man, might understand costly dress and self-presentation—that is, personal display—to be their duty.[11]

Brontë satirizes this contradiction with a heavy hand where the Brocklehursts are concerned, but she cuts Jane a good deal more slack. When Rochester takes her as his bride-to-be to the silk warehouse, in order to provide her with a trousseau, he tries to foist on her "a rich silk of the most brilliant amethyst dye, and a superb pink satin" (296). She tastefully opts for a "sober black satin and pearl-gray silk," announcing her changed station through fabrics too costly to purchase on her governess's salary, but muting the message by sending it in neutral colors. She has good reasons to resent, as she does, "being dressed as a doll by Mr. Rochester" (297), not the least of which involve his assertion of a masculine power she regards as tyrannical and enslaving: "I thought his smile was such as a sultan might, in a blissful and fond moment, bestow on a slave his gold and gems had enriched."[12] Her recoil from the exhibitionistic display he tries to impose on her takes an explicitly economic form: she thinks, "If I had but a prospect of one day bringing Mr. Rochester an accession of fortune, I could better endure to be kept by him now"

(267). She determines to write to her rich uncle John in Madeira, through whom the right to display herself in silks and jewels might prove to descend to her by inheritance instead of through the achievement of marrying up.

She now permits herself to meet Rochester's eye, which during this prenuptial shopping spree "most pertinaciously sought mine; though I averted both face and gaze." We have already seen the mixture of fear and desire in Jane's averted gaze. Does she perhaps fear that in meeting his look now she might succumb prematurely to the temptation to appear in this dazzling finery? She chides him: "You need not look in that way. . . . If you do, I'll wear nothing but my old Lowood frocks to the end of the chapter." Both her banter and her avoidance of his gaze provoke him to exclaim, "Oh, it is rich to see and hear her! . . . Is she original? Is she piquant? I would not exchange this one little English girl for the Grand Turk's whole seraglio—gazelle-eyes, houri forms, and all!" (297).

Nor, he makes clear, would he exchange this "little English girl" for all the women of continental Europe, represented metonymically by the French opera dancer Céline Varens and her successors, the "unprincipled and violent" Italian Giacinta and the "heavy, mindless, and unimpressible" German Clara (338). These are the lovers in whom he seeks some kind of refuge after his intemperate and unchaste West Indian wife has shamed him "in the eyes of the world" (334) and made him long to go "home to God" —or, at least, to Europe. Bertha, a woman suspiciously "in the style of Blanche Ingram" (332), gives him a taste of what can go wrong when one marries a fine woman who dazzles by being "splendidly dressed" and by "lavishly display[ing]" all her "charms and accomplishments" to a whole circle of admiring men. Among her "giant propensities" (334), the one that should have tipped him off is her propensity for display, which instead worked a dangerous seduction: "I was dazzled, stimulated: my senses were excited; . . . I thought I loved her" (332). By contrast, the "little English girl" whom Rochester would not exchange for the Grand Turk's seraglio is most "rich to see" when she is renouncing the display he seeks to impose on her. What he terms "originality" is simultaneously constructed as a distinctively English, nonaristocratic version of ideal femininity.

Notes

1. Janet Gezari covers some of the material in this paragraph in her nuanced and very differently inflected reading of *Jane Eyre*, but she does so in the service of a reading in some way at odds with my own: she reads the novel as the "triumphant progress of a heroine who has been denied the right to look and punished by the looks of others"; see Gezari, *Charlotte Brontë and Defensive Conduct: The Author and the Body at Risk*, 88. I am inclined to see Jane as being from the beginning permitted *only* to "look on and listen" from a position of obscurity, like her author in her governessing days.

2. Freud acknowledges the semantic problem of the term *passive* with respect to the drive: "Every instinct is a piece of activity; if we speak loosely of passive instincts, we can only mean instincts whose *aim* is passive" ("Instincts," *SE*, 14:128).

3. Gezari notes that "Jane is the only Brontë heroine whose art is visual and celebrates the visible world" (*Charlotte Brontë*, 67).

4. Gaskell, *Life*, 198, quoting the biographical notice that Charlotte appended to the second edition of *Wuthering Heights* and to Anne Brontë's *Agnes Grey* (1850).

5. David Allen, *The Fear of Looking, or Scopophilic-Exhibitionistic Conflicts*, 109–10. Freud observes in *Five Lectures on Psycho-Analysis* that scopophilia is the origin, in its active form, of curiosity, and in its passive form, of "the impulsion to artistic and theatrical display" (*SE*, II:44).

6. One might argue that Jane's paintings therefore domesticate the sublime—as indeed they do. But perhaps we should ask what this means, rather than merely accepting the assumptions behind the issue that has long troubled Brontë criticism—at least since Richard Chase argued in "The Brontës" that both novels "domesticate" the mythic, rebellious, larger-than-life energies in which they traffic. Contemporary feminist discourse has reinterpreted the domestic sphere as a crucial part of an industrial-capitalist economic and social world—rather than a refuge from it, as nineteenth-century ideology represented it, one in which women exercised agency and power. I hardly need point out that

a simple reversal, a privileging of domesticity in separatist terms as a special space where women hold sway, gets us nowhere; I merely want to question the assumption that Brontë's domestication of the sublime, of myth, of rebellious energies, and so on, is necessarily a step backward, a kind of selling out. Her project is to reinvent domesticity and the ideals that go along with it, and if we simply scoff at Jane Eyre's insistence late in the novel to St. John Rivers that "domestic endearments and household joys" are "the best thing the world has" (416), it may be because we accept that "domestic" means "debased." Doing so is surely the privilege of those who can take domesticity for granted—as Harriet A. Jacobs might have been pointing out in proclaiming, near the end of her autobiographical narrative, published in 1861: "Reader, my story ends with freedom; not in the usual way, with marriage. . . . The dream of my life is not yet realized. I do not sit with my children in a home of my own. I still long for a hearthstone of my own, however humble" (*Incidents in the Life of a Slave Girl: Written by Herself*, 201.)

7. See Susan Fraiman, *Unbecoming Women: British Women Writers and the Novel of Development*, chapter I ("Jane Eyre's Fall from Grace"), on the importance of working-class characters in Jane's self-definition.

8. Pierre Bourdieu, *Distinction: A Social Critique of the Judgement of Taste*, 7, 31, I.

9. Leonore Davidoff and Catherine Hall, *Family Fortunes: Men and Women of the English Middle Class, 1780–1850*, 75.

10. In *The Best Circles: Society, Etiquette and the Season*, Leonore Davidoff writes: "By effectively preventing upper- and middle-class women from playing any part in the market, any part in public life whatsoever, the Victorians believed that one section of the population would be able to provide a haven of stability, of exact social classification in the threatening anonymity of the surrounding economic and political upheaval" (16). In *Nobody's Angels: Middle-Class Women and Domestic Ideology in Victorian Culture*, Elizabeth Langland extends this role beyond the "policing" of social boundaries, observing that midcentury social manuals advise men "to marry a woman who will solidify or better her husband's social position with appropriate status display" (30).

11. Davidoff, *Best Circles*, 57; emphasis in the original.

12. For a compelling reading of the way this orientalist language of slavery co-opts racial and colonialist struggle in the name of middle-class feminism, see Susan L. Meyer, "Colonialism and the Figurative Strategy of *Jane Eyre*," 247–68.

Works Cited

Allen, David W. *The Fear of Looking: or, Scopophilic-Exhibitionist Conflicts.* Charlottesville: University Press of Virginia, 1974.

Bourdieu, Pierre. *Distinction: A Social Critique of the Judgment of Taste.* Translated by Richard Nice. Cambridge: Harvard University Press, 1979.

Chase, Richard. "The Brontës: A Centennial Observance." *Kenyon Review* 9 (1947): 487–506.

Davidoff, Leonore. *The Best Circles: Society, Etiquette, and the Season.* London: Croom Helm, 1973.

Davidoff, Leonore, and Catherine Hall. *Family Fortunes: Men and Women of the English Middle Class, 1780–1850.* Chicago: University of Chicago Press, 1987.

Fraiman, Susan. *Unbecoming Women: British Writers and the Novel of Development.* New York: Columbia University Press, 1993.

Freud, Sigmund. *Five Lectures on Psycho-Analysis.* In Freud, *Standard Edition,* 11:3–55.

———. "Instincts and Their Vicissitudes." In Freud, *Standard Edition,* 14: 111–40.

Gaskell, Elizabeth Cleghorn. *The Life of Charlotte Brontë.* London: J. M. Dent and Sons, 1971.

Gezari, Janet. *Charlotte Brontë and Defensive Conduct: The Author and the Body at Risk.* Philadelphia: University of Pennsylvania Press, 1992.

Jacobs, Harriet A. *Incidents in the Life of a Slave Girl: Written by Herself.* Edited by Jean Fagin Yellin. Cambridge: Harvard University Press, 1987.

Langland, Elizabeth. *Nobody's Angels: Middle-Class Women and Domestic Ideology in Victorian Culture.* Ithaca: Cornell University Press, 1995.

Meyer, Susan L. "Colonialism and the Figurative Strategy of *Jane Eyre.*" *Victorian Studies* 33 (1999): 247–68.

"That Stormy Sisterhood"

Portrait of the Brontës

HELENA MICHIE

◆　◆　◆

THIS, THE ONLY SURVIVING portrait of the three of them, groups them forever around phallic absence, the organizing principle, the painter, their brother. Branwell's decision to erase himself from this painting of his sisters only draws attention to the figure that once represented him, now alluded to by a vertical swath of yellowish paint. In so vividly depicting his own absence, he turns himself—hesitantly—into a phallic presence, into the column that comes to stand, in Charlotte's portraits of Brocklehurst and St. John, for the sin of male arrogance. Branwell under erasure reminds us in a way no signature could that he is the painter, that his sisters sit in reference to him. Branwell's arrogance, however, is no simple thing; his sisters will leave their mark, and he will leave his through scarring them; Emily's biography is especially marked by Branwell's entrances and exits, his delirium tremens, his drunkenness, his genius, and his shameful death that some say showed the way for Emily's own.

This sisterhood stands in the shadow of the brother. Branwell arranges his sisters, flattens their faces, their differences; it is hard

FIGURE 1. Branwell Brontë's painting of his sisters, c. 1835. *Courtesy of the National Portrait Gallery, London.*

to tell Anne from Emily. The portrait reminds us eerily of an earlier effort by Branwell to capture his sisters' likenesses: the so-called "gun group." In this sketch Branwell does not erase himself; he sits again between two sisters, the third figure to the right of center, holding a gun. In this sketch Brontë scholars can literally not tell Anne from Emily; the argument over the sisters' identity rages today. There is no doubt over the identity of Branwell; he is the one with the gun on his knee. In the finished portrait there is also no room for debate; Branwell is the one who isn't there. The gun, like Branwell, suggests itself through its absence, through the juxtaposition of painting with sketch; like Branwell, the gun speaks more loudly through its absence. The painting becomes the portrait without the gun. The gun in the sketch, the gun that perhaps never was in the painting, marks Branwell off from his sisters, cuts Charlotte, to the right of her brother, off from Emily and Anne to his left. Both the column of yellow paint and the gun draw the viewer's eye to Branwell and up along a vertical plane. The gun adds mass to his body; the vertical swath of paint makes him taller, the tallest, taller than all of his sisters although we are told by Mrs. Gaskell that Emily was the "tallest person in the house except her father."[1]

The painting plays—perhaps it would be better to say works— with difference, sameness, and opposition. It allows for very little difference between Emily and Anne; their faces point solemnly, almost sullenly, in the same direction; their linked gazes remind us of Ellen Nussey's observation that the two sisters were like twins. Across the painting, across the obliterated body of Branwell, Charlotte sits plump and square. The painting has cracked along the lines where it was once folded; the sisters look out to the spectator from behind a grid of cracks that cuts Emily and Anne off from Charlotte and severs Anne's chin. The isolation is prophetic; Charlotte alone will survive—for a few important years. She will represent the Brontës, tell the stories of her sisters. She will never intrude upon the twinning of her two younger sisters, will never fully understand their need for each other. If there is a place for difference within this sisterhood, which does not reside in the figure of the brother, it is in the face and body of Charlotte. If we look below the grid, to where the sisters' bodies disappear into the textured darkness of their dresses, we see only one hand. It is Charlotte's: the hand that will, after the deaths of Anne and Emily, destroy manuscripts, add prefaces to published works, choose from among their possessions and their writings those that will survive into what will quickly become the cult of the Brontës.

If the painting inscribes for posterity the difference between the Brontë sisters and their brother, and the difference between

FIGURE 2. Branwell Brontë, "The Gun Group" portrait of the Brontës. *Courtesy of the Brontë Parsonage Museum.*

Charlotte on the one hand and Emily and Anne on the other, it only echoes and foreshadows a litany of verbal portraits handed down to us from friends, pupils, enemies, and biographers of the sisters who were simultaneously so startlingly alike and so spectacularly different. To remove Branwell from the picture, to repress his maleness, his paintbrush, and his gun is still to have to face difference. The voices that speak to us of the Brontë sisters speak in comparatives; it is against and across each others' bodies that each sister really begins to take shape. Emily was the tallest, Anne, the most delicate looking, Charlotte the plainest, Emily the prettiest,[2] Emily, or perhaps Charlotte, the practical one. These sisters come in degrees, can be ranked: Emily was taller than Anne who was taller than Charlotte; we must resort here to superlative as well as comparative forms Charlotte died young, Anne died younger, Emily died youngest of all—except for those who would not enter the picture if it were not for "the Brontë sisters" as institution: Branwell, Maria, and Elizabeth, and, of course, first of all, the mother of these famous children.

Winifred Gerin on Charlotte: "[She was] admittedly the least attractive of the three Miss Brontës." (Gerin, p. 106)

Pupil Laetitia Wheelwright comparing Emily to Charlotte: "I simply disliked her from the first; her tallish, ungainly ill-dressed figure contrasting so strongly with Charlotte's small, neat, trim person, although their dresses were alike." (Gerin, p. 130)

Pupil Louise de Bassompierre comparing Emily to Charlotte: "Miss Emily était beaucoup moins brillante que sa soeur mais bien plus sympathique." (Gerin, p. 131)

Elizabeth Gaskell on the question of relative genius: "[M. Heger] rated Emily's genius as something even higher than Charlotte's." (Gaskell, p. 230)

Winifred Gerin on Emily's and Anne's poetry: "It would be unfair to Anne to make a literary comparison." (Gerin, p. 173)

Elizabeth Gaskell on Anne's "shyness" and Emily's "reserve": "I distinguish reserve from shyness, because I imagine shyness would please, if it knew how, whereas reserve is indifferent whether it pleases or not." (Gaskell, p. 162)

Locked together in their infancy, the sisters and their brother lived out Victorian strictures on family closeness. They collaborated on the creation and articulation of imaginary kingdoms. When they were forced to separate, they continued to tell each other stories of their kingdoms in letters. As adults, the sisters and the brother diverged, took different routes to fame and—famously—to the grave. The sisters planned to open a school together; the brother went to London to become a painter and ran immediately back home. He took up drinking and drugs, his sisters renamed themselves, and published—again together—a volume of poetry. Their first pieces of adult fiction were written side by side, came into the world together as productions of a sisterhood at once meek and powerful. The writing of the first round of Brontë novels was an experiment in sisterly unity; the publication of the novels made visible the cracks in that sisterhood. Public reactions to the novels officially inscribed the language of sisterly difference. We must now begin to speak differently of the sisters.

Charlotte's first novel, *The Professor*, was rejected, while *Wuthering Heights* and *Agnes Grey* were eventually accepted. Charlotte wrote most of her second novel, *Jane Eyre*, alone, away from the parsonage, in Manchester, where Elizabeth Gaskell, unknown to her, was writing *Mary Barton*. Charlotte was in Manchester in the first place because she had been, in this instance favorably, compared to her sisters; she was chosen to nurse her father through an eye operation, to obtain lodgings in an unfamiliar city, and to talk to the doctor in attendance, because she was considered to be the most social of the three painfully antisocial sisters. *Jane Eyre* was published in six weeks, long before her sisters' novels, which had been accepted earlier, came out. When Anne's and Emily's unscrupulous publisher rushed to publish *Wuthering Heights* and *Agnes Grey* to take advantage of *Jane Eyre*'s immense success, the two novels were thought to be immature productions of the author of *Jane Eyre*. *Wuthering Heights* was dismissed as unspeakably coarse; *Agnes Grey* was dismissed with very little notice. The official verdict on both novels, as well as on her sisters' other works, was Charlotte's.

Charlotte on *Wuthering Heights:* "Whether it is right or advisable to create beings like Heathcliff, I do not know: I scarcely think it is."[3]

Charlotte on *The Tenant of Wildfell Hall:* "The choice of subject was an entire mistake."[4]

Charlotte on whether to publish a posthumous edition of her sisters' poems: "an influence stronger than could be exercised by any motive of expediency, necessarily regulated the selection. I have, then, culled from the mass only a little poem here and there. The whole makes but a tiny nosegay, and the colour and perfume of the flowers are not such as fit them for festal uses."[5]

We read Emily's and Anne's works through Charlotte's painstaking comparisons, through her letters, remarks, and prefaces—through the first Brontë biography, Elizabeth Gaskell's memorial to the surviving sister, Charlotte. We read Emily's and Anne's corpus as we read their bodies, through Charlotte's disfiguring spectacles, through her excisions, omissions, and silences. What happened to Emily's second novel, already well in progress by the time of her death? Was it Charlotte or Emily who destroyed it, who made us read *Wuthering Heights* as a single burst of novelistic genius? Charlotte silences Emily's genius as a writer in the very novel that serves as a memorial to her; in *Shirley*, Charlotte has the narrator claim that the heroine, based by Charlotte's own admission on her sister Emily, will never be a writer.

Who can resist comparing the sisters to each other? Who can resist the structure of opposition, the grid of difference and sameness? We feast on the differences between the sisters, on the arguments and differences that arose among them. Biographers chart their shifting alliances: Emily and Anne were spiritual "twins," Branwell initially preferred Charlotte to his other sisters, but Charlotte turned away from her brother and toward Emily when Branwell turned to drink. Emily defended Branwell; Anne tried to reform him. Charlotte preferred Emily's company to Anne's and brought Emily with her to Belgium in spite of Emily's history of excruciating homesickness. Emily could not forgive Charlotte for "happening" upon a manuscript of her poems or betraying her real identity to publisher George Smith. Emily and Anne refused to take their work to Charlotte's publisher even when it became clear that Newby, who published *Wuthering Heights* and *Agnes Grey*, was dishonest and stingy. Charlotte betrayed her preference for Emily in a final comparison between her sisters' deaths: "(Anne's) quiet, Christian death did not rend my heart as Emily's stern, simple, undemonstrative end did. I let Anne go to God, and felt He had a right to her. I could hardly let Emily go." (Gerin, p. 261)

These sisters internalize the idiom of comparison; they come to life with respect to each other, sometimes without respect for each other. Women in their books take their lives from other women: Jane triumphs because she is not Blanche, not Georgiana, not Eliza. Lucy Snowe triumphs because she is not the Cleopatra or the women portrayed in that series of lifeless domestic pictures,

"La Vie D'Une Femme." Cathy Linton is born on the deathbed of her mother, that other Cathy Linton, who died struggling against the name they both share. Sisterhood is powerful but not easy: sisters are exaggerated and parodic opposites like the flirtatious Georgiana and the sanctimonious Eliza, indistinguishable from each other, like Diana and Mary Rivers, or jealous rivals like Isabella and Cathy, sisters in and under Edgar Linton's law— and again under the equally powerful and perhaps more demonic law of Heathcliff.

Is it enough, with Virginia Woolf, to say "Jane liked Chloe" or even "Charlotte loved Emily"? Surely even without the specter of Branwell it is more complicated than that. But the specter of Branwell intrudes anyway; these sisters are not alone; they do not represent themselves, their bodies, and their faces to us. They stare out of the portrait in different directions, their bodies held a little awkwardly: is this a failure of physical grace? Of sister love? Of brotherly loyalty? Or is it—simply—a failure of genius on the part of the painter that these sisters look so wooden, so separate? Certainly it is not Branwell's fault that the paint cracked, producing scars that run along his sisters' faces. Or could he, who was so inept at preserving his own dignity, his own life, have done better at preserving his sisters for immortality? Perhaps more important, could Charlotte, into whose capable hands the painting probably fell—again, we do not know what those hands were doing with the documents in the case—have made with those same hands a sisterhood less cracked, less stormy? Could she have given us another Emily, another Anne, another series of portraits in words?

We cannot hope to reconstruct the Brontë sisterhood as it was, but we can hope not to simplify its energies, its allegiances, its passions. It is perhaps worth noting that Charlotte Brontë conceived of passion itself in a sororal idiom. Speaking of a literary "sister" about whom she had mixed feelings, Charlotte once wrote that in *Emma* (Charlotte's last piece of work, a fragment of a novel, was to bear the same name), Jane Austen "ruffles her reader by nothing vehement, disturbs him by nothing profound: the Passions are perfectly unknown to her; she rejects even a speaking acquaintance with that stormy Sisterhood." (Peters, p. 285) Charlotte's acquaintance with passion and with sisterhood pervades her novels, her letters, and her life; it is the complex relation between passion and sisterhood that must be understood before her readers, and before feminist critics in particular, can appreciate the full complexity of her legacy.

Notes

1. Winifred Gerin, *Emily Brontë* (Oxford: Clarendon Press, 1971), p. 35.

2. Elizabeth Gaskell, *The Life of Charlotte Brontë* (Harmondsworth: Penguin Books, 1975), p. 87.

3. Charlotte Brontë, "Editor's Preface to the New Edition of *Wuthering Heights*," reprinted in Emily Brontë, *Wuthering Heights* (New York: W. W. Norton, 1972), p. 12.

4. Charlotte Brontë, "Biographical Notice of Ellis and Acton Bell," reprinted in *Wuthering Heights*, p. 6.

5. Margot Peters, *Unquiet Soul: A Biography of Charlotte Brontë* (New York: Atheneum, 1986), p. 308.

Jane Eyre in Later Lives

Intertextual Strategies in Women's Self-Definition

PATSY STONEMAN

◆　◆　◆

"NO ONE WHO HAD ever seen Catherine Morland in her infancy would have supposed her born to be a heroine." The opening of Jane Austen's *Northanger Abbey* (1818) offers a challenge to an earlier literary convention that a heroine should be beautiful, good, and accomplished, an ideal to be aspired to rather than the real, dirty, ignorant girl Catherine Morland proves to be. The debate was still vigorous in the 1840s when Charlotte Brontë protested to her sisters that she would take a heroine as small and plain as herself and make her as interesting as the most beautiful and accomplished heroine of conventional fiction.[1] Both the "idealist" and the "realist" approaches to literature, however, are based on a mirror-like concept of the reading process. The "idealists" assumed that the reader, by identifying with an image of perfection, would become more perfect herself. The "realists," on the other hand, assumed that readers needed above all confirmation of their own imperfect existence.

Ideals, of course, are themselves subject to historical change; Charlotte Brontë's "realist" heroine has become an ideal of nonconformity for later readers. Valerie Grosvenor Myer argues that "Jane Eyre has been an inspiration and example to generations of clever girls. . . . She is the first defiantly intellectual heroine in English literature."[2] Her defiance, moreover, is as important as her intellect. The playbill for a Children's Theatre Company production of *young jane eyre* in Minneapolis (1988) reads:

> Ten-year-old Jane is thrust into a frightening . . . orphanage. But the waif's spirit does not succumb. A passionate testament to the courage and fortitude of youth, the power of love, and the eternal promise of a brighter tomorrow.[3]

This "testament," moreover, speaks beyond the white Anglo-Saxon world. Patricia Duncker quotes O. C. Ogunyemi as evidence that *Jane Eyre* as a "feminist utopia is for white women only"; but Maya Angelou writes:

> When I read the Brontës, I was a small black girl in the dirt roads of Arkansas during the depression. The society was against me surviving at all, but when I read about Heathcliffe [*sic*] and Jane Eyre, white society in that mean town had no power against me.

Tsitsi Dangarembga's heroine Tambudzai, a black child in Rhodesia, also "read everything from Enid Blyton to the Brontë sisters, and responded to them all. . . . Thus," she says, "began the period of my reincarnation." In the Brontë Parsonage Museum at Haworth there is a handwritten comment from a Japanese woman called Hideko Maki on a Japanese stage production of *Jane Eyre*; she likes the production because the woman director, Kazue Kontaibo, "has the same feeling on Jane Eyre, Charlotte Brontë as I have: She respects and loves Jane (Charlotte)'s dauntless, bracing way of life." Barbara T. Christian, a black Caribbean woman, shares this response:

> Disturbed as I was by Brontë's portrayal of Bertha, I none-theless loved *Jane Eyre* and identified with plain Jane. . . . Despite the cultural differences between her world and mine . . . I saw that her life too was sharply constrained. . . . Jane

and I shared something in common, even as the mores of her society, even as the physical geography of her world were alien to me.[4]

The need for identification with literary models lies behind the 1970s phase of feminist literary criticism known as "Images of Women" criticism. Arlyn Diamond, in *The Authority of Experience*, asks for "authentic" pictures of women's lives, because she cannot "recognise [her]self, or the women I know" in the female characters of male writers. "Authenticity," however, easily shades into idealism: Cheri Register, writing in 1975, asks that "a literary work should provide *role-models*, instill a positive sense of feminine identity by portraying women who are 'self-actualising, whose identities are not dependent on men.'" Maurianne Adams, in *The Authority of Experience*, actually quotes a famous passage of *Jane Eyre*—"Women feel just as men feel; they need exercise for their faculties and a field for their efforts as much as their brothers do"—to prove precisely this point. This "authentic realism" movement was partly discredited in the 1980s by poststructuralist critics who found the "mirror theory" of literature naive. Toril Moi, for instance, compares it with the misguided aims of socialist realism: "instead of strong happy tractor drivers . . . we are now presumably, to demand strong happy *women* tractor drivers."[5]

Maurianne Adams's model of reading is not, however, a static one: "Every time we rethink and reassimilate *Jane Eyre*," she writes, "we bring to it a new orientation." Adult rereading of *Jane Eyre* is "unnerving," she says, because we do not encounter the same novel which "we were engrossed by in our teens or preteens, when we saw in Jane's dreadful childhood . . . our own fantasies of feeling unloved and forever unloveable." As adult women, for instance, we have to come to terms with the precise kind of "happy ending" offered by the novel. Each of the women I quoted as making Jane Eyre her heroine has, in fact, made a complicated negotiation between recognition and "unnerving" difference. Pat Macpherson, for instance, considers how Jane can be a "heroine" both for her and for her students twenty years later; she concludes:

What [my students] and I shared in *Jane Eyre* was a reading of ourselves, present-to-future, that half-described and half-prescribed our course out of lost girlhood to the resting place of fulfilled womanhood. . . . From real women we learn . . . the limits of female space and power in the world as it presently is constituted. . . . From fiction, we learn how far we might push the limits of our own space and power.

For Barbara T. Christian this negotiation of sameness and difference extends over race and culture as well as over time:

To read is not only to validate the self but also to participate in "the other's" view of the world, the writer's view. Or why read? Writing and reading are means by which we communicate with one another, as Audre Lorde would say, "bridge the joinings."[6]

Maggie Berg, in her book, *Jane Eyre, Portrait of a Life*, argues that *Jane Eyre* itself provides a model for this process of negotiation. "In the red-room," Berg argues, "Jane sees herself as a rebellious slave, a hunger striker, the 'scape-goat of the nursery.' . . . 'No doubt,' says the autobiographer [Jane] in retrospect, 'I was a precocious actress.' " Jane's "self-dramatization" here is equivalent to her looking into literary mirrors for an image of herself, just as Angelou, Dangarembga, Maki, Kontaibo, Christian, and Macpherson look into *Jane Eyre*. "This first identification of oneself in a mirror," Berg goes on, "is regarded by Jacques Lacan as the most decisive stage in human development, constituting the awareness of oneself as an object of knowledge. Although the reflection is a misrepresentation, because static, it nevertheless confers the mark of adulthood: self-consciousness." It is from this position of self-consciousness, achieved through repeated part-mirrorings of her self, that Jane is able to contribute to the symbolic construction of her identity. As Berg puts it, "that Jane is the author of her own story is the single most important yet most neglected aspect of the novel."[7]

In the rest of this chapter I want to argue that although readers may not consciously register the importance of Jane's status as author of her own story, the control of narrative plays a crucial part in the process of self-definition in those women's texts in which *Jane Eyre* functions as "intertextual archetype," and that this is true whether we look at relatively sophisticated examples of twentieth-century texts by women or more popular writing.[8] All the texts I shall discuss confirm Maggie Berg's perception that Jane's significant legacy lies *not in her attainment of the object of her desire—experience or love—but in her control of the process of writing.* Moreover, they suggest that women's self-definition is a process in which the "mirrors" which they look for in older texts sometimes turn monstrous, so that the writer must use language to separate herself from these mothers or sisters who are at the same time too much like themselves and too horribly unlike what they want to be. The aggressive aspects of this process are present even without reference to Bertha Mason, Jane's mirror and monster within Charlotte Brontë's text. Bertha does not figure in this chapter because my focal texts do not themselves refer to her. This "not-said" is of course important, but to say it would make a different argument

The Game by A. S. Byatt (1967) and *The Waterfall* by Margaret Drabble (1969) were each written by a woman who, like Charlotte Brontë, shared a childhood fantasy world with siblings. Byatt and Drabble are sisters who appear, fictionally transformed, in each other's novels; in Byatt's novel one of the fictional sisters also writes a novel about a fictional family fantasy. The connections between "life" and "fiction" are here unusually convoluted, but it is commonly accepted that intertextuality is not confined to the printed page. John Hannay, in *The Intertextuality of Fate*, argues that the knowledge of generic plots like that of romance fiction constitutes a modern sense of "fatedness": "we 'know what comes next,' " he says, "because we recall analogous stories and so discern the proleptic logic of the one we are reading"—or living. In each of these texts, Jane Eyre functions as a "generic plot," transmitted both direct and by means of an intertextual chain, which for A. S. Byatt included another Brontë-inspired text, *The Brontës Went to Woolworths* by Rachel Ferguson (1931). "I read *The Brontës Went to Woolworths*," Byatt writes:

when I was ... a very well-read schoolgirl whose imaginary life was considerably livelier, more populated and more interesting than her real one. I was intrigued by the title, which seemed to suggest some impossible meeting of the urgent world of the romantic imagination and the everyday world of (in my case) Pontefract High Street.[9]

For all these writers "the urgent world of the romantic imagination" offered more than "the everyday world"; moreover, it was a world shared with siblings.

For Charlotte Brontë, the family fantasy which she describes in a poem, "We wove a web in childhood ... ," lasted well into adult life. At the age of twenty, she knew her Angrian characters as well as her brother and sisters; her daydreams were a resource so valuable that she provides it for her heroine in *Jane Eyre*. As a governess in Thornfield Hall, Jane describes how "my sole relief was ... to open my inward ear to a tale that was never ended—a tale ... quickened with all of incident, life, fire, feeling, that I desired and had not in my actual existence." Like Antonia Byatt on Pontefract High Street, Jane Eyre's daydreaming stems from an unsatisfying life, and she was not alone. The heroine of Julia Kavanagh's 1850 novel, *Nathalie*, also "listened invariably to the wonderful and endless romance, which her own thoughts had framed from the dreams that haunt the brain and trouble the heart of longing and ardent youth."[10]

In fact, Freud, in *Creative Writers and Day-Dreaming* (1908), argues that "every single phantasy is the fulfilment of a wish, a correction of unsatisfying reality." Florence Nightingale made the same observation in the 1850s; in her essay "Cassandra" she imagines a Victorian family group and asks, "Mothers, how many of your sons and daughters are *there*, do you think, while sitting round under your complacent eye? ... Is not one fancying herself the nurse of some new friend in sickness; another engaging in romantic dangers?" Nightingale sees that "it is the want of interest in our life which produces" daydreaming. Moreover, like Freud, she sees its connection with creative writing: "What are novels?" she asks. "What is the secret of the charm of every romance?"

Her answer is twofold: novels provide scope for thoughts and feelings, and they liberate the heroine from "family ties." Nightingale has perceived what the Marxist-Feminist Literature Collective put in rather different terms in 1978; in women's Victorian writings, they say, "the devised absence of the father represents a triple evasion of . . . class structure, kinship structure and Oedipal socialisation."[11]

Both Nightingale and the Marxist-Feminist group argue like Jane Eyre that "human beings . . . must have action; and they will make it if they cannot find it."[12] On the other hand, Jane's dreams seem to be satisfied by Mr. Rochester, just as Elizabeth Barrett Browning writes:

> I lived with visions for my company,
> Instead of men and women, years ago . . .
> . . . Then THOU didst come . . . to be,
> Beloved, what they seemed . . .
> (*Sonnets from the Portuguese*)[13]

Freud, too, argues that while men's fantasies are mostly ambitious, women's are mostly erotic. For Rachel Ferguson's heroine of the 1930s, the fear that Jane Eyre's ambition is just a smokescreen for erotic desire—which leads, of course, straight back to domesticity—makes Jane into a "monster" rather than a "mirror." Deirdre Carne, the first-person narrator of *The Brontës Went to Woolworths*, is a bright young thing who, like Ferguson herself, earns her living as a journalist. She seems to have achieved Jane Eyre's dream of reaching "the busy world, towns, regions full of life." Yet she and her sisters, just like Elizabeth Barrett, "live . . . with visions . . . instead of men and women." Their fantasy life is much more "real" than the office she never describes. It seems that they have escaped the private house of the past only to be repelled by "the public world . . . with its jealousy, its pugnacity, its greed." Virginia Woolf described women of this period as "between the devil and the deep sea," and for the Carne sisters, the Brontës represent "the devil" which they must and cannot escape.[14] Judith Kegan Gardiner argues that "twentieth-century women writers . . . often . . . communicate a consciousness of their identity through paradoxes of sameness and difference," and *The Brontës Went to Woolworths* is paradoxical in this way; the Carne sisters copy the Brontë sisters by inventing "a tale that was never ended," but they also fear them as spinsters ruled by erotic compulsions. The youngest sister's governess, Miss Martin, who dreams of marrying the curate, is a cruel parody of Charlotte Brontë, and when the sisters visit Haworth the Brontës, as table-tapping ghosts, appear really menacing. It is, I think, the modern women's fear of regression which allows the Brontës to figure as monsters in a text which also mirrors their fantasy lives; they occupy the position which, in more recent women's fiction, is taken by a "bad mother." Judith Kegan Gardiner argues that "the mother-villain is so frightening because she is what the daughter fears to become." In intertextual terms, the Carne sisters fear being "characters" in a story in which they "know what comes next," in which the "bad mother" is their "author." Their self-authored fantasies are thus a more vital aid in gaining control over their lives than the work they do in the "busy world." Refusing the Brontës as authors, they use them as characters in their own stories. The Brontës "go to Woolworths" because only in that way can the Carne sisters be authors of their own lives.[15]

This apparently whimsical story has a disturbing side to it which shows intertextuality not as an academic concept but as a battlefield where writing subjects struggle for control. A. S. Byatt's *The Game* has a similarly sinister atmosphere, but whereas in Ferguson's novel modern sisters use their shared fantasy against the Brontë threat, in Byatt's novel a childhood game shared by sisters becomes an adult fight to the death. Freud suggests that

> a phantasy . . . hovers . . . between . . . the three moments of time which our ideation involves . . . some provoking occasion in the present . . . which . . . arouse[s] one of the subject's major wishes . . . a memory of an earlier experience . . . in which this wish was fulfilled; and . . . the future which represents a fulfilment of the wish.[16]

In *The Game* the "provoking occasion" is a television series, seen separately by both sisters, presented by a man who had been part of their youthful game; but neither their memories nor their "wishes" are at all clear. Linda Anderson argues that Freud's sense of connection between past and present was much more complex than his "daydreaming" essay suggests; he "came to believe that memories were [themselves] . . . phantasies, constructed out of wishes and their repression." Thus "the neurotic for Freud was someone who could not tell their own story."[17]

In *The Game*, Cassandra, the elder sister, is an Oxford don; Julia a successful novelist. Cassandra is celibate; Julia is married; but their desires cannot be reduced to Freud's categories of erotic or ambitious wishes. Freud himself concedes that the categories are "often united," and Jacques Lacan, developing Freud's theory of "displacement," argues that objects of desire are always relatively arbitrary, since desire is a process of infinite deferral.[18] Since the gap between the subject and the object of desire is bridged, if at all, by language, it is appropriate that the sisters in Byatt's *The Game* strive not for specific objects but for transient victories in the battle for self-representation. Judith Kegan Gardiner argues that "literary identifications . . . derive some of their undoubted power from analogy with earlier mental states" such as "infantile identifications with parental figures," and in *The Game*, the academic Cassandra finds a literary "mother" in Charlotte Brontë, who "had seen the Duke of Zamorna leaning against a school mantel-shelf and had felt exhilarated and faint" (p. 219). Cassandra's sister Julia, however, uses both Cassandra and Charlotte Brontë not as "mothers" but as "daughters" in her own novel, in the sense that Gardiner suggests, that "the hero is her author's daughter." Ironically, a fictional reviewer praises Julia's "sympathy for her central character, Emily, the lady don," whose "imaginative life" suggests "Charlotte Brontë's passion for the Duke of Zamorna." Julia's "sympathy," however, has left no space for Cassandra to "write herself." If, as Gardiner argues, "female identity is a process," Cassandra's use of Charlotte Brontë had been a strategy in that process; but Julia's novel "identifies" her sister in the sense of fixing her to that image. Cassandra's mirror turns into a monster. "There is," she knows, "nowhere I shall not drag this grotesque shadow" (p. 230). So she kills herself. Julia is not unscathed—"all her life Cassandra had been the mirror . . . that proved her existence; now, she had lost a space and a purpose" (p. 235)—but she has won the battle for reality, which proved to be a battle of words. Cassandra's real death comes in the final sentence where, "closed into crates, unread, unopened, Cassandra's private papers bumped and slid" (p. 238).[19]

In Fay Weldon's stage adaptation of *Jane Eyre*, Branwell, Emily, and Anne are on stage throughout, helping Charlotte to write her story. Charlotte becomes Jane from time to time and the staging also identifies young Jane, her pupil, Adèle, and all the orphans of Lowood. The audience is thus made to feel that Jane's sense of isolation is an illusion, for all round her are girls and women each separately sharing the same experience. In *The Private Self*, Susan Stanford Friedman suggests that women's autobiography is characterized by this same sense of sharing. Drawing on Nancy Chodorow's theories, Friedman argues that whereas male autobiography requires "a conscious awareness of the singularity of each individual life," women's autobiographies "often explore their sense of shared identity with other women," feeling themselves "very much *with* others in an interdependent existence." This theoretical perspective raises a problem for the texts I am dealing with. Friedman acknowledges that women's "sense of shared identity . . . exists in tension with a sense of their own uniqueness," and Gardiner points out that "the word 'identity' is paradoxical in itself, meaning both sameness and distinctiveness." The Fay Weldon play foregrounds this paradox by representing to us as similar women who, in the "mother-text," are separate. In each of my texts, however, "sameness" itself is the threat. In Margaret Drabble's novel, *The Waterfall*, the heroine, Jane, feels that her cousin Lucy is "my sister, my fate, my example: her effect on me was incalculable"; but she is "tired of all this Freudian family nexus." Similarly Cassandra in *The Game* feels that she and Julia have been "too real to each other, sharing the same thoughts. . . . In an ideal state they should be no more and no less real to each other than anyone else."[20]

Carol Gilligan, in her book about women's ethical decision making, provides an explanation for this troubling unsisterliness.

Like Susan Friedman, Gilligan uses Chodorow as her theoretical base, but unlike Friedman she argues that women, precisely *because* they have more fluid ego-boundaries than men, tend to experience ethical problems with individuation, whereas men experience problems with relationship. Interviews show that the women who feel happiest with their lives are those who feel that they have made their own decisions—even if afterwards they feel they were wrong—rather than being "a character in someone else's story." This could explain both the unpleasantly aggressive strategies by which my fictional sisters free themselves from the "grotesque shadow" of their monstrous symbioses, and the fact that the novels end on a fairly positive note.[21] Even Jane Gray, in *The Waterfall*, who begins as "the heroine of a life that has no story," stealing Charlotte Brontë's story to depict herself as suffering in "some Brussels of the mind," ends by writing "a very good sequence of poems" from her fear that her lover was dying.[22] The fact that he doesn't die underlines the extent to which our stories can be liberated from our lives—or vice versa. The generic texts of tragic love, of comic romance, are each susceptible to interception, and, like Derrida's postcard, can be diverted to other destinations.

Although these texts consistently confuse Jane Eyre with Charlotte Brontë, there are important differences between them. Jane, a fictional heroine, writes her own life; she is happy with the decisions she has made and sees herself as a character in her own story. If Charlotte Brontë had written her autobiography, it is likely that she would have written not of her passionate desire but of her life as a dutiful daughter. When Robert Southey gave his famous advice that "literature cannot be the business of a woman's life," Charlotte replied that her ambition had all been "senseless trash"—but she also began writing *Jane Eyre*. Stevie Davies describes this as a process "whereby words (a sign in themselves of loss . . .) are liberated from their original conditions to be inscribed in the form of a homeopathic . . . remedy for the very conditions they record." Charlotte Brontë did not write her life, she wrote her daydream, composed of Freud's three elements: the memory of loss, of mother, sisters, lover; the present "provoking" fear that her father too would die; and her future wish for a lover embodying mother, sisters, father. But we may note that, in Charlotte's daydream, Jane's "sisters" (Diana and Mary) stay at a distance. Fay Weldon, rewriting *Jane Eyre* as a modern woman, sees sisters everywhere; Charlotte Brontë dreams herself as an orphan. Nancy Friday, in *My Mother My Self*, suggests that what we need is precisely sisters (or mothers) "at a distance." We need the "web" of relatedness, but we also need to be authors of our own stories. Charlotte Brontë's daydream, anchored in the past but launched into the future, becomes our past, the mirror by which we know ourselves, but, read as our future, the mirror turns monstrous. "We wove a web in childhood," Charlotte Brontë wrote; but "the web is sticky," wrote Antonia Byatt. If "female identity is a process," we must recognize that the moment when web turns to fly-trap and mirror to monster is also part of that process; the hope is that it forms a "provoking occasion" for new daydreams, a new construction of past, present, and future.[23]

The Game and *The Waterfall* are novels of the 1960s; they are, moreover, sophisticated productions. Jane Eyre, however, has played her part in provoking that same movement from identification to self-consciousness in more popular fiction. Despite feminist relish for Jane as rebel, most modern reproductions of *Jane Eyre* have tended to domesticate her story, to emphasize its closure and to focus on her childhood experience not as "mad cat" but as victim. Moreover, in spite of an apparent growth of feminist consciousness, critics and commentators outside academia still focus on the content of the story rather than its process. Fay Weldon's 1988 stage play, for instance, was meant to dramatize not just Jane's story but Jane's making of her story, and the female reviewer for the *Irish Sunday Tribune* saw that Charlotte, Emily, and Anne were there on stage to "tell us how the book might have been written." The *Daily Telegraph* reviewer, by contrast, thought that "the device of the peripheral family observing the action . . . is an irrelevant intrusion."[24]

Recognition of the writing process, on the other hand, appears in unexpected places. In 1990 *Good Housekeeping Magazine* launched a competition to rewrite the end of *Jane Eyre*, recognizing its force as a catalyst for new writing rather than as a role model. In 1988 the sixteen-year-old winner of a Brontë Society writing competition enacts the negotiation between identification and writing as her essay, "A Brontë Childhood," begins in the first person as Charlotte Brontë, but shifts to the third person:

> Charlotte put down her pen. . . . She thought of all the dreams and aspirations they had had, and of her governess sisters and broken brother. As she thought a new emotion swept her tiny body, and fired by a new wave of hope she resolved to urge herself and sisters and brother to follow their common passion: the written word.[25]

The shift in narrative position here can be seen to mimic the move described by Maggie Berg from the mirror phase of literary identification, in which this writer writes "as" Charlotte, and the "self-consciousness" from which she recognizes the distance between them, bridged by the writing process.

Sheila Greenwald's novel for teenage girls, *It All Began with Jane Eyre*, is built around this movement from identification to writing. The young narrator, Franny Dillman, tells how, because her life was less interesting than fiction, she tried to fit the people in her life into roles provided first by *Jane Eyre*, and later by modern stories, scandalizing her family by imagining passion, incest, and abortion among her relations. Eventually a literary friend persuades her to read *Jane Eyre* not just for its story but for its author's commentary: "It is vain," Franny reads at last, "to say human beings ought to be satisfied with tranquility; they must have action; and they will make it if they cannot find it." Forced to confront the reasons for what she has done, she also realizes that writing is a kind of action; the last line of the novel repeats the first as she sits down to write, "My mother thinks it all began with *Jane Eyre* . . ." Sheila Greenwald's novel is not subtle, but it suggests that the processes familiar to feminist academics as "writing the self" or "searching for subjectivity" are proceeding on a broad front. The Franny Dillman who writes her own story occupies the same position as the critic Pat Macpherson, who affirms that "in identifying with Jane Eyre as the subject, the narrator,

the moral agent of her own experience, I practiced how to become the nervy heroine, rather than the confused victim, of my
own experience."[26]

Interestingly, even a Mills and Boon novel which misreads Jane
Eyre as conformist rather than rebel nevertheless shows its heroine in this active negotiation with the earlier text. In *Devil Within*,
by Catherine George, the heroine conceives Jane Eyre to be a
timid Victorian spinster:

> The fictional Mr. Rochester in *Jane Eyre* was a pussycat com-
> pared with the dour, unfriendly man who had met her
> today without a word of welcome. Not that she was any
> Jane Eyre, either, decided Claudia—it would take more than
> a bit of boorish behavior to put her off life in this idyllic
> spot.[27]

Claudia's self-construction involves rejection of what, to her, is
the Jane Eyre image of sexual propriety: "her attitude had been
one of antediluvian rectitude, like some Victorian prunes-and-
prisms spinster drawing her skirts aside from contact with man's
baser instincts" (p. 171). If one reads for the outcome of the story,
Devil Within is reactionary in feminist terms, ending with Claudia
"deeply satisfied" with the prospect of marrying "one of those
chauvinists who consider woman's place is in the home" (p. 191).
There is no doubt, however, that Claudia does go through the
process described by Maurianne Adams and Pat Macpherson, of
matching herself against a partially accurate mirror image. For
Claudia, liberation and change are constituted by a less "Victorian" attitude to sex, and although sophisticated feminists may
feel that the permissiveness of the 1970s was a dead-end for
women, there is still a measure of self-assertion to be read in her
recognition of advance from an earlier model of male–female
relations: "It was hard to recognise the grim, dour Mr Rochester
in this elated male creature who was occupying her bed in such
flagrant nudity" (p. 190).

In "The Death of the Author," Roland Barthes has written
that "a text is made of multiple writings . . . entering into mutual
relations of dialogue, parody, contestation, but there is one place

where this multiplicity is focused and that place is the reader, not, as was hitherto said, the author."[28] It is not stupidity which prompts Catherine George, like Rachel Ferguson, to read *Jane Eyre* as a threat from the past, but the need to assert difference. *Jane Eyre* is a fascinating text because it compels generations of readers, in different historical circumstances, to measure themselves against Jane in confronting afresh the question, "What will you give in return for love?" The answer will depend, not on the author, but on the reader, and the compulsion to work through afresh the struggle of Jane Eyre leads the reader to something more like Jane's own process of self-narration than a simple process of mirroring. Whatever the outcome of these endlessly repeated struggles, this process whereby readers become writers of their own lives is, as Pat Macpherson puts it, "the psychosocial stuff of which identity is made."[29]

Notes

This chapter is a condensed version of material which appears scattered through several chapters in Patsy Stoneman, *Brontë Transformations: The Cultural Dissemination of Jane Eyre and Wuthering Heights* (Hemel Hempstead: Harvester Wheatsheaf, 1996).

1. See Elizabeth Gaskell, *The Life of Charlotte Brontë* ([1857] Harmondsworth: Penguin, 1975), p. 308.

2. Valerie Grosvenor Myer, *Charlotte Brontë: Truculent Spirit* (London: Vision Press, 1987), p. 108. See also Elaine Showalter, "Looking Forward: American Feminists. Victorian Sages," *Victorian Newsletter* 65 (Spring 1984), pp. 6–10, on the influence of Victorian novels as modern feminist role models.

3. Playbill/poster for *young jane eyre*, Children's Theatre Company, 2400 Third Avenue, South Minneapolis, MN 55404 (8 Jan–27 Feb 1988).

4. O. C. Ogunyemi, *Signs* 11, 1 (Autumn, 1985), p. 66; see Patricia Dunker, *Sisters and Strangers: An Introduction to Contemporary Feminist Fiction* (Oxford: Blackwell, 1992), pp. 24–7; Maya Angelou, Virago publicity leaflet for *Reading Women Writers*, a learning resource produced by the National Extension College (September 1991); Tsitsi Dangarembga, *Nervous Condi-*

tions (London: Women's Press, 1988), pp. 93, 92; Hideko Maki, MS note to Japanese program for *Jane Eyre*, directed by Miss Kazue Kontaibo, 1978 (in Brontë Parsonage Museum Library, Haworth); Barbara T. Christian, "Response to 'Black Women's Texts.'" *NWSA Journal* I (1) (1988), pp. 32–3.

5. Arlyn Diamond and Lee R. Edwards (eds.), *The Authority of Experience: Essays in Feminist Criticism* (Amherst: University of Massachusetts Press, 1977), p. 68; Cheri Register, "American Feminist Literary Criticism: A Bibliographical Introduction," in Josephine Donovan (ed.), *Feminist Literary Criticism: Explorations in Theory* (Lexington: University Press of Kentucky, 1975), p. 20; Maurianne Adams, "*Jane Eyre*: Woman's Estate," in Diamond and Edwards (eds.), *The Authority of Experience*, p. 145; Toril Moi, *Sexual/Textual Politics* (London: Methuen, 1985), p. 8.

6. Adams, "Woman's Estate," pp. 140–1, 137; Pat Macpherson, *Reflecting on Jane Eyre* (London: Routledge, 1989), p. xii; Christian, "Response." pp. 34–5.

7. Maggie Berg, *Jane Eyre: Portrait of a Life* (Boston: Twayne, 1987), pp. 37–8, 24.

8. Umberto Eco, "Casablanca: Cult Movies and Intertextual Collage" (1984), in David Lodge (ed.), *Modern Criticism and Theory* (London: Longman, 1988), p. 447.

9. A. S. Byatt, *The Game* ([1967] Harmondsworth: Penguin, 1987); Margaret Drabble, *The Waterfall* ([1969] Harmondsworth: Penguin, 1971); John Hannay, *The Intertextuality of Fate: A Study of Margaret Drabble* (Columbia, Mo.: University of Missouri Press, 1986), pp. 1–2; Antonia Byatt. "Introduction" to Rachel Ferguson. *The Brontës Went to Woolworths* ([1931] London: Virago, 1988), p. iii.

10. Charlotte Brontë, *Jane Eyre* ed. Margaret Smith ([1847]) Oxford: Clarendon Press, 1973), ch. 12; Julia Kavanagh, *Nathalie: A Tale*, 3 vols. (London: Henry Colburn, 1850), vol. II, p. 138.

11. Sigmund Freud, "Creative Writers and Day-dreaming" (1908) in James Strachey (ed.), *The Pelican Freud Library*, vol. 14 (Harmondsworth: Penguin, 1985), pp. 134–5; Florence Nightingale, "Cassandra" (1859), in Ray Strachey, *The Cause* ([1928] London: Virago, 1978), p. 397; Marxist-Feminist Literature Collective, "Women's Writing: *Jane Eyre, Shirley, Villette, Aurora Leigh*," in Francis Barker et al. (eds.), *The Sociology of Literature: 1848* (Colchester: University of Essex, 1978), p. 188.

12. Brontë. *Jane Eyre*, p. 110.

13. Elizabeth Barrett Browning, *Poems* (including *Sonnets from the Portuguese*) (London, 1850), No. XXVI.

14. Brontë, *Jane Eyre*, p. 110; Virginia Woolf, *Three Guineas* ([1938]. Harmondsworth: Penguin, 1977), p. 86.

15. Judith Kegan Gardiner, "On Female Identity and Writing by Women," *Critical Inquiry 8* (Winter 1981), pp. 354, 356, Note 18; J Hannay, *Intertextuality of Fate*, pp. 1–2.

16. Freud, "Creative Writers," p. 135.

17. Linda Anderson, "At the Threshold of the Self: Women and Autobiography," in Moira Monteith (ed.), *Women's Writing: A Challenge to Theory* (Brighton: Harvester Press, 1986), pp. 54–5.

18. Freud, "Creative Writers," p. 135; Anika Lemaire, *Jacques Lacan*, trans. David Macey (London: Routledge, 1970), p. 87.

19. Gardiner, "On Female Identity," pp. 356, 349; A. S. Byatt, *The Game*, pp. 24, 219, 230, 235, 238.

20. Fay Weldon (adaptor), *Jane Eyre*, directed by Helena Kaut-Howson, first presented at Birmingham Repertory Theatre in 1986; Susan Stanford Friedman, "Women's Autobiographical Selves: Theory and Practice," in Shari Benstock (ed.), *The Private Self: Theory and Practice of Women's Autobiographical Writings* (London: Routledge, 1988), p. 44; George Gusdorf, "Conditions and Limits of Autobiography" (1956), quoted in Friedman, pp. 34, 38; Gardiner, "On Female Identity," p. 347; Drabble, *The Waterfall*, pp. 114, 130; Byatt, *The Game*, p. 97.

21. Carol Gilligan, *In a Different Voice: Psychological Theory and Women's Development* (Cambridge, Mass., and London: Harvard University Press, 1982); Byatt, *The Game*, p. 230; see Joanne V. Creighton, "Sisterly Symbiosis: Margaret Drabble's *The Waterfall* and A.S. Byatt's *The Game*," *Mosaic* 20:1 (Winter 1987): 15–29.

22. Sandra Gilbert and Susan Gubar, *The Madwoman in the Attic: The Woman Writer and the Nineteenth-Century Literary Imagination* (London and New Haven: Yale University Press, 1979), p. 39; Drabble, *The Waterfall*, pp. 84, 233.

23. Elizabeth Gaskell, *Life of Charlotte Brontë*, pp. 173–4; Stevie Davies, *Emily Brontë* (Hemel Hempstead: Harvester, 1988), pp. 89–90; Nancy Friday, *My Mother My Self* ([1977] London: Fontana, 1979), p. 67; Byatt, *The Game*, p. 230; Gardiner, "On Female Identity," p. 349.

24. Mary O'Donnell, "Difference between Passion and Page 3," *Sunday Tribune*, 9 Dec 1990; Peter Mortimer, "Theatre North: No Plain Jane," *Daily Telegraph*, 20 April 1988.

25. Catherine Tillotson, "A Brontë Childhood," Brontë Parsonage Museum Haworth National Essay Competition for Schoolchildren, 1988, printed by the Brontë Society.

26. Sheila Greenwald, *It All Began with Jane Eyre* (New York: Dell Publishing, 1980), pp. 47, 122–3; Macpherson, *Reflecting*, p. xiii.

27. Catherine George, *Devil Within* (Richmond, Surrey: Mills and Boon, 1984), pp. 37, 171, 191, 190.

28. Roland Barthes, "The Death of the Author," in David Lodge (ed.), *Modern Criticism and Theory* (London: Longman, 1988), p. 171.

29. Macpherson, *Reflecting*, p. xii.

Romance and Anti-Romance

From Brontë's Jane Eyre to Rhys's Wide Sargasso Sea

JOYCE CAROL OATES

◆ ◆ ◆

J EAN RHYS'S HAUNTING and hallucinatory prose poem of a novel, *Wide Sargasso Sea* (1966), boldly tells the story—authentic, intimate, and unsparing, because first-person confession—of Mrs. Bertha Rochester, the doomed madwoman of Charlotte Brontë's *Jane Eyre.* Yet Rhys's novel is more than a remarkably inspired tour de force, a modernist revision of a great Victorian classic: it is an attempt to evoke, by means of a highly compressed and elliptical poetic language, the authentic experience of madness—more precisely, of being driven into madness; and it is a brilliantly sustained anti-romance, a reverse mirror image of Jane Eyre's and Rochester's England. Rhys's sympathy is fully with the innocent Creole heiress who is married off to the visiting Englishman, Rochester, and trapped in a loveless (but not, it seems, atypical) marriage: born Antoinette, she is rebaptized Bertha by her husband, and brought back to England, to Thornfield, to be kept in captivity like a wild animal. When Jane Eyre is surprised by the "Vampyre" in chapter 25 of Charlotte Brontë's novel, Bertha has become a savage, "fearful and ghastly," and possessed of a "dis-

colored" and "lurid" visage; glimpsed more closely, she is not a
human figure at all, but bestial, repellent. ("It grovelled, seemingly on all fours; it snatched and growled like some strange wild
animal: but it was covered with clothing; and a quantity of dark,
grizzled hair, wild as a mane, hid its head and face.") Yet the first
Mrs. Rochester, in Rhys's novel, is despised by her Englishman
husband precisely because she is beautiful, and because, in the
frank sensuousness of her beauty, she is aligned with the "magic"
of the West Indies which he finds treacherous. One way of life,
one vision, makes war upon its opposite; for all of the West Indies
is dismissed by Rochester as dreamlike and unreal, just as, by
extension, all of the non- (or anti-) English world must be dismissed by the English, before it can be conquered and exploited.
(Rhys's novel is set in the 1830s and 1840s.)

Near the fragmentary conclusion of *Wide Sargasso Sea*
Antoinette-Bertha at last catches a glimpse of the girl who will
succeed her as Rochester's wife: Jane Eyre is a "ghost" with
streaming hair. ("She was surrounded by a gilt frame," Antoinette
says mysteriously, "but I knew her.") Inhabiting contrary worlds,
one woman is a savage to the other; the other, a ghost. Rochester,
that most masculine and romantic of heroes, might link them.
But of course the Rochester of Brontë's novel differs radically
from the Rochester of Rhys's. Even more radically, the prose
styles of the two novels differ, giving voice, or voices, to the
extraordinary distance between the Victorian sensibility and that
of the twentieth century. A novel is a phenomenon of language,
and much that we imagine we *see* and *feel* and *believe* about a
fictional world is really a consequence of what we *hear:* what is
communicated to us by way of prose rhythms and the artful
structure of sentences, paragraphs, chapters. Meaning is carried,
if not precisely embodied, by a novel's voice: how is the story
being narrated is as significant a question as who is narrating it
or what it says.

One of the most remarkable elements of *Jane Eyre* is simply Jane's
voice. As the romantically complicated plot evolves the reader is
allowed to understand that the *story* is actually *history*; Jane Eyre,

wife and mother, in 1819, is recounting the events of 1799–1809 in assured, masterful, distanced prose that may brilliantly depict scenes of despair, passion, and intense physical appetite but never lapses from its authoritative tone. From her authorial vantage point, the second Mrs. Rochester is capable of prodigious feats of summary ("Hitherto I have recorded in detail the events of my insignificant existence: to the first ten years of my life, I have given almost as many chapters. But this is not to be a regular autobiography: I am only bound to evoke memory where I know her responses will possess some degree of interest; therefore I will pass a space of eight years almost in silence. . . ."); she assesses herself without self-pity or sentimental illusion, as plain, Quaker-like, yet touchingly hopeful that some "fairer era of life was beginning" at Thornfield ("Externals have a great effect upon the young. . . . My faculties, roused by the change of scene, the new field offered to hope, seemed all astir. . . . It was not my habit to be disregardful of appearance, or careless of the impression I made: on the contrary, I ever wished to look as well as I could, and to please as much as my want of beauty would permit. I felt it a misfortune that I was so little, so pale, and had features so irregular and so marked. . . .") The technique is perfectly suited to Brontë's intention, for her heroine has triumphed by the novel's end, having resisted the temptation of outlaw romantic love (with the yet-married Rochester) and the rather more subtle temptation of a passionless "Christian" life of devotion (with the ascetic St. John Rivers). At the time of the novel's narration the plain Quakerish governess has become wed at last, *properly wed*, to the man she loves. Mystery is resolved or dissolves into something approaching ordinary human happiness. As Robert Graves said of Lewis Carroll's Alice, so it might well be said of Brontë's inimitable Jane—she is the heroine of her race.

Much of the power of *Jane Eyre* derives from a dialectic strategy, which the author unobtrusively pursues on several structural levels. For instance, in the largest, most spacious sense the novel is about character stimulated into growth—remarkable growth—by place: Jane Eyre, orphaned and presumably defenseless, and a mere girl, discovers the strength of her personality by the challenges of several contrasting environments—the Reed household, where she is despised; Lowood School, where she discovers a model in Miss Temple; Thornfield, where she cultivates, with agreeable naturalness, a measure of sexual power; Whitcross, where, at last, she acquires the semblance of a family; and Fern-dean, Rochester's retreat, a manor-house of "considerable antiq-uity . . . deep buried in a wood," where she is at last wed. Just as these places differ greatly from one another, so Jane differs greatly in them, though the dramatic "expansion of soul" she experiences in the Reed household has affected a permanent change in her. Brontë's sense of human personality is that it is pliant, fluid, and living, in immediate (and often powerful) response to its sur-roundings; not that it is stable and determined, as if sculpted in marble. And it is the case too that Jane Eyre is a heroine in a "heroic" mold, as susceptible as any man to restlessness and ennui when opposition fails to provide a cause for struggle. (Grown bored at Thornfield, for instance, before the arrival of the master, Jane longs for a power of vision that might overpass the limits of her sequestered life, peaceful and pleasant as it is. Very like the unnamed governess in Henry James's *The Turn of the Screw*, Jane walks agitatedly about, alone, "safe in the silence and solitude," and eager for adventure: which is to say, romance. Women are supposed to be calm, generally, Jane says, but women feel pre-cisely as men do, requiring exercise for their faculties, and suf-fering from stagnation. On the third floor of Thornfield she paces about, not unlike Bertha in *her* backward-and-forward move-ments, allowing "my mind's eye to dwell upon whatever bright visions rose before it—and, certainly, they were many and glow-ing; to let my heart be heaved by the exultant movement, which, while it swelled it in trouble, expanded it with life; and, best of all, to open my inward ear to a tale that was never ended—a tale my imagination created, and narrated continuously; quick-ened with all of incident, life, fire, feeling, that I desired and had not in my actual existence." Jane is Charlotte Brontë speaking of the mesmerizing experience of writing *Jane Eyre*.

It is interesting to note that Brontë characteristically introduces a situation meant to provoke conventional associations on the part of the reader (to whom Jane is relating her history), and then, within a paragraph or two, deftly qualifies or refutes it. The narrative's dialectic, then, constitutes a plot-motion of its own, quite apart from Jane's activities. A thesis of sorts is presented, but, if we should respond to it, the narrator will set us right: for she is always in control of her narrative. What *seems to be* rarely *is;* even when Rochester disguises himself as a fortune-telling gypsy, in one of the novel's more improbable sequences, Jane alone suspects "something of masquerade."

For instance, Jane's story begins with a blunt statement: "There was no possibility of taking a walk that day." The shrubbery is leafless; the winter sky overcast; the rain penetrating; Eliza, John, and Georgiana, and the despised orphan Jane, are cooped up together in the house. But, should the reader automatically respond to this atmosphere of privation, Jane immediately says: "I was glad of it: I never liked long walks." Excluded from Christmas celebrations in the Reed household, Jane describes the festivities and exchanges of gifts she missed; then says: "To speak the truth, I had not the least wish to go into company." Given what is known of Charlotte Brontë's grief at the deaths of her older sisters at school, when she was a very small child, the dialectic of chapter 9 is all the more dramatic: for here the typhus epidemic at Lowood Orphan Asylum is set against an unusually idyllic spring, and while disease, death, gloom, hospital smells, and the "effulvia of mortality" predominate, Jane, untouched by the disease, is frank about her enjoyment of the situation. Forty-five out of eighty girls are affected; some go home to die, and some die at school, like Helen Burns, and are buried "quietly and quickly"; but the ten-year-old Jane, clearly no child-heroine in a novel by George Eliot or Charles Dickens, is capable of responding to the bright May sunshine and the "majestic life" that is being restored to nature. She delights in her newfound freedom to ramble in the wood, and to eat as much as she likes, perhaps for the first time in her life: with very little Victorian sentiment, but with a refreshing air of truthfulness, Jane notes that her breakfast-basin is better filled because the sick lack appetite. Even the death of Helen Burns is sparely treated; and Jane's close questioning of

Helen's religious convictions does not appear resolved. ("Again I questioned; but this time only in thought. "Where is [Heaven]? Does it exist?")

Jane Eyre is remarkable for its forthright declaration of its heroine's various passions and appetites. Unlike Lucy Snowe of *Villette*, whom she superficially resembles, Jane Eyre does not need to cultivate a "healthy hunger": she is ravenous with appetite at Lowood, and, when she flees Thornfield, in the brilliantly sustained nightmare of chapter 28, she is in danger of literally starving to death. In the latter scene, Jane responds at first like any romantic heroine, imagining a Wordsworthian sort of solace in the moorland: "Not a tie holds me to human society at this moment—not a charm or hope calls me where my fellow-creatures are—none that saw me would have a kind thought or good wish for me. I have no relative but the universal mother, Nature: I will seek her breast and ask repose." Outcast that she is from human society, Jane knows herself loved by nature, to which she clings with an ingenuous "filial fondness": "Tonight, at least, I would be her guest—as I was her child: my mother would lodge me without money and without price. I had no more morsel of bread. . . . My hunger, sharp before, was, if not satisfied, appeased by this hermit's meal." As her reverie continues Jane speculates about God, a *He* set beside nature's *She:* "We know that God is everywhere; but certainly we feel His presence most when His works are on the grandest scale spread before us: and it is in the unclouded night sky, where His worlds wheel their silent course, that we read clearest His infinitude."

Next morning, however, Jane wakes to extreme hunger and begins to suffer the humiliation, mounting very nearly to physical terror, of near-starvation. Charlotte Brontë renders this painful interlude with such convincing authority that one cannot doubt she wrote from firsthand experience, as her earliest biographer Mrs. Gaskell suggests; few scenes in English literature are so harrowing as those in which Jane overcomes her pride to beg for food and is given a crust of bread, or food meant for hogs, or is rebuffed altogether. ("I blamed none of those who repulsed me.

I felt it was what was to be expected.") Hunger has become real to Jane in a way that the comforting platitudes surrounding "Nature" and "God" are not. (One is reminded of the "thin, haggard, and hollow-eyed" Lucy Snowe, that past mistress of deprivation who, confronted with a Renoir-like portrait of a voluptuous female—ostensibly Cleopatra—responds with the spiteful bitterness of any involuntary ascetic. Brontë is so incensed by this "enormous piece of claptrap" that, for some paragraphs the often-soporific prose of *Villette* is enlivened by genuine passion: "I calculated that this lady . . . would infallibly turn from fourteen to sixteen stone. She was, indeed, extremely well fed: very much butcher's meat—to say nothing of bread vegetables, and liquids—must she have consumed to attain that breadth and height, that wealth of muscle, that affluence of flesh. . . . She had no business to lounge away the noon on a sofa. She ought likewise to have worn decent garments; a gown covering her properly.")

No aura of mystery or exoticism accrues to Rochester's visitor from the West Indies, Richard Mason: in Jane's eyes he is sallow and unmanly, with something in his face that fails to please—"His features were regular, but too relaxed: his eye was large and well cut, but the life looking out of it was a tame, vacant life." When, later, Jane is brought into Bertha Mason's presence, and mockingly introduced to Rochester's wife, she naturally feels no kinship—in truth very little human sympathy—for the woman who has become a beast, beside whom *she* appears to distinct advantage. Though she charges Rochester with cruelty in so despising his mad wife, claiming that the woman cannot help being mad, she cannot identify with her in any way; and she readily forgives Rochester his curious and ungentlemanly behavior regarding both the legitimate Mrs. Rochester and herself—whom he had hoped to marry dishonestly. (It is even the case, as Rochester suggests, that Bertha Mason deserves her fate, for, from the very first, her nature was wholly alien to his, and her tastes obnoxious: "her character ripened and developed with frightful rapidity; her vices sprang up fast and rank . . . ; her excesses had prematurely developed the germs of insanity"—which is to say,

Bertha Mason is suffering from the tertiary stage of syphilis.) But the legitimate Mrs. Rochester, along with Thornfield Hall itself, will soon be destroyed in a refining fire.

The tensions of an interior dialect necessarily resolve themselves as *Jane Eyre* moves to its conclusion. It is sometimes said that the Whitcross section, of nearly one hundred pages, is an unfortunate digression in the novel's plot; but the carefully rendered sequence is required for symmetry's sake. Brontë's strategy is to balance one kind of temptation with its reverse (if Rochester is all romantic passion, urging her to succumb to emotional excess, St. John Rivers is all Christian ambition, urging her to succumb to a spiritual asceticism of which she is incapable); and the miraculously realized "family" of Diana, Mary, and Rivers himself is a benign adumbration of the novel's original household, in which Jane was despised by Eliza, Georgiana, and the loathsome John Reed. Rochester, following the novel's interior pattern, must be altered in some respect, but it is erroneous to read his blinding as a species of "castration"—as that perennial cliché of Brontë criticism would have it. Not only is the blind and crippled Rochester no less masculine than before, but, more significantly, it was never the case that the virginal Jane shrank from either her master's passion or her own: the issue was not Jane's alleged timidity in the face of Rochester's manly desire, but her shrewd understanding that, should she become his mistress, she would inevitably lose his respect—for Brontë's sensibility is unfailingly realistic here. (In this Jane is no hypocrite: she is simply an intelligent young woman of her era who has learned well from Rochester's own testimony. And who can doubt that, given the terms of Victorian prejudice, and the double standard which Jane herself never questions, she is absolutely correct in refusing to "yield" to her impassioned lover as she does? Romantic and idealistic as Jane so frequently is, she is at bottom the most pragmatic and reliable of persons.)

"Reader, I married him," Jane announces in the novel's last chapter: the tacit message being that *"I"* married *"him"*—not that *"he"* married *"me"* or even that *"we were married."* Jane Eyre is herself still, autonomous and self-defined; but even this concluding chapter ends with a curious aside to St. John Rivers, away in India "laboring for his race" and anticipating his "incorruptible crown." In fact it is St. John's grim, exultant language that closes the story: " 'Amen; even so come, Lord Jesus!' "

Wide Sargasso Sea, written more than a century later, defines itself immediately as a novel less of character than of destiny. Its subject is really a mysterious region of the soul into which persons and historical events and objects drift and are lost in stasis: a "Sargasso Sea" of the interior life, impressionistic for all the authority of its detail, its shimmering linguistic beauty overlaid by an air of irrevocable doom. Rhys's novel, though primarily narrated by its heroine, could not have been titled *Antoinette Cosway* (paralleling *Jane Eyre*) because Antoinette is no more in control of her dreamlike narrative than she is in control of her life. Things happen to her: if she acts it will be impulsively and unwisely, like the beautiful gigantic moths that fly into candle flames and die. Unlike Jane Eyre, who both knows her personal history and what she should think about it, Antoinette barely "knows" her story at all. Her passive, unjudging, highly emotional nature registers events but cannot summarize them for us, so that, as readers, we are meant to feel both fascination and impatience. Like the visiting Englishman Rochester, we may equate the childlike Antoinette with her West Indian landscape, which *must* harbor meaning, for all its lushness: for are we not fated to insist upon an interior, spiritual meaning in all human encounters? Rochester, newly recovered from his fever, thinks: "It was a beautiful place—wild, untouched, above all untouched, with an alien, disturbing, secret loveliness. And it kept its secret. I'd find myself thinking, 'What I see is nothing—I want what it *hides*—that is not nothing.' "

Jean Rhys, born in the Windward Islands, where she lived until the age of sixteen, could not have failed to read Brontë's famous romance from a distinctly alien and skeptical perspective. Why did Rochester marry a Creole heiress and bring her back to England? What might have been the circumstances of their meeting? Could it really have been true, even in fictional terms, that he had never loved her? When Antoinette tells Rochester on the day before their wedding that she is frightened of the future, because "you don't know anything about me," she is a West Indian speaking to an Englishman; and though Rochester immediately protests, of course she is correct. (Rochester's unacknowledged motive for marrying is mercenary.) Each views the other as a sort of looking-glass figure, inhabiting an inaccessible world. To Antoinette the very idea of London is dreamlike; to Rochester, the islands for all their beauty are "quite unreal and like a dream." Antoinette's fragmentary tales, told to Rochester, have only the effect of arousing anxiety in him. "Well, what happens?" he asks characteristically. And then again: "Is that the story?" But Antoinette's impressionistic recollections are offered as aspects of her inchoate childhood, memories of events she herself has imperfectly understood "Do you think . . . that I have slept too long in the moonlight?" she asks her bridegroom.

Wide Sargasso Sea is the fifth of Jean Rhys's novels, and Antoinette Cosway shares a number of characteristics with earlier Jean Rhys heroines, but in this novel the protagonist, for all her isolation, is emblematic of an entire way of life. If she is passive and easily victimized, this has been true of other members of the decayed Creole "aristocracy," including Antoinette's own mother; if she suffers from a kind of sporadic amnesia, this too is typical of her people. Since the freeing of the slaves in the Islands, the white landowners have lived in a state of undeclared war, forced to employ former slaves as servants and utterly helpless without them. In this sickly and dreamlike atmosphere in which an old ruling class is no longer really ruling, a tremendous expenditure of psychic energy goes into denying what is self-evident: that the white families are in danger of being murdered at any time. Paranoia, that most terrifying of mental derangements, may be the most intelligent response to life at the Coulibri Estate, since its opposite, a hysterical form of denial, will be suicidal. ("They are children," Antoinette's deluded stepfather says, "they wouldn't hurt a fly." "Unhappily children do hurt flies," says Aunt Cora.)

Just as Charlotte Brontë's authorial voice in *Jane Eyre* informs us of the assumptions about reality and our capacity for absorbing it in which educated readers of the early of mid-nineteenth cen-

tury believed, so does Jean Rhys's oblique, elliptical, rather un-
inflected voice tell us a great deal about twentieth-century expectations. If the atmosphere of Rochester's Thornfield is blighted
in some mysterious way, what other approach for Jane Eyre than
to confront the mystery, to puzzle over it, to pursue it?—the
tacit assumption being that mystery will be satisfactorily resolved.
(It is significant that, soon after her arrival at Thornfield, the
impetuous young governess climbs into the attic of the manor
house, that she might survey the grounds "laid out like a map.")
In Antoinette's similarly blighted atmosphere no direct assault is
possible, since the gravity of the political situation is resolutely
denied, and a child of Antoinette's nervous sensitivity cannot fail
to respond to nuances of meaning and vaguely glimpsed horrors
her elders seem incapable of observing. Even after the worst has
happened—the estate burned, the idiot child Pierre killed, Mrs.
Mason hopelessly insane—Antoinette must continue to live in
her poisoned atmosphere as if it were not poisoned: as if it were,
simply, the world.

In so ominous and undefined a setting, fear naturally blossoms
at any time, provoked by any stimuli. And Rhys's finely honed
language communicates both the logic of this fear and its ubiq-
uitousness. No casual relationships between "events" and "results"
can be named, for one day a horse is living, the next day he is
dead, said to be poisoned. But perhaps (so the child Antoinette
reasons) if she tells no one about it, it might not be true. Where
in Jane Eyre's imagination all things of significance are related to
one another in a universe in which God means well, in Antoinette's experience nothing is predictably related and emotions like
terror may spring suddenly from the most innocent of sources:

> Our garden was large and beautiful as that garden in the
> Bible—the tree of life grew there. But it had gone wild.
> The paths were overgrown and a smell of dead flowers
> mixed with the fresh living smell . . . Orchids flourished out
> of reach or for some reason not to be touched. One was
> snaky looking, another like an octopus with long thin
> brown tentacles bare of leaves hanging from a twisted root.

Twice a year the octopus orchid flowered—then not an inch of tentacle showed. It was a bell-shaped mass of white, mauve, deep purples, wonderful to see. The scent was very sweet and strong. I never went near it.

In recitation this logic may appear mad, like that expounded by a character in one of Lewis Carroll's dream landscapes; but at the Coulibri Estate it is perfectly reasonable. And no less reasonable is Antoinette's childish terror at an imagined image:

> One day when I was waiting [in Christophine's room] I was suddenly very much afraid. The door was open to the sunlight, someone was whistling near the stables, but I was afraid. I was certain that hidden in the room (behind the old black press?) there was a dead man's dried hand, white chicken feathers, a cock with its throat cut, dying slowly, slowly. Drop by drop the blood was falling into a red basin and I imagined I could hear it. No one had ever spoken to me about obeah—but I knew what I would find if I dared to look. Then Christophine came in smiling and pleased to see me. Nothing alarming ever happened and I forgot, or told myself I had forgotten.

(As for the practice of obeah, or voodoo as it is called in Haiti— what can any white observer learn about it? Years later, married to Antoinette, Rochester reads about native superstitions in a book called *The Glittering Coronet of Isles*—"A zombi is a dead person who seems to be alive or a living person who is dead"—but when he questions one of the natives he is told not to believe in such foolishness. And it is not clear whether obeah is black magic— or merely the cunning use of vegetable poisons.)

Imagined more as a prose poem than a novel of conventional technique, *Wide Sargasso Sea* so perfectly mirrors its heroine's fragmentary vision that a sensation of genuine malaise is communicated to the reader. Paragraphs follow one another without evident connection; dialogue begins and breaks off; conversations are overheard by the narrator but granted no emotional consequence. In terror of knowing too much Antoinette knows too little—and what she refuses to know will result, in part, in her disastrous marriage. ("I remember that after my mother's funeral, very early in the morning . . . we went home to drink chocolate and eat cakes. She died last year, no one told me how, and I didn't ask.") Only once does she surprise us by coolly defining herself—"Antoinette Mason, née Cosway, Mount Calvary Convent, Spanish Town, Jamaica, 1839"—but she does so only because she is sewing in the schoolroom, while Mother St. Justine reads barbaric tales to the girls from *The Lives of the Saints.* (The convent school has its own saint, Innocenzia, a fourteen-year-old girl now dried to a skeleton, and hidden beneath the chapel altar.)

Antoinette is incapable of seeing and assessing herself, though the reader infers, from Rochester's reluctant desire for her, that she is an uncommonly beautiful young woman. But his response to her beauty fills him with self-loathing: she is a part of his fever dream, his sickness, his acquiescence to the least noble aspects of himself. Indeed, in Rochester's English eyes, there is even something repulsive about Antoinette's very beauty: "Her eyes . . . are too large and can be disconcerting. She never blinks at all it seems to me. Long, sad, dark alien eyes. Creole of pure English descent she may be, but they are not English or European either," Rochester thinks shortly after their wedding. And her Island fatalism challenges his superficial Christian piety: for when he blandly says that he believes in God, Antoinette replies that it doesn't matter what they believe because they can do nothing about it—they are helpless as moths flying into candle flames, swept dead off the table.

After Rochester is given a poisonous "love potion" by the desperate Antoinette, the ambivalent passion he feels for her turns irrevocably to hatred. He in turn practices a sinister sort of magic upon her by renaming her Bertha and refusing to acknowledge her love for him. And though their marriage is over, he will not relinquish her: "She's mad but *mine, mine.* What will I care for gods or devils or for Fate itself," he thinks.

I hated the mountains and the hills, the rivers and the rain.
I hated the sunsets of whatever color, I hated its beauty and

its magic and the secret I would never know. I hated its indifference and the cruelty which was part of its loveliness. Above all I hated her. For she belonged to the magic and the loveliness. She had left me thirsty and all my life would be thirst and longing for what I had lost before I found it.

Once Antoinette-Bertha is brought to England, to Thornfield, and placed under Grace Poole's care, she descends rapidly into madness. Her new world is totally unreal to her, a cardboard house in which nothing of consequence can happen. Time speeds up; times are rapidly jumbled; in a brilliant hallucinatory sequence Antoinette sees into the near future in which she will set a fire and destroy Thornfield—and herself.

I dropped the candle I was carrying and it caught the end of a tablecloth and I saw flames shoot up. As I ran or perhaps floated or flew I called help me Christophine and looking behind me I saw that I had been helped. There was a wall of fire protecting me but it was too hot, it scorched me and I went away from it. . . . I ran up the last flight of stairs and along the passage. I passed the room where they brought me yesterday or the day before yesterday, I don't remember. Perhaps it was quite long ago for I seemed to know the house quite well. I knew how to get away from the heat and the shouting. . . . When I was out on the battlements it was cool and I could hardly hear them. I sat there quietly. I don't know how long I sat. Then I turned round and saw the sky. It was red and all my life was in it.

But Bertha Rochester's pathetic death will make Jane Eyre's life possible—if one follows the logic of fictional legend.

Suggested Reading

◆　◆　◆

Adams, Maurianne. "Family Disintegration and Creative Reintegration: The Case of Charlotte Brontë and *Jane Eyre*." In *The Victorian Family: Structure and Stresses*, 148–79. Ed. Anthony S. Wohl. New York: St. Martins, 1978.

Armstrong, Nancy. "Captivity and Cultural Capital in the English Novel." *Novel* 31 (1998): 373–98.

Auerbach, Nina. "Charlotte Brontë: The Two Countries." *University of Toronto Quarterly* 42 (1972): 328–42.

Beaty, Jerome. *Misreading Jane Eyre: A Postformalist Paradigm*. Columbus: Ohio State University Press, 1996.

Bellis, Peter J. "In the Window-Seat: Vision and Power in *Jane Eyre*." *English Literary History* 54 (1987): 639–652.

Berman, Carolyn Vellenga. "Undomesticating the Domestic Novel: Creole Madness in *Jane Eyre*." *Genre* 32 (1999): 267–96.

Bewell, Alan. "*Jane Eyre* and Victorian Medical Geography." *English Literary History* 63 (1996): 773–808.

Boumelha, Penny. *Charlotte Brontë*. Bloomington: Indiana University Press, 1990.

Case, Alison. *Plotting Women: Gender and Narration in the Eighteenth- and*

Nineteenth-Century British Novel. Charlottesville: University Press of Virginia, 1999.

Chase, Richard. "The Brontës, or Myth Domesticated." In *Forms of Modern Fiction*, 102–13. Ed. William V. O'Connor. Minneapolis: University of Minnesota Press, 1948.

Chow, Rey. "When Whiteness Feminizes . . . : Some Consequences of a Supplementary Logic." *Differences* 11 (1999–2000): 137–68.

Dale, Peter Allan. "Charlotte Brontë's 'Tale Half-told': The Disruption of Narrative Structure in *Jane Eyre.*" *Modern Language Quarterly* 47 (1986): 108–29.

Dale, Peter Allan. "Heretical Narrative: Charlotte Brontë's Search for Endlessness." *Religion and Literature* 16 (1984): 1–24.

David, Deirdre. *Rule Britannia: Women, Empire and Victorian Writing.* Ithaca, N.Y.: Cornell University Press, 1995.

Donaldson, Laura E. "The Miranda Complex." In *Decolonizing Feminisms: Race, Gender, and Empire Building*, 13–31. Chapel Hill: University of North Carolina Press, 1992.

Dunn, Richard. "The Natural Heart: Jane Eyre's Romanticism." *Wordsworth Circle* 10 (1979): 197–204.

Ellis, Kate, and E. Ann Kaplan. "*Jane Eyre*: Feminism in Brontë's Novel and Its Film Versions." In *The English Novel and the Movie*, 83–94. Ed. M. Klein and G. Parker. New York: Ungar, 1981.

Franklin, J. Jeffrey. "The Merging of Spiritualities: Jane Eyre as Missionary of Love." *Nineteenth-Century Literature* 49 (1995): 456–82.

Gibson, Mary Ellis. "The Seraglio or Suttee: Brontë's *Jane Eyre.*" *Postscript* 4 (1987):1–8.

Gilbert, Susan. "*Jane Eyre* and the Secrets of Furious Lovemaking." *Novel* 31 (1998): 351–72.

Glen, Heather, ed. *The Cambridge Companion to the Brontës.* Cambridge: Cambridge University Press, 2002.

Heilman, Robert B. "Charlotte Brontë, Reason, and the Moon." *Nineteenth-Century Fiction* 14(1960): 283–302.

Judd, Catherine A. "Male Pseudonyms and Female Authority in Victorian England." In *Literature in the Marketplace: Nineteenth-Century British Reading and Publishing Practices*, 250–68. Ed. John O. Jordan and Robert L. Patten. Cambridge: Cambridge University Press, 1995.

Kaplan, Carla. "Girl Talk: *Jane Eyre* and the Romance of Women's Narration." *Novel* 30 (1996): 5–31.

Kaplan, Cora. " 'A Heterogeneous Thing': Female Childhood and the

Rise of Racial Thinking in Victorian Britain." In *Human, All Too Human,* 169–202. Ed. Diana Fuss. New York: Routledge, 1995.

Kreilkamp, Ivan. "Unuttered: Withheld Speech and Female Authorship in *Jane Eyre* and *Villette.*" *Novel* 32 (1999): 331–54.

Levine, Caroline. " 'Harmless Pleasure': Gender, Suspense, and *Jane Eyre.*" *Victorian Literature and Culture* (2000): 275–86.

Levy, Anita. "*Jane Eyre,* the Woman Writer, and the History of Experience." *Modern Language Quarterly* 56 (1995): 77–95.

Litvak, Joseph. *Caught in the Act: Theatricality in the Nineteenth-Century Novel.* Berkeley: University of California Press, 1992.

London, Bette. "The Pleasures of Submission: *Jane Eyre* and the Production of the Text." *English Literary History* 58 (1991): 195–213.

Marcus, Sharon. "The Profession of Author: Abstraction, Advertising, and *Jane Eyre.*" *Publications of the Modern Language Association of America* 110 (1995): 206–19.

Massé, Michelle. "Looking Out for Yourself: The Spectator and *Jane Eyre.*" In *In the Name of Love: Women, Masochism, and the Gothic,* 192–238. Ithaca, N.Y.: Cornell University Press, 1992.

Michie, Elsie. " 'The Yahoo, Not the Demon': Heathcliff, Rochester, and the Simianization of the Irish." In *Outside the Pale: Cultural Exclusion, Gender Difference, and the Victorian Woman Writer,* 46–78. Ithaca, N.Y.: Cornell University Press, 1993.

Pell, Nancy. "Resistance, Rebellion, and Marriage: The Economics of *Jane Eyre.*" *Nineteenth-Century Fiction* 31 (1977): 397–420.

Perera, Suvendrini. *Reaches of Empire: The English Novel from Edgeworth to Dickens.* New York: Columbia University Press, 1991.

Politi, Jina. "*Jane Eyre* Class-ified." *Literature and History* 8 (1982): 56–66.

Ratchford, Fanny E. *The Brontës' Web of Childhood.* New York: Columbia University Press, 1941.

Ratchford, Fanny E., with the collaboration of William C. DeVane. *Legends of Angria.* New Haven: Yale University Press, 1933.

Roy, Parama. "Unaccomodated Woman and the Poetics of Property in *Jane Eyre.*" *Studies in English Literature* 29 (1989): 713–27.

Schacht, Paul, "*Jane Eyre* and the History of Self-Respect." *Modern Language Quarterly* 52 (1991): 423–53.

Senf, Carol. "*Jane Eyre:* The Prison-House of Victorian Marriage." *Journal of Women's Studies in Literature* 1 (1979): 353–59.

Sternlieb, Lisa. "*Jane Eyre:* 'Hazarding Confidences.' " *Nineteenth-Century Literature* 53 (1999): 452–79.

Vanden Bossche, Chris R. "What Did *Jane Eyre* Do? Ideology, Agency, Class and the Novel." *Narrative* 13 (2005): 46–66.

Williams, Carolyn. "Closing the Book: The Intertextual End of *Jane Eyre*." In *Victorian Connections,* 60–87. Ed. Jerome McGann. Charlottesville: University Press of Virginia, 1989.

Winnifrith, Tom. *The Brontës and Their Background.* New York: Barnes and Noble, 1973.

Yaegar, Patricia. *Honey-Mad Women.* New York: Columbia University Press, 1988.

Yeazell, Ruth B. "More True Than Real: Jane Eyre's 'Mysterious Summons.' " *Nineteenth-Century Fiction* 29 (1974): 127–43.

Zlotnick, Susan. "*Jane Eyre,* Anna Leonowens, and the White Woman's Burden: Governesses, Missionaries, and Maternal Imperialists in Mid-Victorian Britain." *Victorians Institute Journal* 24 (1996): 27–56.